The Folklore of Texan Cultures

PUBLICATIONS OF THE TEXAS FOLKLORE SOCIETY
NUMBER XXXVIII

In Commemoration
THE AMERICAN BICENTENNIAL
1776-1976

The Folklore of Texan Cultures

Edited by

Francis Edward Abernethy

Music Editor

Dan Beaty

University of North Texas Press
Denton, Texas

Preface

PIED BEAUTY *(ETC.)*
   —Gerard Manley Hopkins *(et al.)*

Glory be to God for dappled things—
   (For black, white, yellow, red)
For skies of couple-color as a brindled cow;
   (And for various mixtures thereof: breeds and redbones,
      mestizos and mulattoes)
For rose-moles all in stipple upon trout that swim:
   (For Greasers and Gringos—Japs, Jigs, and Czechs)
Fresh-firecoal chestnut falls; finches' wings;
   (Polacks and Bohunks—Kikes and Coonasses)
Landscape plotted and pieced—fold, fallow, and plough;
   (Fredericksburg and Falfurrias—Nederland, Norse, and
      Nacogdoches)
And all their trades, their gear and tackle and trim.
   (Pirogues and lederhosen, roundups and rodeos.)

All things counter, original, spare, strange;
   (Eating kolaches and collards, pizza and boudain
      all in the same town is not ordinary)
Whatever is fickle, freckled (who knows how?)
   (Nor is listening to a black man talk French to a
      Japanese rice farmer)
With swift, slow; sweet, sour; adazzle, dim;
   (From the Big Thicket to Big Bend—cypress to sagebrush—
      Panhandle to Port Isabel)
He fathers-forth whose beauty is past change; Praise him.
   (This land is rich in the strength of its people. Praise Him.)

This land is rich in the strength of its people and their pride and their dignity. It is rich because the blood of the strongest mixed with the strongest before it went back to the dust which nurtured it.

The pioneers of Texas traveled a long road before they got here.

Outcasts and dispossessed in their own lands, some of them, they died in the coming and died again in the lonesomeness of this strange and alien country. A hundred different shades between blond and black put down roots that cracked rocks and opened up the tight, black gumbo and red clays, roots that strained for a hold and reached down in panic to find moisture before they died. Many perished in storm and drouth, but those that lived have provided shade and comfort for a land that needed them. Their fruit has generated their kind, and the earth still catches their strong and vital seed.

The culture of this land is rich with the variety of its people. All colors, shades, and kinds have mingled with the flow and have made their languages, customs, and cultures into the state we call Texas. Some have melted into the flow but many remain and still celebrate their cultural identity, finding in their histories a source of strength and personality. Theirs is a pride founded on the knowledge that their tribe still lives and has survived all the rigors of discernible time.

We are emerging from the dreadful anonymity derived from the myth of the melting pot. The individual in a society crawling-thick with people cannot afford to conceive of himself as a part of the great goo of a nation; the ego cannot afford it. Assembly-line mass-produced people, housing developments, and shopping centers create a numbing sameness that shrivels the soul. The result and the reaction has been a rediscovery of the cultural variety and personality that has not only been a part of the individual's history but the country's as well.

And this is where the Institute of Texan Cultures comes in. It has shown us our infinite variety.

The seed for the Institute was planted by Governor John Connally in 1965, when he promised a major Texas exhibit for San Antonio's Hemisfair. He had been inspired by a recent visit to the National Institute of Anthropology and History in Mexico City. In the same year he prompted the legislature to appropriate money and hired architects and consultants for the establishment of a permanent Texas exhibit.

In 1966 Henderson Shuffler, the Director of the Texana Program at The University of Texas, was appointed as consultant to determine the character of the Texas exhibit, a character in which he decided to tell the story of Texas in terms of its people and their ethnic diversity. This was to become the Institute of Texan Cultures, established by law in 1967 as a permanent State educational institution. It was made a part of the University of Texas System in 1969 and became a division of the University of Texas at San Antonio in 1973.

In 1967 Shuffler was appointed Executive Director of the Institute, money was appropriated for its completion, and the race was on to beat the April 6, 1968, deadline and opening of the Hemisfair.

A dedicated staff within those few months tracked down and assembled the arts and crafts and souvenirs of all the surviving cultures that make up the culture of Texas. They took photographs, shot movies, and collected pictures that told the histories of twenty-six ethnic groups whose histories seen all together were the real history of Texas, stripped of the boisterous bravado of the Texas stereotype.

To add to the already saturated year of 1968, the Smithsonian Institute invited the Texas Institute to co-sponsor the Festival of American Folklife, held annually on the Mall in Washington, D. C. O. T. Baker, the projects manager at the Institute, was in charge of this operation and within a very few weeks recruited the ethnic representatives for this grand show.

The success of Texas' role in the Festival of American Folklife provided the incentive for the founding of the Texas Folklife Festival, which opened initially on the Institute grounds on September 7, 1972. The annual Festival, under O. T. Baker's direction, covers four days of the second weekend in September, includes over two thousand participants and entertains more than seventy thousand visitors. Almost every ethnic group in Texas is represented with its music, dancing, food, arts, or crafts.

The Institute of Texan Cultures and the Texas Folklife Festival are now established and vital forces in the state. The Institute is continually broadening its services to schools and the general public. It publishes a periodical and a series of pamphlets on Texan Cultures and on its special historical exhibits. For general circulation it has movies, slides, film strips, and illustrated shows, all of which can be obtained at minimal cost. It is the state's only repository for an indexed collection of historical documentary pictures. And it sponsors courses and teachers' seminars on ethnic history.

These are the tangible results of its purpose and labor. Its greater contribution is less measurable in terms of things produced.

What the Institute has done mainly is to focus the public's eye on what our history and our culture have really been made of, a beauti-

Henderson Shuffler (left) and O. T. Baker (right).

ful conglomerate of colors and cultures who have lived together a century and a half and who have survived their differences to create an exciting Texas. In a season of ethnic conflict the Institute has shown that diversity does not have to be divisive, that each culture can and should live its own life style proudly. It has shown that the heightening of the dignity of one culture does not depend on the lessening of the dignity of another group nor on provincial ethnocentricity. The Institute has shown that a man and a tribe and a culture can afford to be what they peculiarly are in a country that is strong enough and confident enough to enjoy the excitement and the entertainment of diversity.

I fell in love with the Institute on first sight in 1968, have dated her several times since then, and keep up with her by regular correspondence.

This volume is the Texas Folklore Society's contribution to the American Revolution Bicentennial celebration. The fulfillment of the American dream is illustrated repeatedly in the stories of impoverished immigrant families who in succeeding generations produced their country's social, political, and intellectual leaders. This nation's greatest beauty lies in its multi-cultural heritage, and much that has gone into the pot is fortunately still unmelted. In spite of the great melters and levelers—advertising, TV, movies, radio—we are thankful that we still do not talk, dress, or act alike. And we can be thankful that this nation is still blessed with the visible and audible remains of the old stock who brought to it all their strength and personality.

The Texas Folklore Society is deeply appreciative of the assistance, both financial and moral, given by the Texas College Bicentennial Program under the directorship of Edgar L. Roy, Jr., and we thank the American Revolution Bicentennial Commission of Texas for permission to use the state's Bicentennial seal.

In addition to the assistance given by the Texas College Bicentennial Program, financial support for this volume was given by the Temple Foundation of Diboll, the George and Mary Josephine Hamman Foundation of Houston, the Pollock Foundation of Dallas, the Harris and Eliza Kempner Fund of Galveston, and the Tellepsen Foundation of Houston. We appreciate the altruistic spirit with which they gave and recognize that without their help we could not have produced the book in its present form.

From the very first Laura Simmons, Pat McGuire, and the rest of

Texas Folklife Festival.

The Institute of Texan Cultures.

the Institute of Texan Culture's Research Department have assisted and guided the production of this book. We love them for it.

I want to thank the contributors to this volume. Many of them were writing on assignment and had to start from scratch on their research and field work. These writers are a beginning. Texas has a tremendous supply of both folklore and folklorists among its many ethnic groups. This wealth of talent and material has barely been tapped. The still existing primary materials should be the source for further profitable research in Texas folklore. In 1916 George Lyman Kittredge, the Society's godfather, said that Texas was the folklorist's happy hunting ground. It still is.

The Society thanks Dr. Ralph W. Steen, president of Stephen F. Austin State University, and Dr. Roy E. Cain, head of the English Department, for their moral and material support. The Society's secretary, Mrs. Martha Dickson, did the hard work for this annual, and there is no way (except to raise her pay) to thank her for all she did to get this book ready to go forth into society. And I am deeply in debt to Henderson Shuffler, O. T. Baker, and the Institute of Texan Cultures.

Francis Edward Abernethy
Nacogdoches, Texas
June 27, 1974

Contents

The Cultures of Texas

By R. HENDERSON SHUFFLER,
Director, Institute of Texan Cultures

THE TEXAS FOLKLORE most of us know about is as limited and fragmentary as our history books used to be. Its characters are almost wholly Anglo-American and its setting restricted to the Western frontier. We have generally ignored the rich heritage of lore and legend which came to us from all ages and all parts of the world with the immigrants who peopled our land from the time of the first Texan to the present. This book makes a beginning on correcting the situation.

In modern times we have added a few touches of Mexican and Negro lore and hit a glancing blow at the rich German lode in our heritage. But what about the rest? Texas is, and always has been, one of the most cosmopolitan spots on earth, a crossroads of humanity, peopled by a polyglot assortment of immigrants and the descendants of immigrants from the far corners of the globe. All of them brought their own special customs, traditions, dances, songs, and folktales, adding to the flavor of the heritage which now belongs to all of us.

The first Texans, our anthropologists believe, were Asian hunters, ancestors of the American Indians. They followed the elephant herds across the Bering Strait somewhere near the end of the last Ice Age and drifted down from Alaska to the hunting grounds of Texas. That was between twenty thousand and forty thousand years ago.

By the time the first Europeans landed on Texas soil in the sixteenth century there were some fifty tribes of descendants of these first-comers here. They differed from each other in stature, color, language, and customs even more than the assorted types of Texans do today. Their lore, while having a common background in nature, varied in detail as widely as their other characteristics. Most of the rich product of their many generations of struggle for survival on Texas soil has been buried, but it remains to be mined by the careful researcher.

The mass influx of settlers into Texas starting in 1821 almost wrote "finis" to the story of the Indian Texan. Almost. From an estimated 15,000 in 1835, our Indian population dropped to 470 in the census of 1900. But, by 1970, the figure was back up to 18,132. How much of this can be attributed solely to the birthrate, it is hard to say. In 1900 most Texans did not admit to any Indian blood; in 1970 it was fashionable.

We still have two resident tribes, whose customs can be observed first-hand and whose lore can be learned by word of mouth. These are the Tiguas of Ysleta del Sur, a suburb of El Paso, and the Alabama-Coushatta of deep East Texas. In addition, there is the inter-tribal council of the Dallas-Fort Worth area. Its ten thousand members came to Texas from reservations all over North America. The lore of the Indian is not lost, just misplaced in the rush of "progress."

If they had been men from another planet, instead of just from another age, the Spaniards could have had no more shocking impact on Texas than they did when they first landed here. To the Stone Age Indians these Medieval men were as strange as if they had come from outer space.

The Spaniards brought into the Texas wilderness the first guns and gunpowder, armor and weapons of metal, and, most terrifying of all, the horse. They brought strange new diseases, even more deadly than their armed and mounted phalanxes.

More revolutionary, still, were the customs and ideas of these new-comers. They built permanent structures of wood and stone, introduced crops and strange domesticated animals to sustain them, and recorded their history and the dreams of their wise men in papers and books. Strangest of all was their religion and the iron-willed determination of the Spaniards to cram it down the throats of any who survived their conquests.

In nearly three centuries of dominion over the land we now call Texas, the Spaniards left an indelible mark. The names of our rivers and mountains, the language and bloodlines of a fifth of our people, our architecture, foods, customs, and laws all bear their mark. We owe the basic elements of our entire ranching tradition to these adventuresome conquerors.

Most of us know about Estevan, said to have been the first black man to come to Texas. He arrived with Cabeza de Vaca in 1528. Few, however, realize that Negroes accompanied most of the Spanish expeditions of exploration and conquest north of the Rio Grande. It has been a well-kept secret that nearly fifteen percent of the settlers who moved into Texas from Mexico in the eighteenth century were "of broken color," bearing varying mixtures of Negro blood. They were freedmen, often educated, and occasionally wealthy, mixing freely in business, society, and marriage with the Spanish, Indian, and Spanish-Indian segments which made up the rest of the "civilized" population.

Practically all of the Negro lore we have preserved in Texas stems from those who came as slaves before the Civil War. Still to be mined is the rich lode of lore of the free men of color of the three centuries of Spanish Texas and that of the goodly number of freedmen who migrated here from the United States of the North in the Mexican colonial period.

Nobody has been particularly impressed by the Italian influence on Texas. Yet, there were Italian adventurers in the earliest Spanish and French expeditions of exploration and a small but steady stream of Italian immigration throughout the Spanish period. Today such pockets of Italian settlement as the fruit-and-grape-growing community of Montague County, the rich agricultural settlement along the Brazos from Hearne to Navasota, and the large Italian colonies in Houston and San Antonio preserve the special flavor of this phase of our heritage. The Italian Texans have enriched our music, sculpture, and our appreciation of fine wines and foods. Some of their early customs, such as that of throwing silver dollars at a plate during a wedding celebration (if you broke the plate you could dance with the bride, but all the dollars became the property of the newly-married pair) and the charitable Altar of St. Joseph each March 19th, have practically disappeared, but are a definite part of our lore.

The Mexican, part Spanish and part Indian, gave us some of the flavor of both, as well as a very special tradition of his own. Accompanying the Spaniards in their first penetrations of Texas, as soldiers and settlers, priests and mission helpers, the mestizos were an important element of the Texas population throughout Spanish and Mexican times and are still so today. Their descendants and a host of immigrants who followed them, represent about a fifth of our total population. In South Texas their percentage is much higher; in many localities, predominant. Possibly no other element of our population has contributed so much to the special flavor of life and tradition which distinguishes things Texan from those of other states.

The Cultures of Texas   xxi

Our French influence has been almost as elusive and subtle as their role in our history. Actually the short-lived attempt at French settlement in 1685, led by La Salle, was significant only because it forced the Spanish to begin a serious effort at settling the territory. Still, it left its mark on the phony tradition of "Six Flags Over Texas" and an imposing statue of La Salle at Navasota, near the spot where he may (or may not) have died. Equally ephemeral were the colonization attempt at Champ d'Asile on the Trinity and the brief reign of the pirates, Louis Aury and the Lafitte brothers, at Galveston Isle.

The brief utopian experiment called La Reunion, at Dallas in 1854-58, left a more lasting mark. When the colony dispersed, its members stayed in Dallas. It is no accident that this city became a fashion center and a symbol of sophistication and worldliness in Texas during the next century. It even, for a time, supported a periodical called *Beau Monde.*

The strong French influence at Weatherford and in the ranch country west of that city in the last quarter of the nineteenth century has practically disappeared. Still, from 1876 to 1896 Weatherford was headquarters of the Franco-Texan Land Company, which played a significant role in opening up West Texas as far out as Sweetwater.

The only obvious French influence in Texas today is to be found in the Alsatian village of Castroville and the Acadian colonies of the Beaumont-Port Arthur-Orange triangle.

Whether by Teutonic tenacity or sheer weight of numbers, the German Texans have preserved more of their old world customs and traditions than any other group of European origin. Throughout the Hill Country and in a cluster of communities in Austin, Washington, and Fayette Counties, there are strong imprints of the original German culture, in language, foods, lifestyles, and architecture. Fredericksburg, in its annual re-enactment of its Easter Fires ceremony, keeps alive one of our most fascinating folktales of German Texan origin.

The entire modern tradition of the family Christmas, the decorated tree, and the giving of gifts was brought here by these people. The Germans have been in Texas longer and in greater numbers than most other types of Texans. A few adventurers showed up in Spanish times, and a steady flow of immigration started in Austin's first colony in 1831, when Friederich Ernst settled near San Felipe on the Gotier Trace. The organized immigration sponsored by the Mainzer

Adelsverein between 1844 and 1848 brought thousands of farmers, scholars, artists, and professional men to the raw Texas frontier. An estimated half-million Texans today are of German ancestry.

The Irish, English, and Scots who came directly to Texas were so closely related to the vast flood of immigrants from the United States of the North, whom we call, for want of a better name, Anglo-Americans, that they were soon lost in the general population and are difficult to trace. The Irish, however, did come first as organized colonists in 1833-34 and concentrated their settlements on the coastal prairie in what are now San Patricio and Refugio Counties. Later a small but steady stream of individuals came to add their special touch to the arts, education, finance, architecture, and fighting forces of Texas. A few, like the indestructible Pegleg Ward and indomitable Dick Dowling, became genuine Texas folk heroes.

The English, whose empresarios Stephen Wilson, Richard Exter, John Charles Beales, and Jonathan Ikin were monotonously unsuccessful in the 1920's and 1830's, did supply us with the last great colonizers, the Peters family, in the 1840's. But the greatest impact on our lore, as well as on our history, came from the wealthy Englishmen who bought cheap Texas lands and opened up West Texas to large-scale ranching. It would be hard to top some of the tales that have grown up around the Baron Tweedmouth and his associates of the Rocking Chair Ranche Company, who rode across their vast West Texas acreages wearing formal riding habits, topped by bowlers, and earned the lasting distaste of the neighbors by referring to all cowboys as "cow servants"; or the Seventh Earl of Ayelsford, who ranched near Big Spring and won the undying admiration of his neighbors by doing everything in a grand free-wheeling "Texan" style. He bought the local hotel in order to be sure of rooms for his numerous guests, the meat market in order to get the mutton he wanted for his table, and the leading saloon in order to insure a steady supply of his favorite spirits.

The Scots, James Grant, Arthur Wavell and John Cameron, were no more successful as colonizers than the English, and no modern Texas area can be identified as having their distinctive mark. Still, they gave us folk figures in the dashing Ewing Cameron, hero of the "black bean" affair, and Jesse Chisholm, the half-Scotch half-Cherokee trail blazer. It was a Scot, Robert Bontine Cunninghame-Graham, whose career was reshaped by his Texas experience, who, in turn,

The Port of Indianola.

Map of Texas by Mitchell, 1837.

influenced the course of Texas lore and letters. This dashing descendant of Scottish kings was twenty-seven years old when he came to Texas in 1879 with a few thousand dollars and dreams of building a ranch empire. In San Antonio he made the acquaintance of a Mexican con man who supposedly owned vast holdings in West Texas. They stocked the area and built a headquarters. The Comanches promptly burned the buildings and drove off the cattle. Graham turned to writing to recoup his fortunes. J. Frank Dobie always said his style was more affected by that of Graham than by that of any other writer. His complete collection of Graham's works is an important section of the Dobie library at The University of Texas in Austin.

The Dutch, the Danes, and the Belgians came to us in small numbers, but each contributed a special spice to the Texas cultural stew. A Dutch con man who had absconded with tax collections in the old country showed up in Texas very early. Hendrick Nering Bogel posed in the New World as Philipe Enrique Neri, the Baron de Bastrop. He was a master at dealing with Spanish colonial officialdom through flattery and bribery. Without his aid the Austins would never have secured their first grant. He is still a vague figure in our history, more legend than fact, but unquestionably deserves the title of Godfather of Anglo Texas. A more discernible modern mark of the Dutch may be seen at Nederland, near Beaumont, where descendants of an 1895 colonizing group keep alive the Dutch traditions with a very attractive museum and even more attractive Dutch delectables.

Danevang in Wharton County is still definitely Danish in accents, foods, and customs. Founded in 1904 by the Danish Folk Society of America, it has become a prosperous agricultural community with the most successful cooperatives in the state.

The Belgians have concentrated in an area on the edge of San Antonio, where they operate some of the profitable truck farms in Texas. A close-knit community, they have preserved many of their original customs, games and special foods.

Polish engineers and artillerymen were among the Napoleonic veterans who built Champ d'Asile, and others played heroic roles with Fannin at Coleto and with Houston at San Jacinto. Their mass migration to Texas began in 1854, with the settlement of Panna Maria. That quaint hilltop village in Karnes County is today the oldest Polish settlement in North America. From this "mother settlement" these hard-working, hard-playing folk have spread throughout South Texas, into the Hill Country and into the far Western Panhandle. Spicy Polish sausages and tasty beet and pickle soups have added new life to many jaded Texas menus, as have Polish folk songs and dances to many local celebrations. While the Poles have broken through their earlier ethnic barriers to intermarry with other elements of the population and have been readily assimilated into the mainstream of Texas life, they cling proudly to their special heritage. It is estimated that there are around a quarter of a million Texans of Polish descent today.

Only a few thousand Swiss have settled in Texas since the Rueg brothers, Louis and Henry, came to Nacogdoches in 1821. Still in Texas, as in international circles, a few Swiss can make a considerable impact. Dallas, which acquired a number with the French at La Reunion, has had a Swiss Mayor (Benjamin Lang) and an active Swiss Society, bell-ringers and all. Swiss Avenue is still one of the choice old residential streets of the city. In Galveston, the great old Rosenberg Library stands as a monument to the beneficence of a Swiss immigrant who rose to Texas riches, while in Houston the Hermann Park and Hermann Hospital do the same. There is no Swiss concentration in Texas today and no longer do we boast an active Swiss society.

Though few Czechs came before the mid-nineteenth century, they have come by the thousands since then. Their concentration in ethnic clusters throughout the blackland belt has made them a distinctly visible phase of our cultural mix. Many Texans are familiar with Czech foods, particularly the delicious fruit-stuffed kolaches which are the pride of every Czech housewife. Costumes, music, dancing, and athletic games from the old country have been preserved in the Texas setting. Major Czech settlements can be found around Corpus Christi, Bryan, La Grange, West, Ennis, and Dallas. Villages established in Czech farming communities where the old language can still be heard include New Bremen, Fayetteville, Hostyn, Dubina, and Praha.

Although the Swedes started coming to Texas several years before the Norwegians and have come in about twice the number, they are not as easily located and identified. The Swedes came in smaller groups over a longer period of time, and melted into the general population. The Norwegians, in a more organized migration, began settling in Bosque County in 1854. Today a large area in the county, including the towns of Meridian, Norse, and Cranfills Gap, are predominantly Norwegian. In this "little Norway of Texas," the Norse language, foods and customs are still preserved. There are concentrations of Swedes in the Austin-Round Rock area, in McCulloch County near Brady, and around Stamford, Lyford, Fort Worth, Dallas, and Waco.

From the Mediterranean coast, the Greeks, Lebanese and Syrians have come in rather surprising numbers, adding an exotic flavor to the Texas stew. All formed tight-knit communities, centered around their churches. Even today they traditionally maintain close contact with their own communities and resist marrying into other groups. The Greek and Syrian Texans are generally concentrated in the larger towns and cities, while the Lebanese are scattered throughout small towns as well. Thrifty, fun-loving people, all have preserved their old traditions in music, dancing, foods, and customs and are beginning, just now, to share them with the rest of us.

The number of Texans of oriental ancestry has always been small, but highly visible. The three hundred Chinese workmen brought to the Brazos Valley in 1870 to build a railroad from Calvert to Dallas aroused much interest and curiosity. When the railroad was finished they were welcomed back to the Brazos plantations as laborers. In time, they melted into the predominantly black labor force. Today in the Calvert-Hearne area there are many dark-skinned Texans with Chinese names and oriental eyes. Other Chinese railroad workmen scattered throughout West Texas after building the railroads from California. Few traces of them are left in the small towns, but some of the patriarchs of the Chinese in the cities are descended from this group. The late General John J. "Blackjack" Pershing is a folk hero of the Chinese Texans of San Antonio. He established this community by rescuing several hundred Chinese from the vengeance of Pancho Villa in 1916 and settling them near Fort Sam Houston. The general's picture can still be seen in the family shrines of San Antonio Chinese Texans and his memory is preserved in such interesting names of their children as Blackjack Wong and Pershing Yuim. The older Chinese communities are close-knit, centered around churches and clubs.

In contrast, the new waves of students, scholars, and professional people which have come from China since 1940 have been rapidly assimilated into the mainstream of life in our cities.

Though slightly more numerous than the Chinese, the Japanese Texans are less noticeable. With the exception of old rice-growing settlements near Webster and Orange, few large Japanese communities exist in the state. In the larger cities the Japanese have maintained some cohesion through their clubs and societies.

A large and important segment of the Texas population throughout our history has been Jewish. Though this religion-centered cultural group cuts across all nationalities and shares the lore of all the countries from which its people came, it also has a distinctive flavor of tradition and custom all its own.

There are other groups, some of imposing numbers, whose history and lore are yet to be explored. There were Russian farmers in Texas during the days of the Republic, and a steady stream of Russian immigrants has come since. The Yugo-Slavs at Galveston and the Portuguese in the fishing towns nearby form interesting communities, as do the remnants of the Wends, around Serbin in Lee County. Practically unknown to most of the rest of us are the Gypsies, who come to light in numbers only at the time of an important wedding or funeral. When we know more about all of these, our knowledge of the full-flavored folklore of Texas will be more complete.

Until a comparatively few years ago, the trend was for the sons and daughters of immigrants to turn away from the old ways, abandon the language and customs of their forefathers, and become as typically "American" as possible. Under the spell of the old "melting pot" myth, we all strove to be more and more alike. But in recent times there seems to have been some reversal of this foolish process.

Maybe we have begun to realize that conformity, ethnic or individual, is a curse. We may also have begun to raise the question of who should set the pattern by which we should all standardize ourselves.

At any rate, in the last generation we have had a strong revival of diverse origins. We have begun to appreciate the influence of our varied hereditary backgrounds on each of us as individuals, groups of us with common ancestry, and all of us as Texans.

The strongest evidence of this trend and the most effective mechanism for its enhancement has been the resurgence of ethnic societies and the colorful celebrations in which they display their respective heritages. In almost any part of Texas at almost any time of year, you will find one of these very special Texas celebrations under way.

If you have gourmet taste buds, the Norwegians will tempt you with the bountiful Smorgasbord held each November at Norse, in Bosque County.

Probably next in pure delight for the discerning palate are the many German festivals. The Berges Fest, in June, at Boerne, A Night in Old Fredericksburg on the third Saturday in July, or the ten-day Wurstfest at New Braunfels in November will fill the bill. The Brenham Maifest, the second weekend in May, offers parades and pageantry, and the Easter Fires Ceremony at Fredericksburg on Easter Eve combines history, lore, and religion. The Polka and Waltz Festival on two days in July at La Grange is half Czech and half German, with the common denominator of music and dancing.

The Poles at White Deer annually offer their wares to the Panhandle in a special festival. In the larger cities, observance of Polish Constitution Day, each May 3rd, brings out the musicians, dancers, foods and the fun-loving Polish community. Columbus Day, October 8th, brings together the Italians in Houston, Galveston, and San Antonio. Less formal, but even more fun, are the monthly spaghetti suppers at the local Columbus Halls. The National Polka Festival, on the first weekend in May at Ennis, is one of the best Czech festivals in the State. The annual Kolache Bake by the Christian Sisters of Taylor Brethren Church, at Taylor, is considered a gourmet's must.

Aptly named is the Greek Funstival, a fun-filled celebration put on in San Antonio, Houston, and Dallas each October. Even more exotic are the reedy music and torso-tossing dances of the Lebanese, whose celebrations are scattered throughout the year in San Antonio, Austin, El Paso, and Houston.

San Antonio's famous fiestas are genuinely Mexican in flavor and tradition. The most elaborate, nine delightfully festive days each April, includes parades, rich pageantry, the crowning of a short-reigned King, river rides, oratorical contests, a pilgrimage to the Alamo, and finally, the "Nights in Old San Antonio."

A genuinely bilingual and bi-cultural event occurs at Laredo and Nuevo Laredo on Washington's Birthday. Balls, dinners and other socializings bring together the people of Mexico and Texas in a warm expression of international friendship. Another celebration in which Texans of both Anglo and Mexican ancestry join is the Cinco de Mayo observances at Goliad, which include a pilgrimage to the birthplace of General Ignacio Zaragoza. More distinctly Mexican, though a few Anglos participate and many attend, are the Charro Days at Brownsville, during the pre-lenten season.

There are three distinct types of French Texans, each with its own special celebration. The Cajuns of the Beaumont-Port Arthur area stage an annual Crawfish Festival at Port Arthur. Quieter and slower paced are the annual Saint Louis Day Homecomings each August in Castroville. Different from either of these are the annual Bastille Day (July 14) balls sponsored by L'Alliance Francaise in the cities.

There are also three very different centers for Indian ceremonies and celebrations. The Alabama-Coushatta, on their reservation near Livingston, run a year-round show for tourists. At Ysleta del Sur, a suburb of El Paso, the Tiguas celebrate the day of their patron, St. Anthony, on June 13th. For a wide variety of Indian music, dances, and ceremonies there are the gatherings of the Inter-Tribal Council near Dallas, where people from many tribes throughout the country gather once a month.

You can see the Scots at a Gathering of the Clans each October in Austin and The Gathering of the Scottish Clans, on the weekend nearest November 11th at Salado.

In Houston, the Youth Club of the Chinese-American Citizens Alliance stages an annual Scholarship Ball, entertaining the public with a very sprightly team of young dancers called the Ricksha Riders. Probably the largest Jewish festival in Texas is sponsored by the Congregation Agudas Achim of San Antonio, during the citywide Fiesta each April. This traditional festival is celebrated also, on a smaller scale, at synagogues in Dallas, El Paso, Houston, and Galveston.

Anglo celebrations throughout Texas are so numerous and varied that there's no way of keeping up with all of them. Two of the most ambitious are the Fort Griffin Fandangle, near Albany on two successive weekends in June, and the summer-long presentation of "TEXAS" in Palo Duro Canyon. Older events still going strong are the Old Fiddlers' Reunion on the last Friday in May at Athens, the XIT Rodeo and Reunion in early August at Dalhart, the Texas Cowboy Reunion at Stamford each July 4th, the Cowboys' Christmas Ball at Anson, and the Texas Independence Day ceremonies at the town of Washington. Equally historic in nature are the "Come and Take It" celebration at Gonzales in October and San Jacinto Day at the San Jacinto battlefield.

Almost every community with old or historic houses holds an annual trek. Notable are the Jefferson Pilgrimage each Spring, the Anderson-Montgomery trek in the summer, and the Magnolia Homes at Columbus in May.

For sheer off-beat fun, you can find such events as the Heart of East Texas Fox Hunt at Center each October, the East Texas Yamboree at Gilmer, the Sidewalk Cattlemen's Association gathering at Madisonville in June, the annual rattlesnake hunts in March at Big Spring and Sweetwater, and the combined Rattlesnake Hunt and Antique Show at Coleman. Canyon stages an annual Husband and Hog Calling Contest, while nearby Muleshoe has the world's only Mule Shoe Pitching Contest. No matter where you are in Texas, at what time of year, there's a refreshingly unusual celebration of some kind going on nearby.

Of course, if you want to see a cross-section of them all, in one big statewide celebration of our Texas diversity, you can attend the annual Texas Folklife Festival staged by the Institute of Texan Cultures at San Antonio each September.

The Cultures of Texas xxxi

THE INDIANS

Chief Kicking Bird, Kiowa.

Four Tigua Indian scouts, 1880. Courtesy A. Griffen.

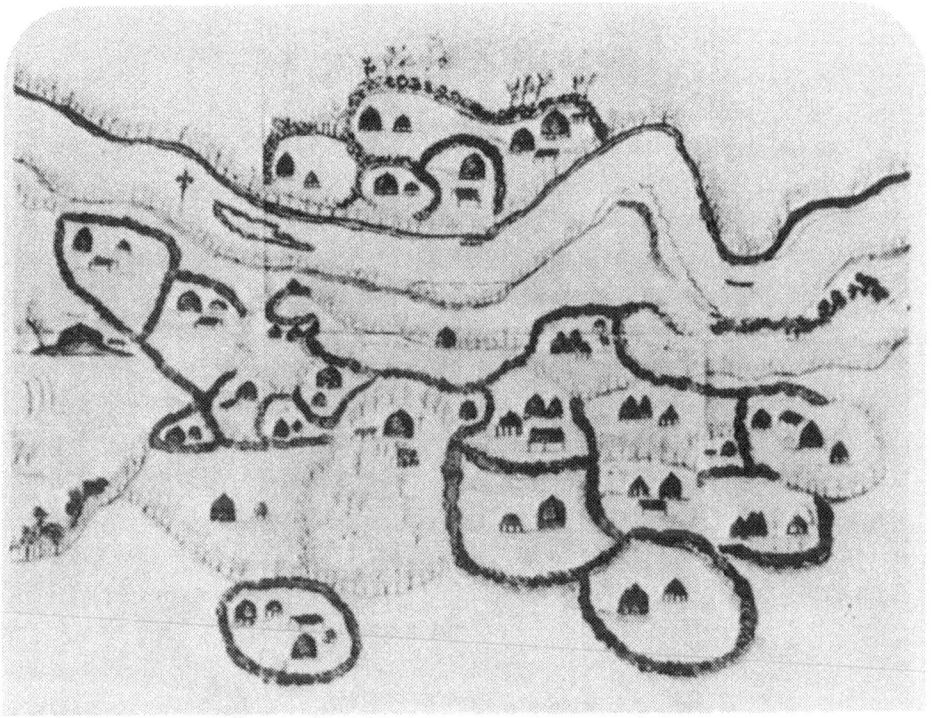

Map of Caddo village, 1691. Courtesy Archivo General de Indias de Sevilla.

Elders of the Tigua tribe. Courtesy A. Griffen.

Courtesy Western History Collection, University of Oklahoma.

Maggie Poncho, Alabama-Coushatta.

Chief Fulton Battise, Alabama-
Coushatta.

Texas Folklife Festival.

Early Texas Indian Songs and Tales

By EDWIN W. GASTON, JR.

For 25,000 YEARS in Texas the Indian was the land's, but the land was never his. Proprietorship eluded him at first by his own choice. So rapidly did the nomadic aborigine shift from place to place in pursuit of the Pleistocene camel, horse, and mammoth providing his table meat, that he had no need for a deed to the real estate. Then, to the ancient Indian's more settled descendant, the sanctity of private property meant a mystical unity between man and the land as much as it did the hunting rights of man to the land.

As practiced, the concept represented what John Graves calls living *in* rather than *on* the country. It was part of a larger belief that everything in nature contained an inner quality, a spiritual counterpart with supernatural force that could exert good or evil influence upon earthly affairs. The Indian thus strived to live in harmony with nature—both external and internal—not only for his physical survival, but also for his spiritual welfare.

Tribal rivalry over hunting privileges confuses the perspective. So, too, do the Indian wars with the white intruder. Nevertheless, the Indian aspired not to ownership of the land, but simply to the right of continuing 250 centuries of occupancy in unison with the place that he lost in fewer than four centuries.

The loss of the land by the Indian finally was a matter of dispossession. Squatter's rights, the Anglo-American later called it. The native Indian extended a disproportionately generous amount of hospitality to the sixteenth century European explorer. In return then and later, after his hospitality had turned to hostility against the hordes of European and Anglo-American settlers, he suffered the decimation of his ranks by imported firearms and disease. The Indian in the main had departed the Texas scene by the twentieth century.

Today the Indian's meager bequest consists of a few names that he gave to Texas and some of its parts, scattered artifacts that put life here among the earliest in the New World, two minor reservations separated by the six-hundred-mile expanse between Livingston on the east and El Paso on the west, and the stereotyped notions that he was either a blood-thirsty savage or a romantic child of nature. What is notably missing are plentiful examples of his early folk literature—songs and tales that were central to his life because the songs usually were inextricable from the theories and practices of his religion and the tales provided his entertainment.

It is possible, nevertheless, to fit together bits and pieces into an overview of early Texas Indian folk literature. Such a perspective, as previously suggested, reveals the basic purpose of songs to be religious and of tales to be entertainment. Songs, for example, sought power over invisible life forces toward numerous ends: (1) to praise the gods and seek their help; (2) to explain life and death; (3) to work cures; (4) to stimulate fertility in man and nature; (5) to promote hunting; (6) to bring victory in battle; (7) to arouse love; (8) to quieten noisy children; (9) to chronicle tribal life and thought. Illustrative is the Cherokee song containing a formula to destroy life:

> Listen! Now I have come to step over your soul.
> You are of the wolf clan. Your name is Ayuiuni.
> Your spittle I have put at rest under the earth.
> Your soul I have put at rest under the earth.
> I have come to cover you over with the black rock.
> I have come to cover you with the black slabs, never to reappear.
> Toward the black coffin in the Darkening Land your path shall
>   stretch out.
> So shall it be for you.
> The clay of the upland has come [to cover you].
> Instantly the black clay has lodged there where it is at rest at
>   the black houses in the Darkening Land.
> With the black coffin and the black slabs I have come to cover
>   you.
> Now your soul has faded away.
> It has become blue.
> When darkness comes
> Your spirit shall grow less
> And dwindle away,
> Never to reappear. Listen![1]

Perhaps the foremost characteristics of Texas Indian song were clarity and concision of expression. Those features invite a comparison between Indian song and the Japanese *Haiku,* and enabled the

Indian song to anticipate twentieth-century imagistic verse. Further, they underscored the importance that the Indian ascribed to the *word*. The *word*, as Margot Astrov and others have shown, constituted a force "not only to perpetuate but also to actuate, to bring about change, and to create."[2]

Unique among thinkers of the western world, then, the Indian attributed supreme power and, especially, recreative ability to the *word*. When a tribal shaman administered a potion to a sick Indian, he chanted incessantly like a prehistoric Oral Roberts, "Heal! heal! heal!" His religion placed the burden of healing upon the chant—the words— more than the medicine. As a Navajo priest, the Texas Indian's western neighbor, once sang, "I hold my word tight to my breast."[3]

Early Indian songs could be composed by anyone. But once a song, as distinct from a tale, had been composed, it became the property of either the composer or a group with which he was affiliated. There thus existed a kind of primitive copyright arrangement under which the composer or his group had to give permission—and often receive recompense—before a song could be used by others.

Indian song ordinarily was accompanied by drums and occasionally flutes and rattles. In fact, it was composed in such a way that, in Mary Austin's apt simile, the lyrics, melody, and movement fit as closely as the "water of a river with its own ripples." But despite its rhythmic quality, song seldom rhymed. It did, however, have repetitional patterns, as in this excerpt from the Apache "Songs of the Masked Dancers":

> The living sky black-spotted;
> The living sky blue-spotted;
> The living sky yellow-spotted;
> The living sky white-spotted;
> The young spruce as girls stood up for their dance in the way
> of life.[4]

Probably the nearest approximation to Indian song form in the Anglo-American tradition, then, has been that deriving from free verse.

This free verse quality, in fact, made song shade into prose in early Indian folk literature probably more often than it did in the folk literature of any other people. It also established a strong correlation between the religious function of song and the tale. One Caddo tale, for example, explains the origin of death and the part played in it by the coyote. A Cherokee tale seeks to explain a facet of existence—the origin of the Pleiades and the pine.

Still another correlation between the religious function of Indian song and the tale may be seen in the tendency of storytellers to borrow gods and heroic personages from songs but then to amplify deeds in ways that the song obviously could not do. And it was in such amplification that the tale took an essentially secular path. The tale basically was intended to provide the Indian's entertainment.

The Indian tale also described the exploits of actual or typical persons who had accomplished notable feats in tribal history. More imaginative examples of the tale dealt with animals humanized in the manner of beast fables such as the later Uncle Remus stories of Joel Chandler Harris.

Combining both the religious and secular functions of the tale, as well as featuring a humanized animal, is the Caddo account of the coyote and the origin of death. According to the story, death originally did not exist upon earth. As a consequence an aboriginal population explosion occurred. That compelled the chiefs, the earliest ecologists on record, to seek a solution to the problem of their people-polluted world. One chief suggested that people might temporarily die and then return to earth. But his proposal was immediately countered by the coyote, who insisted that people should die permanently. The vote of the council, though, favored the less drastic plan.

To institute the plan, the shaman built a large grass house facing the east. People who had died could then come to the house when it was their turn to be restored to life. The house pleased the people even if it provoked the coyote.

The coyote, however, did not give up easily. When the first man died and presented himself at the house to be restored to life, the coyote quickly closed the door. That precluded the man's spirit from entering the house and thus ushered death permanently into man's experience. Nevertheless, the victorious coyote found little satisfaction. Spirits of dead men, he thought ever after, constantly pursued him. At least, that is the supposition of the Indian who noted the coyote's perpetual habit of looking back, glancing apprehensively over one shoulder and then the other. Moreover, the coyote has ever since found himself in a continual state of near-starvation, vexed man refusing to give him anything to eat.[5]

To the pantheon of the humanized coyote in early Indian folk tales may be added rabbits, horses, and other creatures. Their exploits and those of mythologized people made life more entertaining and hence more tolerable along the Gulf, among the woodlands and mountains, and on the plains. And when the tale's function as ancient televiewing is added to the song's office as original church-going, the equation stresses once more the importance of folkloric literature to the lives of the first people of Texas.

[1]James Mooney, *Sacred Formulas of the Cherokees,* 7th Annual Report of Bureau of American Ethnology, Washington, 1891, p. 391.

[2]Margot Astrov, ed., *American Indian Prose and Poetry,* New York: Capricorn Books, 1962, p. 4. Originally published in 1946 as *The Winged Serpent.*

[3]*Ibid.,* p. 3.

[4]Pliny Earle Goddard, *The Masked Dancers of the Apache,* Holmes Anniversary Volume, Washington, 1916, p. 132.

[5]George A. Dorsey, *The Traditions of the Caddo,* Washington: Carnegie Institution, 1905, pp. 15-16.

Religious Beliefs of the Tejas or Hasanias Indians

By ADINA DE ZAVALA

ONE OF THE OLD MISSION PADRES has fully described the religious beliefs of the Hasanias Indians [of Deep East Texas]. Father Isidro de Espinosa [writing in 1746 of his missionary work in East Texas, 1716, 1719, 1721] was very much grieved for them because they had "not the true faith," since in general they were of very good disposition, good to look upon, "well made, and much whiter than the Mexicans and Tlascaltecans, and naturally politic and of good understanding." He was very much surprised by their answers and could not but admire their ingenuity and loyalty in giving reasons for all their rites and superstitions in which their fathers had bred them.

He stated that in all that numerous nation, comprising many tribes of the same idiom and more than fourteen or fifteen dialects, all believed that there is a great Captain in the sky, who is called "Caddi Ayo" or "Captain Above," and that he directs all lives and destinies.

These Indians believe "that in the beginning of the world there was only one woman, and this woman had two daughters—one a virgin. . . . One day when the two sisters were alone without their mother, when the elder was leaning upon the lap of the younger, and the latter was examining her head, they were seized from before and this is what happened. There appeared suddenly a deformed and gigantic man of ferocious aspect, with horns so high that you could not see them, and this was Caddaja—devil or demon—and, seizing the elder sister, he tore her to pieces with his nails, and chewed and swallowed her. Meanwhile the virgin climbed to the top of a very high tree, and when the devil had finished eating the sister, he raised his eyes to look for the maiden, and, seeing her, tried to force her to descend, but, not being able, he commenced (with his teeth and nails) to cut down the tree.

"(When they told me this, I asked why, if his horns were so high, he did not use them at this time, but they were unable to answer me.) The girl, seeing her danger, let herself fall into a deep pond of water at the foot of the tree, and diving in the water she went out very far and made her escape to where her mother was. The giant, in the meantime, began to agitate the water to prevent her swimming out, so as to make her a prisoner; but she made sport of him and finally succeeded in escaping to her mother and told her all that had happened. They went together to the site where the other daughter had died, and, following the track of blood that the devil had made when eating her, they found in an acorn shell a little drop of blood, and, covering it with another shell of the same kind, the mother put it in her bosom and took it to her house, where she put it in a little earthen jar, and, covering it well, put it in a corner. In the night she heard a noise like something gnawing in the jar, and, going to investigate, she found that from the drop of congealed blood had grown a child as large as her finger. She covered it again, and the following night, hearing the same noise, she found the child had grown to the stature of a large man. She was very much pleased. And when he took his bows and arrows and asked for his mother, they told him all the devil had done and he went out to look for him. When he found him he shot him so far with the point of his arrow that he never appeared again. He came to his grandmother and aunt and said to them: 'It is not good to be upon the earth,' and told them that he would now ascend to the 'Cachao,' for so they called the Heaven. He has been there ever since governing the world. And this Caddi Ayo or Captain Above, is the first or highest deity they worship, and they believe that he is able to reward the good and punish the evil which they commit."

These same tribes of the Hasanias have also a particular form of worship with fire. "There is a certain house in which there is a perpetual fire. And there is a certain old man who has charge of it and keeps it alive, and he is the 'Chenesi'—or their grand high priest. They believe that if the fire should go out they would all die. This house which they renovated in December, 1716, is between the Naiches and the Hainai, and is common to both towns and is said to be the house of the 'Great Captain.' It is large, round and made of straw and has a canopy made of mats, and on the bed are three coverings, two of them very small. At each side of the door there are other mats in a roll. Before the bed is a bench with four legs, and upon the bench they are accustomed to place tobacco and pipes, with feathers and earthen vessels which they use in their idolatrous rites for incense. The fire is always made of four very large and heavy tree-trunks and are always placed to point to the four principal winds. The wood is brought and placed in piles outside.

"Here the old men come together for their consultations and war dances, and when they need water for their crops here they meet and make supplication. The ashes from this fire they pile up outside, and when they move the bones of the enemy they have killed, they bury them in these ashes.

"Near this large house are two smaller ones within rifle shot, and they call these two houses 'Coninicis.' These, they say, are two boys, or children, that their Grand Captain sent from the sky that they might be consulted on any doubts. They think these little gods have been in their houses for two years. [It was at the time that the two religions of the Holy Cross were negotiating for entrance to Texas that they made their appearance.] And, according to the Indian interpreter, when their enemies, the Tojienes, burned these houses, they say they saw them go up in the smoke and they have never come down. In these little houses are four little posts with coverings of painted reed grass raised above an altar of wood. Within I found they had four or five plates or dishes of black wood, round and curiously carved, with four feet. Some were made with head and tail of an owl; others with head, tail and feet of an alligator or lizard. Besides this there were many feathers of all sizes and color—plumes of peacocks, white feathers, loosened from the breast; some banners of feathers; crowns of skins; with many bones of cranes that served for flutes and fifes, and some of reed grass; and other instruments that they used to make music for their dances. These little houses were well swept and cared for.

"The house of fire is for the Hanaii and the other tribes of Naiches, Nacogdoches and Nazonis, as the parish church or cathedral [would be to us]. From this, fire is carried to their houses. It is customary for the Naiches and Hanaii to come together in one mosque or house of fire, and for the Nacogdoches and Nazonis to gather in the mosque that is in Nacogdoches. On the principal feasts of the year all the houses or most of them take fire [serve themselves with fire] from that principal house [not that they need it]—but because when it was built they carried it from there and preserved it; and if at any time it should go out, they hold that it is an omen that all the family will die, and [therefore they continue to replenish or] bring it anew from the house of the mosque with great ceremony.

"They fear that the fire will become angry and they bring it the first tobacco, the first fruits of the corn and all their crops and of the meat they kill. They believe the fire created them, although some of them say that man came out of the sea and was scattered throughout the earth by those creatures called Niacaddi—water and fire, but they always go to the fire in all their ceremonies. They say that they were the descendants of bears, others of dogs, others of coyotes, and other animals. Asking them how it was, they answered that their forefathers seeing the evils that the demons wrought transformed themselves into these animals, though at the same time they were rational men, women, and children.

"These Indians have considerable light on the immortality of the soul. They conduct their burials and funerals in this way:

"First they bathe the dead body, dressing it in the best clothes they have, keeping it some hours in its own house where there is in the meantime much moaning. They provide a great quantity of pinole, corn, and all they have to eat. If it is a man, they add his bow, arrows, knife, and other things that he may need—and if a woman, all the womanly implements, mill for grinding, earthen vessels, and so on, because they will need them where they go.

"On asking them where the souls of those who die go, they say that when they go from the body they journey on to the side of the setting sun, and from there they continue on through the air to where the Grand Captain is—Caddi Ayo; and from there they go to stop at a house situated to the south called the house of death (and what is death but eternal life?) and there they imagine, and the old men persuade them, that they are very happy—and that they all remain in the state that death found them, that is if a woman dies nursing a baby, she always walks burdened, and many other erroneous beliefs. But they do not say that husband and wife live in an eternal married life.

"I asked if everybody went to this place without pain, and they said: 'Yes, unless they are wicked.' They have for the wicked, the house of Tescino, that is, the Devil, and there he punishes them severely. They do not believe that adulterers, concubines, thieves, etc., merit this inferno, because they can conceive only of perceptible evil.

"The funerals of those who die in war or absent from home are conducted in this form: They invite all the people for a certain day, and prepare all the food they have at the time. Distant a stone's throw from the house they make a pyre of prepared wood. Men and women seated together on the bed are all mourning, and a captain entering speaks a few words with them and then begins a moaning—we should more properly say a howling—which the mourning women answer. Then seven men go out of the house and, turning their faces to the east, pray, having before them a small vessel with ground and moistened corn; and the petition of the principal old man being finished, they take from the little vessel part of the moistened corn and scatter it to the four winds, and three of them who serve as sponsors of the funeral eat the remainder of the corn, and all return together to the house and renew the clamor. All the captains seat themselves in their order, and the sponsors seat themselves together and offer to an old Santones tobacco and flour, and taking it, he returns to the fire, makes a prayer, and casts some of it into the fire, and returns the remainder to the sponsors. This done, two or three Indians go out and deliver a bow and arrow to the mother or wife of the deceased. Then the Captains, one by one, go offering to the director (or master of ceremonies) some six, some eight arrows, according to the rank or state of each. The women follow giving their condolences, and contributing knives and clothes. Adding to this all the precious things or jewels that belong to the deceased, they roll it all together and cover it with a mat. Meanwhile an old man and a youth are singing in a high key a funeral hymn, and one of the sponsors puts the roll on his shoulders; another carries fire; another a bundle of grass; and going to the funeral pyre they scatter the fire to all parts, and casting on it the mat with the arrows and clothes, reduce them to ashes. Some of the company are now mourning and grieving, while others are laughing and chatting. To crown the function they have a dinner that is free to all the company, and the company is dismissed. They say they do this so that when the soul goes to the house of rest, and the body and soul come together, they may find all that is needed."

Miss Adina de Zavala's summary of Espinosa's description of Tejas Indian beliefs is taken from *Round the Levee* (PTFS I, 1916), Stith Thompson, ed.

The Legends of the Tigua

By THOMAS A. GREEN, JR.

A TRIBE of Indians lives east of El Paso, Texas. They call themselves the Tigua of Ysleta del Sur Pueblo. In the three hundred years following their migration from the pueblo of Isleta del Norte (just outside of Albuquerque, New Mexico) they have built a life rich in ceremony, filled with the reverently told legends of a past built from courage and dignity.

As has occurred far too often, the Tiguas were, in effect, rubber-stamped out of existence due to an accident of history. When the rest of the Pueblos were given reservations by Abraham Lincoln, the people of Ysleta del Sur, residing in the Confederate state of Texas, were left to fend for themselves. This is one reason why, until 1968, few people knew of their existence and fewer people cared. In April 1968, with President Lyndon Johnson's signing of Public Law 90-287, the Tigua people were given recognition and some attempts at restitution have been made.

Contrary to what Stan Steiner has written (*The Tiguas: The Lost Tribe of City Indians*), the Tigua have never been a "lost" tribe in any relevant sense of the word. In the spring of 1972, two weeks after beginning my work with the Tigua, I had the opportunity to take a trip with Pablo Silvas, presently the tribal governor of Ysleta del Sur, and Mathew Padilla, a member of the Isleta del Norte pueblo. After setting the scene as it would be, "and someday when you tell these stories," as it was at that time, "you will say there was a *viejo*, Pablo, who spoke and one called Green who was there," Governor Silvas began to tell of how it had been at the time of "the oldest people." From this beginning until the early hours of the morning when he concluded with, *"Yo soy indio!* I am an Indian, and, you see, this is what no one can take away," there was no hint of being lost. In the legends there was no hint of a lost sense of tradition, and in the man there was no alienation.

Here are some of the stories Pablo tells of "the oldest people" and of the things "no one can take away."

People say that the Tigua ran away with the Spanish after that fight in New Mexico [Pueblo Revolt of 1680], but that is not true. I know, because the oldest people used to tell me. They got here long time before. There were Indians here. There were old pueblos in the sandhills and level places where they would plant at Hueco. That's why the Spanish people don't stop here. That's why they move down to Juarez to stay. They were afraid of the Tigua.

The first people came a long time ago. They followed Coronado— to kill him. Coronado came to New Mexico to take the things the Indians had, to kill the people, even the women and the little babies, but he wore armor and the people couldn't kill him with their arrows. He wore the gold he took from the Indians here on his arms and around his neck, and he wore a crown made out of gold on his head, a *corona*, and that is how he got his name of Coronado, from that *corona*, you see.

So these Tigua people got the idea to kill him, and they followed him. They were like servants and pretended to be afraid, and waited all the time to catch him without his armor on. So one day Coronado decided he would not need to worry about these people any more and he took off this thing he wore over his chest. *Como se dice,* Green?

"His breastplafe?"

Sí. He leave it off, and when they see him, *chinga el cabrón* (Pablo mimed pulling back a bow and releasing an arrow), they shoot him with a poison arrow.

Then when those people kill Coronado, they come back here to Ysleta to live. Maybe they are mad with those people at del Norte because they will not help to kill Coronado, who can say? But that is how the oldest people say we got here.

The Tigua found out that the Comanche was staying over here at the sandhills. That's the way Damacio used to tell me. So during the night time, Bernardo Holguin took some people over there. He don't let them smoke. If they want to smoke, they got to make a little hole, and stay there to smoke, so the Comanche won't see the fire.

On the next morning, early on the morning, Bernardo Holguin, he is the one who opened that fight. There was a Comanche over there. He was watching to see if somebody's coming. Early on the morning, when the sun is just coming up, they shoot the first Comanche over there and they kill him. Then all the Tiguas run to fight with those Comanches and they kill a lot of 'em. Then the Comanches start to run away.

They run through Hueco, and they get in a place over there, they call it *La Sala,* a big cave, but you can only go in by one at a time, and there is a hole in the top of the cave. The Tiguas was tracking behind those Comanches, but when they find them they couldn't get them out.

So they sent some men back over here to Ysleta to get some of that green peppers. They build a fire over that hole in the top of the cave, and dump some of that green chili on it to see if they can get those Comanches out with the smoke, but they couldn't make it.

So then the next morning, the Comanches, they start to sing, because they believe in God, the great spirit, we call him *Abuelito.* Early on the morning, they start to sing. Then it starts to blow, the wind, and they sing a little more, and it comes a little more wind and a little more and more until the whole place got dusty. Dusty! Until they couldn't even see. And so all those Comanches got away from that cave.

If it didn't start to blow on that time, the Tiguas would have killed all the Comanches in that place. That is the way Damacio used to tell me.

Aside from the documentable content of such examples of Tigua oral history, the legends have obviously served as charters or models for action among the tribe. The killing of Coronado is pointed to as earning the Tigua the right to the land they now occupy. The fight for Tigua land rights has been seen by many of my informants to be a direct descendant of Bernardo Holguin's battle with the Comanche. They tell these stories in the same breath with anecdotes of the more recent legal battle.

The Tigua, then, are not—have never been—a "lost tribe.": How can any man knowing what he was, what he is, and where he must go, ever be called lost?

The research for this paper was completed under a grant from the Center of Urban Ethnography at the University of Pennsylvania.

Myths
of the Alabama-Coushatta Indians

By HOWARD N. MARTIN

The Creation of the Earth

In the beginning everything was covered by water. The only living things were a few small animals who occupied a raft floating about on the water. Nothing else could be seen above the surface of the water

One day the animals decided that they wanted to make the land appear; so they called for a volunteer to make the attempt. Crawfish volunteered, and he dived off the raft. The water was so deep, however, that he was unable to reach the bottom of the great ocean.

Three days later Crawfish again tried to reach the bottom, but again he failed. On the third trial, though, he reached the bottom. Using his tail to scoop up the mud, he began building a great mud chimney. He worked rapidly, building it higher and higher, until the top of the mud chimney stuck up above the surface of the water. The mud began spreading to all sides, forming a great mass of soft earth.

The animals looked in all directions. They agreed that Crawfish had done a good job, but they thought that the surface of the earth was too smooth. So Buzzard was sent out to shape the earth's surface. Now Buzzard was a huge bird with long, powerful wings. He flew along just above the top of the soft earth, flapping his wings. When his wings swung down, they cut deep holes or valleys in the soft earth. When his wings swung up, they formed the hills and mountains. When Buzzard didn't flap his wings and just sailed along, he made the level country or plains. And so the surface of the earth is made up of plains, valleys, and mountains.

The Origin of the Alabama-Coushatta Indians

Indians were made from clay down in a big cave under the earth. In this cave they lived a long time before some of them decided to go up to the surface of the earth. After they started upward, they camped three times on the way. Finally, they reached the mouth of the cave.

There they found a large tree standing. The Alabamas and Coushattas went out of the cave on opposite sides of a root of this big tree. Thus, these two tribes differed somewhat in speech, but they have always lived near each other.

At first the Indians would stay outside only during the night, returning to the cave when day came. One night when the Indians were so frightened that they ran back into the cave, they never returned to the surface of the earth. That is why the Alabamas and Coushattas are so few. If the owl had not hooted, then all the Indians would have remained on the surface of the earth, and the Alabamas and Coushattas would have been more numerous.

One day a white man came to the cave and saw some tracks in the sand. He wanted to find out who had made the tracks, so he went to the place three times but did not see anyone. He finally decided to play a trick on these strange people. Early one morning he put a barrel of whiskey near the place where he found the footprints. When the Indians came out of the cave that night to play, they saw the barrel and wondered what was in it. One of them tasted the contents. Soon he began to feel good and sing and dance. Then the others drank also and became so drunk that the white man was able to catch them. After that the Alabamas and Coushattas had to stay on top of the earth and were not allowed to go near the big cave.

Mr. Martin's myths are taken from "Folktales of the Alabama-Coushatta Indians" in *Mexican Border Ballads* (PTFS XXI, 1946), Mody C. Boatright, ed.

THE SPANISH

José Pantalion of Chireno, ca. 1870. Courtesy Ross Pantalion.

Nacogdoches town square, 1882. Courtesy East Texas Collection, Stephen F. Austin State University.

Old Stone Fort, Nacogdoches, 1885. Courtesy East Texas Collection, Stephen F. Austin State University.

The Venerable Antonio Margil. Courtesy East Texas Collection, Stephen F. Austin State University.

Father Francisco Hidalgo. Courtesy East Texas Historical Association.

Antonio Gil Y'Barbo's sword.

Spanish Bluff Crossing, where the Smuggler's and Spanish Bluff Road crossed the Angelina River.

Texas Folklife Festival.

The Spanish on the Moral

By FRANCIS EDWARD ABERNETHY

IF THERE ARE remnants of Spanish rather than Mexican culture in Texas they are in Nacogdoches County in East Texas. The Spanish came to East Texas to settle for the first time in 1690. They left discouraged in 1693. They came again in 1716, this time with a more determined purpose and in significant numbers. They were scared off by the Natchitoches French in 1719. In 1721 Spanish settlers and soldiers came to stay and their descendants are still there, most located in an area that outsiders refer to as The Moral, in the southwestern part of Nacogdoches County.

The story of the Spanish in East Texas begins with the legend of The Lady in Blue, brought from old Spain to New Spain by a Franciscan friar.

Father Damian Massanet was in his late twenties when he landed at Vera Cruz in the New World in 1683. He was a young and vigorous man who wore his brown cassock and knotted-cord belt with the confidence of one who had come to seek and to save and would surely prevail over the heathen. He had a purpose that was as consuming as the gold fever that obsessed Coronado and his children. He was going to bring the Indians into the arms of the Mother Church, a mission that was inspired by the miracle and legend of Maria de Jesus de Agreda, sometimes called The Lady in Blue.

Maria was born into a very devout Catholic family in Agreda in Castille in 1602. She took the vow of chastity when she was eight and when she was sixteen persuaded her parents to convert their house into a convent and take the vows themselves. As a nun in this convent Maria wore no shoes but sandals made of wood or straw. She wore a cassock of coarse brown sackcloth next to the skin, covered by a white habit tied by the knotted cord of St. Francis, and over all this she wore a mantle of blue for the Virgin Mary.

Maria was deeply and mystically contemplative from her youth, and in 1621 when she was eighteen her contemplations became miracles. She began going into trances, and in this state was transported to the New World in a wild and primitive country and moved among savages, who, when she spoke, understood her even though she spoke in Spanish. And when they spoke she understood them even though they spoke in their own language. She visited different tribes during the period between 1620 and 1631, sometimes completing as many as four visitations a day, and she told them about Christ and the Mother and God's wounds and Mary's tears for the suffering of mankind. She was martyred on one visit, receiving many wounds and a crown from God for her suffering. This happened, she said, in the Indian kingdom of the Ticlas, or Theas, in the northeastern part of New Spain. Father Damian concluded that she spoke of the Tejas Indians and the land of the Hasinai Caddoes.

Father Damian was serving the Mission San Salvador in Coahuila at the time that he was collecting information about these Theas, or Tejas, who lived in houses, tilled fields, and worshipped one great sky god whom they called Caddi Ayo, the Great Captain. His chance to meet them came in 1689 when he accompanied Alonzo de Leon on an expedition to search out and destroy all Frenchmen in New Spain. They found the burnt remains of La Salle's fort, and they made their first contact with the Tejas Indians. De Leon reported that the Tejas Indians performed many Christian rites and that the chief asked for missionaries, saying that many years before a beautiful lady in blue had come down from the hills and brought them a new god and told them to go to the white man for more news of this god.

Father Damian was to hear the Tejas story of the Lady in Blue again. In 1690 when he and de Leon went to the country of the Tejas to found missions, the old chief asked for blue cloth to bury his mother in. When asked why, he said that in his mother's day a beautiful lady in blue had come to the village to talk to them and minister to the sick. She had been remembered and venerated by his people ever since.

The end of this part of the legend occurred in 1693. Father Damian founded San Francisco de los Tejas near the Neches River in 1690 and then returned to Coahuila. When he returned the following year he found that although the memory of the Lady in Blue remained in Indian stories her precepts were poorly attended. The Indians were openly hostile toward the Spanish and indifferent to Catholic teaching. Completely disillusioned, Father Damian and his friars left the Tejas in 1693, and San Francisco moldered back into the red dirt on which it was built.

The Lady in Blue legend continued to circulate among the Indians and Spanish of East Texas, and in later years she returned to bring comfort to other East Texas settlers. In the early 1840's, during the late winter and early spring, the Sabine overflowed and isolated many of the river-bottom settlers. The black-tongue plague, or malaria, struck, and whole families sickened and many died. In the midst of the plague a mysterious lady in blue appeared to look after the sick. She stayed and cheered and healed the sick until the plague abated; then she disappeared as mysteriously as she came.

According to other stories the ghost nun still wanders the Camino del Caballo, the old Smugglers Road that skirted the customs and outposts at Nacogdoches. She cries sadly from time to time, perhaps in mourning for the vanished Tejas which she came to save.

The Camino Real—the King's Highway, or the Old San Antonio Road—had its historical beginning during this first period of Spanish occupation. Don Domingo Terán de los Rios, the leader of the 1691 expedition, is reputed to have blazed the road from Coahuila to Mission San Francisco. The trail that ran from there through Nacogdoches and San Augustine to Los Adaes on the eastern frontier had been open many years because of the Natchitoches French trade with the East Texas Indians. St. Denis' use of the road after 1713 gave him a legendary claim to having laid it out. It was well traveled by the time the Spanish began settling along it after 1721.

The history of the Spanish in East Texas begins again in 1716 when the Spanish once more react to the French threat. This time the Spanish established a buffer zone of missions stretching from the Neches River through Nacogdoches and San Augustine to the eastern boundary of Texas near Natchitoches, Louisiana. The folklore of the second phase of Spanish history is dominated by the personality and the legends of Father Antonio Margil de Jesús.

Father Margil was a knotted cord of a man, slim of build but powerful and with the endurance of a Spanish mule. He came to New Spain in 1683 along with Father Damian Massanet and Father Francisco Hidalgo, the friar who maneuvered the Spanish into returning to the East Texas frontier in 1716. Father Margil was twenty-six at the time. During his forty-three years as a Franciscan friar in the New World he walked barefooted from southern Costa Rica to Natchitoches, Louisiana, not once but several times, with side trips to Yucatan in the east and the Sierra Madres in the west. During these years he carried no food, only a staff, a cross, and a breviary, and he wore a skull around his neck to remind him of man's mortality. He ate one meal a day consisting of a broth and some herbs—no red meat or fowl. He took a one-hour siesta but slept only three hours at night, the remaining time being spent on his knees in prayer, sometimes with arms outstretched in remembrance of Christ's suffering. During some of his sermons he scourged himself, mortifying the flesh as an example to his flock, sometimes so brutally that the blood flowed and the people wept.

As a missionary he suffered all the dangers and indignities of a new prophet in a strange land, and the stories of his trials grew into legend. Indians beat him and poisoned him but could not kill him. One tribe tried to burn him but the wood refused to ignite. On his way to Nacogdoches he was chased by hostile Indians who almost caught him when he came to a flooding river. He was carried safely over, however, in the arms of God, and the river has since been known as Los Brazos de Dios, The Arms of God.

By the time Father Margil came to East Texas in 1716 he was already a man of legendary proportions, both to the unlettered Indians and Mexicans and to his own Franciscan Order, which frequently called on him to arbitrate disputes and to occupy high offices. He made the long walk from Piedras Negras to Nacogdoches and Los Adaes, the Spanish mission across from the French fort at Natchitoches, after a bout of illness which his friends had considered terminal, when he was sixty years old, and with a double hernia.

It was as the Guardian of the College of Guadalupe at Zacatecas that he came to Nacogdoches with the Ramon Expedition of 1716, and it was during his first visit that he performed a miracle that has since been a part of the culture of Nacogdoches and its Spanish population.

The years 1717-1718 were drouth and famine years in East Texas and the Indians and the Spaniards suffered terribly from a lack of water. Returning to Nacogdoches from a visitation to the eastern missions, Father Margil knelt in prayer on the banks of La Nana. He prayed to God for relief and rose and struck the bank with his staff. Cool and saving water poured forth from two small springs. Over a hundred years later, in 1828, José María Sánchez described the springs: "On the west bank of *La Nana*, there are a few boulders from which two small springs of cold and clear water flow and keep two circular basins about half a *vara* in diameter and a little less in depth always full. The two springs are known as *los ojos del Padre Margil.*"[1]

The Eyes of Father Margil have since dried up but the story survives. Stephen F. Austin heard the legend and wrote it down in the journal he kept while he was in prison in Querétaro, one of Father Margil's college homes. Austin tells another story of Father Margil's adventures while ministering to the East Texas Spanish. The padre was traveling from Nacogdoches to Bexar when a tiger (panther?) killed his baggage mule. When he learned of the deed the next morning, he made the tiger kneel, and he loaded him with the dead mule's baggage. The tiger carried it all the way to Bexar, where he was unloaded, pardoned, and sent back to his hunting ground. "All this is true," said Austin wryly, "because several old women told it to me in Nacogdoches and Bexar, and we ought not to suppose that Rome would order an engraving to be made of a miracle of the water [referring to the springs] , only to deceive credulous people."[2]

Father Antonio Margil de Jesús finally wore out his tough old body and died at the age of sixty-nine in Mexico City. On that summer day in 1726 all the death bells in New Spain tolled in mourning.

Another legendary character of the 1716-1719 Spanish occupation was the Hasinai Indian maiden Angelina, for whom the river was named. Angelina was taken during the 1690-1693 occupation to the Mission San Juan Bautista on the Rio Grande, where she was educated. She returned to East Texas sometime before 1713, probably with the help of Father Francisco Hidalgo, who was working privately with the French to resettle East Texas with Spanish missions. Angelina met St. Denis and acted as liaison between the French, Spanish, and Indians before and during the 1716 Spanish re-occupation. More romantically, she is reputed to have been the lover of Simars de Bellisle, the young French explorer whom the Hasinai and French rescued from the coastal Atakapan Indians. Bellisle tells in his journal of staying with her in the Hasinai village for several months before obtaining passage to Natchitoches. By this time, 1720, however, Angelina was no longer the "young Indian maiden" of story and picture; she was Indian forty-ish.

This second Spanish occupation of East Texas ended in 1719, when hostilities between Spain and France in Europe prompted a French attack on Los Adaes and an ensuing desertion of all Spanish outposts. When Spain returned for the third time in 1721 under the

Marquis de Aguayo she came determined to stay and backed that determination with soldiers and settlers. The families who came with Aguayo in 1721 were the beginnings of the present-day Spanish in East Texas.

One of the main pieces of Nacogdoches folklore is the widely circulated myth that the Spanish of the Moral and adjoining areas are pure Spanish, descendants of settlers who came here straight from Spain. Spanish family legends relate that the first families came from Spain by way of the Canary Islands to New Orleans. From there they went up the Mississippi to the Red River and then up the Red to Natchitoches, and from there they crossed the Arroyo Hondo to settle in Los Adaes and along the Camino Real toward Nacogdoches. Y'Barbo family tradition brings them directly from the neighborhood of Seville in Andalusía.

Local legends grow from half-remembered experiences that are divided over and over again by generations of leaky memories. Logically, though, they must go back to something historical and satisfy something psychological. The idea of Andalusian origin satisfies an ego desire to have "pure" blood, following the folklore that there is such a thing. The original legend possibly goes back to the fact that the Adaesans neighbored and intermarried with the Natchitoches French, many of whom did come from the old country, landed at New Orleans, came up the Mississippi and the Red, and finally settled around Natchitoches. The history of the East Texas Spanish tells a different story.

In 1720 Spain decided that a settled East Texas was necessary as a buffer zone against the French, and in the following year Aguayo occupied the eastern frontier of Texas at Los Adaes with one hundred soldiers, thirty-one of whom had families. The purity myth is refuted by a survey of 117 conscripts for the Aguayo Expedition who were taken at Zelaya in April, 1720. We can assume that this is typical of other Spanish conscriptions for the expedition. Forty-four were Spanish, seventeen were *mestizos,* twenty-one were *coyotes,* thirty-one were mulattoes, two were *castizos,* and there was one *lobo,* one free Negro, and one Indian. The breed titles refer to various and varying mixtures of Spanish, Indian, and/or Negro blood. Of this group, 107 were taken from the local jail. Of the ten remaining, only one was a volunteer. Their march to Texas began at the hoosgow.[3]

So what we have in the beginning of Spanish settlement in East

Texas is one hundred soldiers, only thirty-one of whom have wives. This leaves the remainder to search where they can for women, and the closest opportunity is across the Arroyo Hondo in French Natchitoches. The result was that many Spanish males took French and French-Indian females, women whose family traditions were French and whose family tales accurately included stories of trips from the Old World to New Orleans and up the big rivers to their new homes on the frontier. Thus French stories were blended with Spanish stories, and because the Adaesans were the dominant culture west of Arroyo Hondo, gradually the tales became Spanish legend.

The Spanish settlers left at Los Adaes were not pure Spanish, or at least they were not any purer than the Americans or any of the other multi-breeds that came to Texas during its settlement. But they were makers, and they survived the French, the Indians and a hostile wilderness, the repressiveness of the Spanish church and state, and finally the hurt of becoming second citizens in their own land. The Spanish in East Texas had less than a hundred years of normal day-to-day living before they were submerged by the Americans, and the brief period was interrupted by a hegira of Biblical proportions.

The story of the Spanish exodus in 1773 and the man who brought them back to Nacogdoches five years later is one of the classic Texas examples of endurance and survival.

Spanish settlement on the Texas frontier had for its official purpose the establishing of a zone of protection against the French. When the zone was no longer needed—after Louisiana was ceded to Spain in 1762—the official view was that the settlers were no longer needed. This was the gist of the Marquis de Rubi's report after his inspection of the frontier in 1767. His recommendation was that the extremities of the Spanish frontier in East Texas be abandoned in favor of a more realistic and defensible northern boundary stretching east to west from Matagorda Bay through San Antonio and Santa Fe to the Gulf of California. The result was that five hundred East Texas Spanish were forcibly evicted from their homes and resettled in the San Antonio area.

The resettlement failed because generations of Spanish had put down their roots in East Texas and because of the tenacity of one man, Antonio Gil Y'Barbo.

The Spanish settlers who were sent to Los Adaes in 1721 had grown from thirty-one families to five hundred people by 1773 and their homesteads followed the Camino Real from Los Adaes to Nacogdoches. Y'Barbo had taken land on the Road just west of the Sabine River on Lobanillo Creek, and by 1773 was the most influential man among the settlers. Although the sign of his comparative wealth and prestige was El Lobanillo, his source of income was a thriving smuggling trade among the French, Indian, Americans, and Spanish, a trade expressly forbidden by the Spanish authorities but accepted as a norm by the colonists.

The Spanish were surviving and expanding and no one was ready to leave his home when the Spanish soldiers began driving them out for the three-month walk to San Antonio in the summer of '73.

The journey to San Antonio was a disaster and their attempted resettlement was never successful. Y'Barbo began a petition as soon as he arrived, requesting permission to return to East Texas. A year and a trip to Mexico City later, with the help of bureaucratic inefficiency and his own determination, Y'Barbo led his people east again in a compromise settlement at Bucarelli, near where the San Antonio Road crosses the Trinity.

From Bucarelli Y'Barbo resumed his illegal trade with the east, and for almost four years the little settlement survived in spite of floods and the general impoverishment. Their eyes were always on their old homeland to the east, though, and in 1779 after a series of Comanche raids, Y'Barbo moved his people back to East Texas in spite of official disapproval. The Spanish settlers stopped this time in Nacogdoches, where they have been ever since.

Antonio Gil Y'Barbo did not pursue a holy vision or miraculously bring forth springs, but his strength and leadership established him as a man of legendary proportions in the history of the East Texas Spanish. His monument is the Old Stone Fort, which he built soon after his return to Nacogdoches in 1779.

In spite of his known extra-legal activities Y'Barbo was officially named as the Lieutenant-Governor of Nacogdoches because he was the only man who could hold the colonists together, deal satisfactorily with the Indians, and maintain some political correspondence with the French and the Americans to the East. One of his contributions was his Criminal Code of 1783.[4] Y'Barbo considered that his people needed strong laws to protect them and their society against the results of its passions. He therefore instituted a beautifully medieval set of ordinances: Against blasphemy, treason, witchcraft, #15: "Any person who shall be found guilty of witchcraft or poisoning, shall be hanged after having been quartered alive." For dueling, bestiality, #25: "Any person who shall have carnal connexion with a beast, shall suffer death, and afterwards have his body burnt with the said beast." For pandering, #26: "Any man who shall assent to the prostitution of his wife, will for the first offense, be exposed in public, being feathered, rubbed with honey, wearing a fool's cap with a string of garlic, and a pair of horns, receive one hundred lashes and be sent to the galleys for ten years; for the second offense, he shall remain in the galleys for life." Other ordinances concerned the usual crimes and vices.

Among the criminal element subject to these laws was one Juan José Peña, called El Bocon, The Braggart. He was an outlaw of unbelievable skill and daring. The story of one series of escapades was sent in a report from Y'Barbo to the governor in 1792.[5]

The crime wave began when Peña robbed an Indian trader of his goods and then stole six horses on his way to Nacogdoches. Y'Barbo captured him and locked him in the Stone Fort. Peña promptly escaped, stole arms and ammunition, a horse and a cow. He tried to rape an Indian girl, but was captured by the Indians, turned over to the Spanish, and this time put in stocks in the Stone Fort. He escaped again and stole clothing, horses, and cows. Farmers in the area of his depredations formed a posse and captured him. This time Y'Barbo chained and stocked him in the Fort. He escaped again, mistakenly broke into Y'Barbo's house, then left town after stealing all the clothes that were drying on lines. He was captured again. When he escaped after this capture he took all the balls and chains and irons he had been tied down with and headed for an Indian camp, stealing horses as he went. Y'Barbo caught him again and placed him in double handcuffs and double ankle chains. He escaped with all irons. He was free for several weeks on this occasion, robbing the area of clothes, arms, and horses. When Y'Barbo caught him this time he sent him to the authorities at San Antonio. There is no further word on El Bocon, but one cannot help but believe that he continued his adventures. A spirit such as his can be eliminated through execution but it cannot be squelched.

Much of the Spanish folklore that remains in Nacogdoches County deals with El Camino del Caballo, the Road of the Horse, or the Old Smuggler's Road.[6] This hidden trail through the deep river-bottom woods was much used by Y'Barbo and his smuggler friends and can still be seen in certain areas. It bypassed the customs station and authorities in Nacogdoches and ran parallel to the Old San Antonio Road. According to tradition it was laid out by St. Denis, who used it for bringing out Texas horses and in his contraband trade with the Indians.

From the opening of East Texas by the Spanish in 1690 until 1845, when Texas joined the Union, Nacogdoches was the gateway and customs collector for all trade coming into the state. Spain absolutely prohibited trade with the French, and Mexico imposed a discouraging tariff. The result was a flourishing contraband trade, which everybody knew about but nobody was able to restrain. Trade policies with the United States were eased during the Republic, but there were still duties to pay—and a century-old smuggling habit to overcome—so the road stayed in use until 1845 when Texas statehood cancelled out customs fees.

Legends of lost and buried treasure are the most prevalent stories surrounding the old road. The old Salinas crossing of the Angelina is now covered by Sam Rayburn Lake. At one time a trail from the Smuggler's Road crossed there to connect with a lower branch of the Camino Real. According to one tale two Dutchmen robbed a Spanish army pack train of its gold and were heading back east with their loot. The soldiers caught up with them near Salinas Crossing and killed one of them. The other man escaped but he had to leave the gold behind. He buried his partner and the gold in the same grave and left the country, never to return as far as anyone knows. The gold is still there somewhere, nestled among the outlaw's moldering bones.

The Indians who lived on Henson's Island near the Spanish Bluff crossing of the Road were reputed to have had much gold which they used in trade with the settlers. They stored their treasure in a cave near the village, and when they died out or drifted off are supposed to have abandoned their wealth. The cave has since fallen in and despite some treasure hunting none of the original gold has reappeared.

Another outlaw who hid out near the Road was jumped by some of his fellows. He had time to hide a "double handful of diamonds and a tow sack of gold in a stump hole" before he escaped. He was killed later, before he told anybody where the treasure was.

There are other legends of pack trains robbed and gold and silver buried along El Camino del Caballo. And there is the legend of the

Lady in Blue, who wanders the Road in mourning for all those who died there and for her Indians who lost their lands and their lives to the white men who traveled the Smuggler's Road.

There might have been something supernatural also about the concept of Manifest Destiny that brought an end to the Spanish in East Texas. Once the Americans started west, nothing seemed to stop them. The Spanish on the Texas frontier, who were supposed to act as deterrents to foreign immigration, barely slowed the Americans down.

Traders and hunters were coming in and through Nacogdoches before 1800. After the Louisiana Purchase in 1803 the rate of entry increased and more were settling in East Texas despite Spain's reluctance to admit their boisterous neighbors. Many Americans believed, or said they did, in the old French claim that the Rio Grande was Louisiana's western boundary. Some did not even go to the trouble to rationalize their greed for new lands to open.

Invasion and rebellion marked the last years of Spain's and Mexico's hold on East Texas: the Gutiérrez-Magee Expedition of 1812-1813 and the James Long Expeditions of 1819 and 1820 both washed through the Spanish colony at Nacogdoches. When the tide receded, a runaway scrape would follow with most of the American and some of the Spanish settlers fleeing across the Sabine to escape retribution from the pursuing armies. When Stephen F. Austin passed through Nacogdoches in 1821 the town's population had been reduced to thirty-six. The Stone Fort, a church, and six houses were all that were left standing. The Spanish had deserted the town, always a political hotbed, for the country, primarily to the Moral area and around Chireno.

Haden Edwards came in 1826 demanding untitled land held by old Spanish colonists for his new American colonists. The Mexican reaction to this high-handedness caused him to initiate the Fredonian Rebellion to free Texas and found the Fredonian Republic. Even Stephen F. Austin marched against him. The Fredonian Rebellion failed but the Battle of Nacogdoches six years later had a large following of American and Spanish colonists supporting it, and this victory cleared the Mexican army out of East Texas forever. The battle also put the Mexican army west of San Antonio, allowing the Texians to gather and group in preparation for the Texas Revolution. By the time of the Revolution in 1836 American residents of the Nacogdoches area were easily able to outvote the old time Spanish.

The East Texas Spanish reacted against the Texas Revolution and the American takeover with the Cordova Rebellion. Vicente Cordova had a ranch east of Nacogdoches on the Camino Real. He had prestige with the Spanish and American colonists alike and fought for their freedom under the Mexican flag. But when he saw that the freedom that the Americans were fighting for was Texas freedom he began to move in a different direction.

In 1835 and in 1836 Cordova had tried to mount an attack against the Texian war party in Nacogdoches, but he could not get the necessary support from the Mexican government.

In 1838 in a belated reaction against Texas Independence he joined forces with the Cherokees and began a rebellion against the Texian forces in East Texas. His attempt was unsuccessful and in the end he was forced to flee to Mexico. The result of the Cordova Rebellion was that some of the Spanish lands were confiscated, and the Spanish who were left were forced into a very low social and political profile.

The Cordova Rebellion was the last flicker of energy and enthusiasm from the Spanish in East Texas, but it was a flame that was only finally extinguished by the Texans. The repressive and frustrating policies of both the Church and the State had dampened Spanish ambitions long before the Americans posed a problem.

The Spanish conquistadors and the padres of the sixteenth and seventeenth centuries came to the New World charged with initiative. They became financially rich with the lands they conquered and spiritually rich by the souls they saved. De Leon and Father Massanet, Ramon and Father Margil, Aguayo and Father Hidalgo: they had the adventurer's spirit and drive and independence, qualities that atavistically cropped up later in such men as Antonio Gil Y'Barbo and Vicente Cordova. For the most part, however, Spanish policy in East Texas was a knee-jerk reaction to French moves, and the settlers were thought of as French-deterrents, not as people trying to build new lives and communities on a new land. Strict conformity and obedience were rewarded. Experimentation and ingenuity in coping with their new environment were punished. Ambition, which frequently rocks the social boat, was discouraged.

Thus it was that when the unrestrainably energetic and boisterously ambitious Americans began tumbling in, the Spanish were no match for them. After 1838 Spanish names crop up from time to time in area politics, but the Spanish as a political block or a social force never had any measurable power. The main group quietly remained on their lands on the Moral and along the Spanish Bluff road. They intermarried in the Spanish community mostly, although there were some marriages with Americans, Indians, and Mexicans from south Texas communities.

Most of the eighteenth century Spanish names—Y'Barbo, Cordova, Arriola, Peña—are still flourishing in Nacogdoches County. The Spanish are a little darker of skin than their Anglo neighbors, and there is still a trace of Spanish accent in their talk. Spanish as a family language, however, began to die out two generations ago. The social separation that existed as late as a generation back is rapidly breaking down, primarily as a result of county school consolidation. The Spanish population inevitably will blend in more and more with the Anglo population, but their pride in themselves and the antiquity of their culture will not let them be totally absorbed in any forseeable future.

The research for this paper was conducted with the assistance of a Stephen F. Austin Faculty Research Grant and with the help of Willie Earl Tindall, SFA Social Sciences Librarian.

[1] José M. Sánchez, "A Trip to Texas in 1828," Carlos Castañeda, trans., *Southwestern Historical Quarterly*, XXIX (April, 1926), 282.

[2] Stephen F. Austin, "The 'Prison Journal' of S. F. Austin," *The Quarterly of the Texas State Historical Association*, II, #3 (January, 1899), 185.

[3] Eleanor C. Buckley, "The Aguayo Expedition into Texas and Louisiana, 1719-1722," *The Quarterly of the Texas State Historical Association*, XV, #1 (July, 1911), 25-28.

[4] Robert B. Blake, *Research Collection in Stephen F. Austin State University Library*, XLV, 244-255.

[5] *Ibid.*, XLV, 240-243.

[6] Edward A. Blount, "Location of the Old Contraband Trace in Nacogdoches County," *Junior Historian*, VI, #3 (1945), 7-11; and Harry G. Petty, "Smuggler's Road," a series of articles published in *The Daily Sentinel* between May and July, 1963.

THE FRENCH

Castroville, ca. 1910. Courtesy Bob Johnson.

Castroville Cotton Gin, Courtesy Dr. M. W. Sharp.

Castroville Blacksmith Barn. Courtesy Dr. M. W. Sharp.

St. Louis Catholic Church, Castroville. Courtesy Miss Ruth Lawler.

Joseph Courand Dry Goods Store, Castroville. Courtesy Dr. M. W. Sharp.

Cajun musicians.

Texas Folklife Festival.

Jambalaya

By JO LYDAY

ON NOVEMBER 7, 1973, the students and faculty of San Jacinto College in Pasadena, Texas, heard a lecture on some recently uncovered documents pertaining to relations between France and the Republic of Texas. The speaker, a writer of fiction under the pseudonym Pierre Nemours, is also an eminent French journalist and historian named Pierre Guillimot. Already interested in Texas history through research for a work on the Alamo written some years ago, Guillimot was recently researching French diplomatic history when he discovered the correspondence concerning the newly formed Republic of Texas. His findings indicate that the French, although they were the first European power to recognize the new republic on September 25, 1839, were nevertheless very cautious to establish diplomatic policies designed to protect an already considerable investment of French capital and French citizens in the area which became Texas.

It is not surprising to find a Frenchman involved in discussing Texas history with a group of native Texans. The lives and fortunes of Frenchmen have been a significant influence in the history of Texas for almost three hundred years, ever since Robert Cavelier, Sieur de la Salle, attempting to lead a group of colonists to the mouth of the Mississippi, inadvertently landed on the Texas coast near Sabine Pass in January 1, 1685. This body of settlers—doomed to suffer incredible adversity through famine, disease, and Indian attacks—later entered Matagorda Bay and then, having lost all their ships, moved inland to Garcitas Creek, where they built Fort St. Louis. After two years of hardships, La Salle organized a party of seventeen men to accompany him overland to Canada. Leaving the fort in January of 1687, the expedition traveled as far as the present town of Navasota, where La Salle's men murdered him in March, 1687.

Perhaps the stories of the few survivors of La Salle's ill-fated group served to discourage other Frenchmen from any concerted effort at establishing colonies in the area during the late seventeenth century and the early eighteenth century. On the other hand, La Salle's presence proved a reminder to the Spanish that a potentially rich holding seemed threatened by the near presence of Frenchmen in Louisiana; and the Spanish made determined efforts to prevent their French neighbors from exploring the territory and from trading with the Indians and the Spanish settlements.

In spite of these Spanish attempts to exclude Frenchmen from New Spain, the border was too difficult to patrol closely, and the French too daring and resourceful to control entirely. For instance, Louis Juchereau de St. Denis explored the upper Red River in 1700; and in 1714 he traveled across Texas to San Juan Bautista. A year later St. Denis made a second visit to San Juan, where he was arrested for smuggling and sent to prison in Mexico City. Released in 1717, he returned to Natchitoches, Louisiana, where he proved an able administrator and diplomat as commander of St. Jean Baptiste, a French outpost. St. Denis negotiated a truce establishing a boundary between French Louisiana and Spanish Texas, encouraged French traders in dealing with the Indians and the Spanish forts and missions, and exerted great influence over the Caddo Indian confederacy.

The intrepid explorers, traders, and politicians of the eighteenth century set the general pattern for French contributions to Texas history. Although they never arrived in large numbers, Frenchmen seemed to be everywhere at fateful moments, making dynamic and significant impressions on the Texas landscape. The gamut of their activities ranged, literally, from the sublime to the ignoble—if not the ridiculous. In the sublime category are the heroic efforts of the Catholic clergy and religious communities to restore the ministry of The Church after the Texas Revolution. No longer the official religion under the Texas Republic, Catholicism suffered the stigma of association with the hated Spanish government. Through the financial contributions of the Society for the Propagation of the Faith at Lyons, France, and the efforts of devoted clergy, the Catholic Church in Texas was reorganized and restored to effective functioning. In addition, Catholic religious communities of French origin established, throughout the state, schools, hospitals, churches, and orphanages, many of which still serve Texans today.

On the ignoble side of the ledger, one must note the Galveston Island piratical operations of Louis-Michel Aury and Jean and Pierre Lafitte. There was even a Frenchman at the Alamo, but he was Louis

(Moses) Rose, the prudent realist who chose to withdraw before the battle rather than to remain and die a hero, thereby becoming in song and legend, "The Coward at the Alamo."

Not all of the French contributions to Texas growth came from individuals, however. Some efforts, with varying degrees of success, were made to establish French communities during the nineteenth century. One of these was in 1818 when the Champ d'Asile colony was established near the site of Liberty, Texas, on the Trinity River. This was not, however, an attempt sanctioned by the French government to build a pure French community, but rather a renegade military venture, led by Frenchmen, but composed of a mixture of ethnic groups committed to one cause: to rescue Napoleon from prison on the island of St. Helena and to see him established as emperor of Mexico. When the Spanish threatened to attack the colony before they were securely established, they fled to Galveston Island, where a hurricane destroyed their temporary camp. Discouraged and frightened of Jean Laffite, some of the group retreated overland to New Orleans. To the remainder, Laffite gave an escape ship after deciding not to turn them over to the Spanish for a reward.

In contrast to the failure of the Champ d'Asile community is the successful venture led by Henri Castro. Ironically, Castro sacrificed his personal fortune to the success of the cause. Although opposed by the French government and by French diplomats in Texas, Castro managed to establish four communities between 1844 and 1847: Castroville, Quihi, Vandenburg, and D'Hanis. While the settlers of three of these were a mixture of ethnic groups, the original colonists of Castroville were immigrants from the French province of Alsace. Even in the twentieth century, this community retains its French flavor, a unique situation which reflects the genuine ethnic pride of the people. Each year on August 25, the St. Louis Catholic Church in Castroville is the center of a patronal festival which involves the entire town and draws thousands of visitors.

With the exception of Castroville, no community today shows the unmistakable stamp of French heritage in the speech, customs, and attitudes of the people; for most of these present-day descendants have been absorbed into polyglot communities where their French identity is lost. For instance, Collins La Croix lives in Houston and does not speak French. He knows that his great, great grandfather was one of three brothers who came to Nashville, Tennessee, from the Alsace-Lorraine Valley. One of these brothers disappeared under mysterious circumstances which no one in the family seems to know about. Collins' father left Tennessee for Texas when he was twenty-one; and Collins never met his father's family until he was twenty-five. Likewise, men with names like Laverne Delaplain, Paul Boudreaux, Robert Crouchet, J. P. Bonnette, and Robert Cailleteau live in the greater Houston area and, but for their names, never think of themselves as French. None of these is ashamed of his French origin, although the loss of ethnic identity may stem from a period of such feeling on the part of a previous generation. Cailleteau has relatives living in Baton Rouge, Louisiana, who still speak French and keep their French customs alive; and Crouchet has a sister living in New Iberia, Louisiana, who is a scholar of both English and French.

Frenchmen who move into Texas and settle at some distance from the Louisiana border seem to slip into the anonymous mass of the urban communities and to cut their ethnic ties. For some this may be a source of regret, or at least, nostalgia. Doris Pitre Aman tells of her father, who was from Dubisson, Louisiana. Orphaned at an early age, Mr. Pitre came as a young man to Texas. His daughter recalls that he often spoke with nostalgic longing of the days when he would go to a *fais de do* to dance all night and then work all the next day. He particularly recalled the warmth and community of the French people and missed the sense of belonging to and being a part of this larger family.

In one area there is a strong French minority which makes itself felt and known. This is in the Golden Triangle along the Louisiana border on the Texas Gulf Coast, and includes the cities of Orange, Port Arthur, and Beaumont. The French people in this area, known as "Cajuns," are descendants of the Acadians—French settlers on the Canadian peninsula of Nova Scotia. "Cajun" is a form reflecting the misunderstanding of "Acadian" by speakers of English. Exiled by the British in 1775, these unfortunate ones were loaded onto ships—families ruthlessly wrenched apart on the shore—and taken away, some to the West Indies and some to the Atlantic coast of North America, many dying aboard ship. Their pitiful story is the subject of Henry W. Longfellow's epic poem, *Evangeline,* which tells of their forlorn wanderings as they sought to find lost relatives. Eventually many of them found their way to French Louisiana, where the climate and people were congenial to their background and experience.

Most of the Cajuns of the Golden Triangle came to Texas from south Louisiana during the two World Wars to work in the defense industries, the huge refineries, or the rice farming areas of the coast. According to Marie Hebert of Deer Park, this migration was actually a huge mistake. An elderly man with a peg leg got lost in a swampy area over on the Louisiana border. He wandered until he saw a light and sought help at a cabin. There he discovered that he was on the Texas side of the border. Meanwhile, Cajuns looking for crawfish to make bisque mistook the tracks of his peg leg for crawfish holes and followed him to Texas.

Delectable food is synonymous with Cajun cooking. As a professional cook, Marie knows most of the favorite Cajun dishes, like Pain Perdu (Lost Bread), Crawfish Bisque, Shrimp Gumbo, Jambalaya, and Boudain. Boudain is a kind of sausage made of pork, pork liver, cooked rice, and seasonings—parsley, salt, pepper, and green onion tops. The boiled meat is put through a sausage mill, mixed with the seasonings and rice, and stuffed into a casing. Like most Cajun dishes, Boudain calls for rice, the staple of the Cajun diet. Most Cajun recipes end with the words, "Serve over cooked rice." One fellow, newly arrived in Beaumont from Church Point, Louisiana, decided to adopt a new sophistication and to disguise his Cajun background. Ordering a hamburger at the local Dairy Queen, he said, "Give me one hamburger, all the way . . . except cut the rice and gravy."

One does not have to be a professional cook to know proper Cajun cooking. Martin (Del) Delahoussaye declares that his grandmother, who raised him over in Lafayette, Louisiana, insisted that the boys learn to cook as well as the girls. According to Delahoussaye, one absolutely essential ingredient for perfect gumbo is Roux, a sauce or gravy made of fat, flour, onions, and water. A cook really cannot tell anyone how to make Roux, Delahoussaye insists; he has to show him until he learns it. Without good Roux, you just do not have gumbo. If one suggests that some people make gumbo without Roux, Delahoussaye is aghast. "Well, some folks make soup and call it gumbo, and they even add tomatoes. Tomato is a bad word for gumbo," he vows with scorn and distaste in his voice. He says that in addition to Roux, some Cajuns add file to their gumbo, a powder made of dried sassafras leaves.

For the Cajun, a good meal is not properly served without wine. Ethelda St. Pe has a recipe handed down in her husband Daniel's family. The recipe indicates the resourcefulness of the displaced Frenchmen as well as the home-centered life of the women. For wild grape wine, grapes are mashed in a crock with equal water. The mixture is allowed to settle four or five days until the pulp rises to the top. Then the juice is squeezed from the pulp and three pounds of sugar are added to each gallon. This mixture remains in the crock for thirty days after the sugar has been added and is skimmed three or four times daily.

Martin Delahoussaye offers further evidence of the adaptability of the Cajuns, specifically in foods and remedies. As a coffee substitute, he says, Sucre Grille is prepared by putting a half cup of sugar in an iron pot and stirring it over the fire until the mixture turns dark brown—almost to the point of burning. Then milk is added to this syrup for an excellent coffee substitute. And for treating a cold, the best cure requires about a dozen new and tender leaves from a young orange tree. These must boil until the water turns yellow. Then a little sugar is added and a little whiskey. This makes a good preventive medicine for the kids to take before school in cold weather; it keeps the blood circulating.

Delahoussaye says the Cajuns are always looking for an excuse to celebrate something. Mardi Gras gives folks a chance to drink enough booze to last through Lent. A wedding offers a *fais de do;* but the wedding must be on Thursday so that the festivities do not carry over onto Sunday, the day of the Lord. After all, Cajuns are trying to establish a new image, Delahoussaye declares. They want to overcome the idea that they are crude or profane; they want to use finesse and sophistication. They, therefore, do not say "cōon′ ass" anymore when they refer to a country Cajun; they say "cŏon ahss′."

La Reunion

By ERNESTINE PORCHER SEWELL

IN SPRAWLING OAK CLIFF, suburb of Dallas, errant boys and girls, and sweethearts too, would tell stories of playing around the "catacombs" built in the white cliffs where the French of La Reunion buried their dead. "We would take our dates out there, daring the ghosts that walked on moonlight nights to frighten us away—and they would," one informant related. Today, the "catacombs" have disappeared. Roy Santerre, heir to the lands of François Santerre, one of the original settlers, laughs at this tale: "No, the French didn't build catacombs. They had a graveyard. That building was a mausoleum that someone started. Never finished it, though. Had columns about forty feet high. It's gone now."

And gone are the remnants of the French way of life that persisted in the Dallas area for a scant decade. One reminder is Fishtrap Cemetery where tangles of brush, old tires, and tin cans hide defaced, overthrown tombstones. This is the neglected gravesite of the French colonists who left Europe in the 1850's to establish their Socialist Utopia near the limestone hills across the Trinity River west of Bryan's log cabin in the village of Dallas. The settlers would fashion willow traps to catch fish in the stream that ran near their chosen burial site. Hence the name Fishtrap Cemetery.

One other memory of the past is preserved. When François Santerre left France, he packed a wooden trunk with his books: a considerable library of French language texts and histories, some children's story books, cookbooks, a book on wine-making, books that glorified the noble savage by Rousseau, James Fenimore Cooper, and Gustav Aimard, an ABCDarium, the first French translation of Chaucer's *Canterbury Tales*, and the writings of political propagandist Fourier. "My favorite was the cartoon book of Bible stories," Mr. Santerre mused. The first Santerre was literate and evidently proud of it, for on each of his six voyages back to France, he packed up all his books and took them along in his wooden trunk. Today this collection is in the research center of The University of Texas at Arlington.

There is one other possible reminder of La Reunion. Overlooking the present turnpike just west of Dallas is a hill of limestone called Goat Hill. According to one resident, the hill is so-named because "long, long ago herds of goats grazed over it." This could be a reference to the herds of the French settlers. "They had better luck at herding their sheep and goats than farming," commented Mr. Santerre.

In 1855 Victor Considérant set sail from Antwerp, Belgium, with an advance guard of 150 volunteers, to be followed by that many more a short time later, all devoted to the ideals of Francis Fourier. Society, according to his socialistic views, must be reconstructed through cooperative endeavor and be self-sufficient. Agriculture was considered the principal industry for the new society. The unit of organization was the phalanx, ideally composed of 1600 members, and each would cultivate allotted portions of the soil. (At La Reunion this portion was 6.4 acres.) Although the members would live in community, it would be possible to enjoy private property and even family life. Theoretically, each man would obey his natural instincts, the primal impulses. Institutions such as the church and school would be abolished. Also marriage. (The folk at La Reunion, however, rejected Fourier's notions about wedlock, preferring to remain within the law. The first wedding, which joined Louise Dessau and a Mr. Jones of Dallas, was performed by a Dallas justice of the peace.) Government of the colony was to be carried on by a director and an assembly chosen in general election. Women were promised political and economic independence, and therefore, voice in the affairs of government. The bookkeeper was the next most important person after the director, for, from the common gain, a fixed share would go to each member; of the remainder 5/12 would go to each member additionally, 4/12 to capital, and 3/12 to talent.

The site in northeast Texas which was the destination of the 150 was dotted with outcroppings of gleaming white limestone cliffs, land reminiscent of that which they had left. The soil was poor in spots but the lush growth of buffalo grass promised good grazing. Springs of clear water trickled from the sides of the cliffs. At the foot of the hills, the virgin soil seemed likely to produce corn, grain, and the vegetables French people like so well. The slopes of the hills appeared ideal for vineyards.

They landed in Galveston. Teamsters and ox-drawn wagons were hired to transport the women and children, baggage and supplies.

The men, attired in long black smocks, little flat berets, wooden shoes, and sporting their week-old black beards, walked alongside, shouting and singing "La Marseillaise" gaily. Among the chosen were bankers, physicians, an architect, distiller, gardener, tinsmith, locksmith, jeweler, scholar, wagonmaker, brewer, cobbler, millwright, lithographer—and a few *cultivateux*. They began building two-room rock and log houses. The large rocks were hewn into shape and rolled into place, where they were set up in a heavy mortar made out of the crushed limestone, a kind of construction they had learned in France. The roofs were of small cedar poles cut from the nearby forests. The poles were laid side by side until the building was covered and spaces between were filled with small rocks. Then a thick coating of the crude mortar was poured on. The women and children moved into the houses and the men lived in the open at first.

The main building, where the governor resided, was of rocks, logs, and "rawhide" lumber—lumber rough-sawed without the bark stripped. The building was forty feet in length with an upper story. A sloping roof extended from the front of the lower story the full length of the building and was supported by small cedar poles, forming an open, dirt-filled porch. The building was then white-washed. The small windows were covered by heavy, plank blinds closed against inclement weather and against marauding bands of Indians. For it was to this building that the settlers "forted up" in case of danger. Furniture consisted of crudely-made tables and chairs, hewn from nearby persimmon groves. West of this building was the commissary. Here was the community kitchen and dining hall with a large fireplace to cook over and wooden counters against both walls. Four long plank tables would be loaded with large bowls of pottage, thick soups, and huge platters heaped with buffalo, deer, turkey, or prairie chickens. After the day's toil, the men would eat and then sit, sipping their wine made from the mustang grapes which grew wild in the forest, and reminisce about France. By the end of the second year, a laundry, a poultry house, a building for making candles, a small office, and two dormitories of eight apartments each were built. There was no church or schoolhouse.

The men worked the fields constantly. Large, wooden-beam prairie plows, drawn by a team of four horses or oxen, turned the virgin sod. Wooden logs roped together formed drags or harrows to smooth the plowed earth. Small grain was broadcast by hand and seed corn likewise was dropped by hand into the deep furrows. They had brought grape cuttings, and peach, pear and apple seeds to start their orchards. The women and children were responsible for gardening the allotted six acres. Their produce was brought to the commissary for storing. Unfortunately they did not know about preserving foodstuffs. Moreover, the arrangement for communal dining did not work out. There were some who would not work but would eat—voraciously. Latecomers would frequently not have food. So a play was carried out whereby each family was allotted certain amounts, and communal dining disappeared.

But life was not all work and no play. One accomplished settler, Alyre Bureau, had brought his piano from France and another had an accordion. All would join in to sing the native songs and every evening concluded with the French National Anthem, "La Marseillaise." One of the colonists wrote this song which became a favorite:

"Les Émigrants"

Première Couplet:

Hélas, nous quittons une terre,
 Où l'on ne sait pas pardonner,
Où l'on demande à la colère
 Ce que l'amour peut seul donner.

Refrain:

Où vont les pauvres hirondellas?
 Frères, il est, dit-on, là-bas,
Un air plus léger pour leurs ailes,
 Un sol plus fécond pour nos bras.

Deuxième Couplet:

Non, plus de sang, plus de misère,
 Nous sommes les gais travailleurs;
Du glaive qui frappait nos frères
 Nous formerons des socs vainqueurs.

Refrain.

"The Emigrants"

Alas, we leave a land,
 Where one does not know how to
  pardon,
Where one demands in anger
 That which love alone can give.

Where fly the poor swallows?
 Brothers, there is, it is said, over
  there,
An air more gentle for their wings,
 A soil more fertile for our toil.

No more blood, no more misery,
 We are the happy workers;
Of the sword (blade) which struck
  down our brothers
 We will make victorious plough-
  shares.

Les Émigrants

Où vont les pauv- res hir- on- del - - - les?

Frèr- es, il est, dit on, là- bas,

Un air plus lég- er pour leurs ai- - - - les,

Un sol plus fé- cond pour nos bras.

1er couplet

Hé- las, nous quit- tons une - ter- re,

où l'on ne sait pas par- don- ner,

où l'on de- mande à la co- le- re,

Ce que l'a- mour peut seul don- ner.

Nous sommes la cohorte sainte   We are the holy cohort
    De ouvriers de l'avenir,   Of workers of the future
Nous allons preparer l'enceinte   We go to prepare the place
    Où nous devons tous nous unir.   Where we must all unite.

Refrain.

Quatrième Couplet:

O'liberté, sois notre guide,   Oh, liberty, be our guide,
    Fraternité, sois notre soeur;   Fraternity, be our sister;
Vivant en paix sour votre égide,   Living peace under your shield,
    Nous bénirons le createur.   We shall bless the creator.

Their most significant celebration, of course, was Bastille Day, July 14, a merry day of song and dance, cake and wine. Roy Santerre remembers all-day picnics on July 14 and speaking on the grounds, but in his memory the accordion and pianos had given way to fiddles. Dances were held regularly on Saturday nights and Sundays. The villagers across the river looked askance at such defamation of the Sabbath, but, as Mr. Santerre says, "Our people were Huguenots. There was no church. Religious life was simply not important in this colony." Besides, dancing on Sunday was customary in France. Some who preferred not to join in the dancing would go into the forest to pick berries and gather nuts in baskets woven from the reeds they found in the swamps. Of course they kept their eyes open for Indians. There were Indians camped near the junction of Elm and the West Fork of the Trinity; there was another camp on Village Creek ten miles away. There was a settlement of Tonkawas about two miles south, friendly but never completely trusted. The settlers had heard stories about an Indian raid on a settlement near Garland in which people had been killed just a short time before they arrived. And there are a few instances of Indian trouble. An occasional raid when the men were in the fields would be stopped by the old men and the children so that the most the Indians ever made away with was a little poultry and a few horses. On one of these raids, the story is told that an Indian attempted to break through a window in the Fort, but a brave woman poured hot water upon him and that ended the assault.

Another menace was the nightly raid by timber wolves and coyotes on the herds. To begin with, they had five hundred horses, cows, oxen, sheep, goats, and hogs. The younger boys were organized to watch and give the alarm. Then the old men would come with their guns to drive the predators away.

"The land along the river was thick forest," Mr. Santerre said. "We often cut wood to sell in Dallas, or shot rabbits. We could get a hundred in a single morning. At the market, they paid us twenty cents apiece. If the market would not buy them, we'd go into Dallas with our hands full of cottontails and peddle them on the street. My father and his brothers told of killing fifty-nine deer on one day's hunt in Mountain Creek area. They supplied the hotels in Dallas with venison—and mustang wine, too," he added.

At harvest time the men with old cradle-scythes cut and windrowed the grain. Women and children gathered the stalks of wheat in large armfuls and tied them into bundles using straw to make ties. Then they would load the bundles upon the high-wheeled ox-carts for hauling to the townsite where they were stacked into tall pyramids. Some of the grain was taken to an old grist mill three miles west where it was made into coarse, brown flour. But industry was not enough. Many enjoyed the fruits of the harvest without doing their share of the work. Besides there were too few skilled in agronomy. François Cantagrel, the director, is said to have exclaimed, "Mon Dieu! I am sent to direct an agricultural colony and have no agriculturists to direct." The clay soil proved unproductive; the winters were severe; the summers given to temperamental weather, late frost and early drouth; pestilence in the form of the hated grasshoppers completed the devastation. The colonists could not pay the six percent interest due the "European American Society of Colonization." This association, which had purchased the seven to ten thousands of acres of land (some at seven dollars per acre) at the White Cliffs site, had also contracted, through the operations of Considérant, for 47,000 acres in Uvalde County. Such extravagant purchases brought on bankruptcy of the company and the subsequent failure of La Reunion. Moreover, as they say, "individualism asserted itself": the land of the free offered many opportunities for each to go his own way.

The entire colony of three to five hundred simply melted away. Some went across the river to settle and prosper in Dallas; some (like the Santerres) chose to remain on the colony site; some went to New

Orleans; perhaps a third, or even a half, returned to France. I am reminded of a favorite saying of my own French immigrant father, pronounced as a truism: "A German will transfer his loyalties to this country, but a Frenchman is always a Frenchman and he will live to return to France." At any rate, by 1858 La Reunion was dissolved.

So, it can be said that the French of La Reunion have not contributed markedly to the folklife of Texas. But in the final assessment, more enduring impressions are recognized in the unrest characteristic of the French, that voices itself in antagonism to autocracy and authority, the deep-rooted desire to strive for their Utopian dreams no matter the cost in industry, and especially, in all that appeals to man's aesthetic sense, the *beaux arts*.

Cajun Lapland

By GORDON BAXTER

WE call Port Arthur "Lapland" because that's where Louisiana laps over into Texas. The French took this territory without ever firing a shot. The secret weapon was dark-eyed Cajun girls—good lookin', good cookin', good lovin'.

Cajun is one of several nicknames given to the Acadian French who were cast out of France as a public service several hundred years ago and who have over-populated the low-lying and swampy areas of Louisiana and Texas. They are noted for their zest for life, love, and boudain sausage and eating crawfish. The less you know about boudain the better you will like it, and as for crawfish, they eat the fatty tail, like small lobster, then shove a thumb up into the body shell and eat what squirts out the eyes.

The Cajun culture here is typified by Landry and LeBlanc, Cessna 180 floatplane pilots out of Lafayette, Louisiana. LeBlanc was standing on a float, propping the engine, when the propeller caught in his suspenders and whirled him five times around and then cast him up on a shrimpboat dock, a smoldering limp heap of rags. Landry shut the engine down, rushed up to LeBlanc and cried out, "Speak to me!"

To which LeBlanc replied, "Why should I speak to you? I passed you five times a minute ago and you didn't speak to me!"

The Longfellow legend of the migration of the Acadian French from Nova Scotia to Louisiana has its historic documentation, but little has been written of the migration of the French from the farms of southwest Louisiana to the refineries of Port Arthur in the 1920s and '30s. As Gulf and Texaco built and grew after Spindletop, they drafted heavily upon the husky dark farm boys from Cajun country. Hired as laborers, many of them put in a lifetime at the plants and rose to supervisory positions. They experienced the pre-union days when management rode hard in the saddle, when hungry men lined the fence during the depression and the bull-gang pushers walked along, looking for muscle, and pointed, "you . . . you . . . and you." They were loyal and stoic in the days of the old dangerous West Side stills, and when the explosion came and smoke darkened the sky and we could hear the rising falling cry of the "wildcat" whistle, they told their wives what the bosses had told them to: "Don't ring the switchboard. If it's your man, we'll call you."

And when the wheel turned later and organized labor rode the saddle, the refineries found that these men had long memories. They became the most loyal of CIO ranks and could stay out on strike forever and enforce their wishes with sudden violence at the gates.

The CIO-management schism is one of the most unfortunate things that ever occurred in Port Arthur. The distrust is still there, the buried hostility, the regrettable end result of hard-nosed Eastern management's failure to ever probe the heart of their fiercely proud and loyal Frenchmen. The union loyalty could have been theirs.

The first man I worked for in radio at Port Arthur was George Crouchet, a Cajun who claimed that he came to Texas by accident. Said he was following a man with a peg leg, poking his finger down in the holes looking for crawfish, and when he looked up he was in Port Arthur. Crouchet made his fortune in Port Arthur too and returned to his native Lafayette and the success he richly deserves as owner of KPEL in his hometown.

I had my fun in those days with the Cajun culture, only time I ever got printed in *Life Magazine* was when they did a story on Dudley J. LeBlanc and Hadacol and I wrote: "My hearing was so bad, I was deaf, until I took Hadacol, then I heard from my brother in Lafayette."

And once when Hank Williams was doing a show in Beaumont I had him as a guest on my KPAC program I called the "Jambalaya." He was intrigued by the name, asked what it meant, (I told him that it was a French stew, mostly ham, that's me), and how to spell it. He wrote this all down, Within a few months of his visit he released his new hit song—"Jambalaya"!

THE MEXICANS

Don Pedrito Jaramillo, The Healer of Los Olmos. Courtesy McGregor Studios.

Vaquero photographs from *Vaquero: Genesis of the Texas Cowboy* by William D. Wittliff.

Arnulfo Castillo.

Texas Folklife Festival.

Vaquero:
Genesis of the Texas Cowboy

By WILLIAM D. WITTLIFF and JOE B. FRANTZ

DON GREGORIO DE VILLALOBOS unloaded the first cattle on the North American continent at the harbor of Vera Cruz in 1521, two years after Hernán Cortez landed with sixteen pure-bred horses. In time, the progeny of those first cattle and horses and the men who chased and herded and worked them over vast open ranges from sure-footed and well-reined ponies would provide Texas and the New World her most enduring legend: The *Vaquero*, the cowworker, the Cowboy.

Gradually horses, cattle, and vaqueros constituted a holy trinity of the deserts and prairies. They formed a continuing equation, in which each was an X factor and none was complete without the others. In Spanish Mexico the *hacendados* perceived that profit awaited those ranchers smart enough to put the three elements together—and so they mounted Indians on horses to herd and handle cattle. As the haciendas grew, the vaqueros learned. Together they all formed a school of range management in which each became both tutor and pupil.

Along the way the vaquero learned how to break a wild bronco, how to saddle and cinch, when to run the horse, when to beat him with a rope, when to coo and soothe and stroke, and how to curb the pony's fractious feelings without completely breaking his spirit. The vaquero learned to braid a lariat, to use rawhide, to hobble without hurting, to protect himself against all the thorns that stick and sting, and to build a saddle that would keep a man astride under the most critical pressures.

The hub of the vaquero's life in the chaparral is his *campo*. It is here that he takes his meals from battered tin plates, here that he makes his bed. It is here that he catches his horses from the *remuda* to begin his day's work; here, too, that he will stand or sit before a campfire as the world grows dark, to smoke and sing and talk of good horses and bad *ladinos* with *compadres* who know, as he knows, what this life is like. Whatever its site, *el campo* is the place as close to a home as the vaquero is likely to find in the chaparral.

The morale of the campo is dependent on *el cocinero del campo*—the cook. Traditionally as salty as the *tasajo*—jerky—he hangs out to dry in the sun, the cocinero must be both versatile and durable, for his duties include everything from preparing three hot meals each day in as many different campsites often miles apart, to repairing wagons and men.

The campo moves almost daily, following the cow work, by means of *el carro del campo*—the chuckwagon. This movable commissary carries the vaqueros' bedrolls, food, water, and extra gear, as well as the cocinero's tools and cooking utensils. The chuckwagon is not a Mexican invention; rather, it evolved during the early days of the big Texas roundups. Charles Goodnight was credited with giving the chuckwagon its greatest refinement, the chuckbox. Within a short time after Goodnight introduced it, this durable cupboard with its drop-down worktable became standard equipment on the grub wagons of all the big cow outfits, from Montana to Mexico. In matters pertaining to cow work, inventions have moved south as well as north across the Rio Bravo, with little regard to national origin.

The remuda, the vaqueros' extra saddle horses, moves with the camp as it follows the cow work. Consisting of five to ten horses for each vaquero, the remuda is tended by the *remudero,* the wrangler. Rising with the cocinero, or earlier, he must round up and drive the remuda to the campo by first light so that the vaqueros can rope out their first mounts of the day. He then loose-herds the remuda to the next campsite, allowing them to graze along the way as time and distance permit.

The remudero is usually an apprentice vaquero—too young or too inexperienced to yet join in the cow work. Occasionally, an ex-vaquero, too old or too stove-up to work cattle any longer, will accept the lowly job rather than leave the chaparral.

Though the remudero tends the remuda, it is the vaquero himself who is responsible for the well-being of each horse in his particular string.

In the early morning the *corrida*—the cow crowd—is "told off," or given directions, by the *caporal.* The vaqueros, individually or in pairs, fan out to points forming a great circle and *la junta de las vacas*—the roundup—begins.

The country is thoroughly combed from all directions and the cattle chased out of the thick chaparral and herded in little groups to a predetermined holding ground. Chasing a ladino out of the chaparral often at breakneck speeds is a treacherous business. Thorns from the mesquite, the blackbrush, and a hundred other spiny species have taken the light from the eye of more than one vaquero. The vaquero's *chaparreras* (adapted from the Spanish brush fenders), his sturdy stock saddle (adapted from the Spanish war saddle) with its strong pommel on which to tie or wrap his rope when he throws cattle, and his noosed loop (purely a vaquero invention; the Spanish used *garrochas*—long poles—to prod the cattle) are all necessary to cow work in the chaparral. The vaquero himself is an invention of the chaparral, as is his well-reined pony.

The holding ground is often near water, where the cattle can be more easily held. By noon, the carro del campo has been moved near the holding ground, and the remuda brought up.

After a lunch of beans, tortillas, and *cabrito* stew, the riders again fan out in search of *las vacas,* leaving two or more vaqueros to hold the cattle already gathered. For days the process repeats itself until the entire herd is thus assembled and ready to drive to the working pens where the cattle will be dipped against ticks, the calves branded and castrated and dehorned. When his work's all done in the chaparral the vaquero returns to *la casa grande*—the headquarters. Nearby is the bunkhouse which the vaquero calls, simply, *la casa.* Inside there is room enough to eat and to sleep and keep a few personal things; and though a roof is welcome when "weather" comes, his better memories still are of *el campo.*

When Texas got interested in the cow business, the Texas cowboy adopted most of the vaquero's accoutrements and methodology of working cattle in big country, adapting here and there to fit his particular needs. He borrowed the vaquero's bandana, lariat, leggings, spurs, saddle, branding irons. He kept some of their technical terms like rodeo, bronco, and sombrero, and he Texanized some good Spanish into such slang words as hoosgow, buckaroo, and mustang, words now universally understood. And he absorbed and modified three hundred years of vaquero experience in handling stock from horseback in unfenced land.

The result was the Texas cowboy, who has become one of the folk heroes of the world as well as of Southwestern life and literature. He made his mark on American history in the years between 1866 and 1900, and the dust that he stirred as he trailed the herds out of Texas to Montana and Abilene and Dodge has drifted all over the world. The cowboy as hero and symbol is as closely identified with the emergence of America as a world power as the chivalric knight is with Europe of the Middle Ages.

Adapted by Francis E. Abernethy from the catalogue to William D. Wittliff's photographic exhibit, *Vaquero: Genesis of the Texas Cowboy*, The Institute of Texan Cultures, 1972.

Charro Jiro Afamado

By ARNULFO CASTILLO
Translation and commentary by INEZ CARDOZO-FREEMAN

I'M going to tell a story which they say is incredible, but it is true.

In 1930 I was still a child of five years, very small but very lively. It happened that my father was invited by some friends who greatly esteemed him, to come and live on their ranch, called Cerro Blanco. It was a very pretty ranch, hidden in the mountains. And as these people had always esteemed my father, with great pleasure my father accepted the offer of those good friends, and we moved to the Rancho del Cerro Blanco.

It really was very pretty and very attractive. The view was admirable, green and very mountainous. The scenery above the green earth was attractive and beautiful because one could appreciate the lovely colors of the perfumed flowers which nature produced. So much so that when the sun came up, no one wanted the day to end so as to continue enjoying the beauty of the lovely colors. And so we felt an incomparable happiness which we had never felt before. And this had happened because they esteemed my father so much.

I also found myself surrounded by many little friends and every day we would go out together to care for the animals. Once we were in the mountains we played peacefully, all running together until the day ended. As the saying goes, "Everyone is happy in his own paradise."

And so, 1930 passed and 1931 began and as always the men of agriculture began to prepare their soil to plant the seed. But the earth remained prepared because the time came to plant the seed and not a drop of water fell from the sky in the whole district. And all the people began to become sad because in these places, if God doesn't send the rain, the people can't live, and so a great calamity began.

They drained the springs that flowed in the mountains, and the cattle began to get sick from thirst and for lack of pasture because everything was dry. But saddest of all were those small cattle ranchers who watched their cattle die of thirst and hunger. And the day arrived when there wasn't water, not even for the people, let alone the animals, because the fathers of the family had to go search for water ten or fifteen miles away and they had to bring it back on their shoulders because where the beasts fell they never got up.

Everywhere the same clamor was heard. One day in July of this same year, an uncle of mine visited us, Jesús Castillo, brother of my father, and he, like everyone else, complained about the calamity, at last asking my father to help him with something so he could continue living. But my father was in the same situation. All he said was, "Brother of my heart, we're all in the same trouble. We cannot help you." And so Jesús continued complaining.

After a long while, a neighbor of ours, whose name was Pimenio Figueroa, arrived, and my uncle, on seeing him, became happy and greeted him and they began to talk about their poverty. And that led them to start talking about hidden treasures. Then my uncle said to Pimenio, "You are suffering hunger and you are so close to the treasure of the Jiro. If I lived here, I would have already gone to ask the Jiro for money."

And Pimenio replied, "No, Jesús, I don't quarrel with the dead because they are things from the other world and the dead should be left in peace. And think about who you are going to face. It is the Jiro. Around here, whenever we hear anyone talk about the Jiro, it makes our skin crawl because those who have seen him pass in the night never have the nerve to meet the Jiro again. That's how it is."

And my uncle replied, "Well, I don't believe a man can be so afraid, least of all you, Pimenio, who serve as a gunman for Guadalupe Villanueva. You have always walked among the bullets but yet you are afraid of a Jiro that is already dead."

Pimenio said, "It's not because I'm so afraid, it's only because he is a spirit and nobody has been able to fight against him."

My uncle Jesús replied, "Well look, Pimenio, I've heard you are a brave man and today I'm hearing the proof and I'm your friend and have never been a killer."

And these words hurt Pimenio very much and Pimenio replied to my uncle, "Well look, Jesús, nobody's going to scare me. Let's get the job done."

Then Pimenio said to my father, "You're the witness, Valente, if we don't return no one is to blame. Everything is for the vision of money." And Pimenio continued talking, "Think well about it, Jesús, before it's too late."

My uncle replied, "Look, Pimenio, you think I'm going to think when I need money? The trick is to get it wherever you find it. I've made up my mind." And they didn't say anything more to each other.

Then Pimenio went out of the house and got a bottle of wine and my father and my uncle and Pimenio began to drink it. They finished this bottle and brought another and continued drinking. But now it was getting dark and Pimenio said to my uncle, "All right, Jesús, night has come. Now is the time when the Jiro comes out and wanders up and down the roads. We should approach his place with care so the Jiro won't come looking for us here. If you really want to go, follow me."

My uncle replied, "Let me bring my rope to tie myself to you in case I become afraid and you won't leave me alone."

Pimenio replied, "Don't worry, I won't leave you."

And they went to the store and each bought a bottle of wine and left for the mountains, the place everyone there knew by a name that is very strange. It is called "The Canyon of Hell," and in just thinking about the name, no one wanted to pass there, especially at night.

But Pimenio and Jesús Castillo had wanted to spend a night in the company of the Jiro, who according to the legend, fought with many when he was alive as well as when he was dead because those who saw him when he was alive said he was a terrible bandit and he buried a great treasure, but it was stained with blood. Also they know that he buried the money with dead men and for this reason no one could get it. They also said that when they took him prisoner, they cut off his head and tied him to the saddle of his own horse, and they let the reins of the horse loose so the horse dragged him until he was finished in pieces. For this reason, those who had had the luck of running into this Jiro were left horrified with fear.

It was close to midnight when Jesús and Pimenio arrived at the Canyon of Hell where they knew the fabulous treasure was, and close to this treasure they found a *capuda encina,* a huge live oak, which made the place more somber. Pimenio and Jesús went and sat at the foot of the trunk of the *encino* because it was said that this was the place where the Jiro shaded himself from the sun.

Once they were seated together at the trunk of the *encino,* Jesús said to Pimenio, "Well, now is the time to tie ourselves so that if you run you have to drag me with you."

And they continued drinking the wine which they had brought, when suddenly, there above them in the canyon they began to hear the bleating of a goat that at the same time came leaping down from rock to rock until it came to where they were seated. It was threatening to butt them and Pimenio and Jesús were paralyzed in that moment. And then it left and they heard again blows from above. But what most tormented them was that all around them the sound of the rattling of chains never ceased. And immediately they heard another loud bellow, but now it was a bull that came after them and threatened to trample them both. Pimenio and Jesús were nearly dead with fear. At last the bull backed away from them but they couldn't get up and the third [thing that happened] was the worst.

Then they began to hear the rattling of the chains as though what was coming was going to jump on them. It was the Jiro that rattled the chains that they had tied him with so he wouldn't get away when they took him prisoner. And he came up between them and then he placed a hand on each of them, and with this they were so frightened that they couldn't ask him for the money. And as they couldn't ask him for the money, well, he left them in peace and that terrible noise ceased.

But Pimenio and Jesús had become dumb with terror and couldn't talk to each other. All Pimenio [and Jesús] could do was to get loose from the rope and cling to each other and get away from that terrifying place, and they went back to the ranch.

But never again did they want to go back to present themselves to the Jiro, nor were they tempted by money that belonged to the dead.

All they did was tell, step by step, about the fright they had had. And my uncle, who wanted money so much, well, he had to go back again to his home with empty hands and the hope that it would rain so he could plant his crops and earn his bread by the sweat of his brow. But I, who never forgot not one episode, write this now. Although it is incredible, it is true.

CORRIDO DE CHARRO JIRO AFAMADO

Voy a cantar esta historia
Del Charro Jiro Afamado,
Que tanta guerro les dió
A los ricos hacendados.

I'm going to sing this story
Of the famous Charro Jiro
Who made so much war
With the rich *hacendados.*

Era un hombre bandolero
Que de día vivía ocultuado,
Pero en la noche salía
A ver los atesorados.

He was a robber
Who hid during the day,
But in the night he went out
To visit the hoarders.

No robaba gallinero
No se robaba el ganado.
El ocupaba su tiempo
En dinero fabricado.

He didn't rob the hen house
Nor did he steal the cattle.
He spent his time
With those who had money.

Charro Jiro Afamado

Arnulfo Castillo   Transc. I. Cardozo-Freeman

Voy a can- tar es- ta his- tori- a,

del charro jiro a- fam- a- do   Que tan- ta guer-ra les

di- o,   A los ricos ha-cen- da- dos.

Todos los ricos decían	All the rich men said
Que era un hombre sangrinario.	He was a blood thirsty man.
Siempre que caíba en una hacienda	Whenever he attacked a *hacienda*
Dejaba un rico colgado.	He left a rich man hanging.
Nadie supo donde vino	No one knew where he came from,
Ni donde era originario.	Nor where he had been born;
Lo único que se decirles	All they said was
Allí murió en Guanajuato.	He died in Guanajuato.
Murió cerca del Ojo de Agua	He died near the Ojo de Agua
Del Rancho del Cerro Blanco,	Of the Rancho del Cerro Blanco,
Bajo una sombra encina	Beneath a dark *encina,*
Allí quedó degollado.	There he was beheaded.
El cuerpo del Charro Jiro	The body of Charro Jiro
Ya una vez de degollado,	Once it was beheaded,
Lo amarron a la silla	Was tied to the saddle
De su ligero caballo.	Of his swift horse.
Luego dieron rienda suelta	Then they loosened the reins
A su ligero caballo	Of his swift horse
Y el cuerpo del Charro Jiro	And the body of Charro Jiro
Se fue cayendo en pedazos.	Went crashing into pieces.
Esta historia sucedió	This story happened
Al fin del siglo pasado;	At the end of the last century;
Tanto le temía los ricos	The rich feared him so much
Que no quierían recordarlo.	They didn't want to remember him.
Dicen que es mucho el tesoro	They say there is much treasure
Que el Jiro dejó enterado,	That the Jiro left buried,
Y por causa deste tesoro	And because of this treasure
El Jiro vive penando.	The Jiro lives in punishment.
En el Rancho del Motivo	On the Rancho del Motivo,
El Rancho del Cerro Blanco,	The Rancho del Cerro Blanco,
To'vía después del muerto	After his death, still
Los ha siguido espantando.	He continues frightening them.
Los que han visto al Charro Jiro	Those who have seen the Charro Jiro
Los hallan agonizando	Are found dying in agony

Por no saber aguantar	Because they cannot endure
A sorpresa del espanto.	The confusion of the horror.
Aunque saben que es un alma	Although they know it is the soul
De un ser que vive penando,	Of a being living in punishment,
Ni el vino les ha servido	Not even wine has helped
Pa' cortarles lo asustado.	To take away their fright.
Adiós, Rancho del Motivo,	Goodbye, Rancho del Motivo,
Adiós, bello Cerro Blanco,	Goodbye, pretty Cerro Blanco,
Donde el Jiro se paseaba	Where the Jiro used to go
Ya después de degollado.	After he was beheaded.
Ya me voy, ya me despido,	Now I go, now I take my leave,
Despensen lo mal trovado.	Forgive this bad composition.
Ya les canté este corrido	Now I have sung you this *corrido*
Del Charro Jiro Afamado.	Of the famous Charro Jiro.

"Charro Jiro Afamado" is a *memorate,* a personal narrative with supernatural elements. Memorates attempt to validate superstitions, in this instance, the belief that the spirits of the dead return. "Charro Jiro Afamado" might also be classified as a *caso,* or belief tale about a personal experience.

"Charro Jiro Afamado" and the *corrido* which it inspired were collected from the folk-poet, Arnulfo Castillo, in September, 1972, who was born in the State of Guanajuato, Mexico, and was a resident of San Juan, Texas, for twenty-four years. He is forty-eight years old. He is unusual as an informant because he is a genuine folk-poet; he represents the source, the wellspring of folk balladry and poetry. Generally, folk sources are unknown, but he is an originator, a genuine poet of the people. With pride he calls himself a *trovero,* or troubadour.

The folk-poet is the voice of the people. He is like a mirror, reflecting through his creation, the values, the hopes, the desires, the beliefs, in other words, the world-view of the people. He differs from the literary poet because he is not removed from the people through formal education and training; often he can neither read nor write. His language is the language of the people and he creates using traditional folk forms and imagery. He is a bearer and preserver of tradition and is often a village chronicler, respected as a wise man among his people.

This narrative and its *corrido* are only one pair of many narratives and *corridos* collected from Arnulfo Castillo which tell of his life and events which occurred while he was growing up in Guanajuato, Mexico. In a very real sense, Arnulfo Castillo has never left Mexico. He may live here in a strange and foreign land but his heart is in his beloved Mexico. In his own words: "One morning, on the tenth of December in 1942, when I least thought of it, they invited me to come live in the North, and without recalling that in my songs that I had composed I always said I was a good Mexican, on this day, I abandoned my land, that little ranch which was the cradle of my childhood, that beautiful and warm land that saw my birth, where men are born with faith in God and the hope of cultivating the earth which is my beautiful Guanajuato. And today, I am getting old. I live in the North but always I remember with sadness and longing my Mexico and my beautiful and colorful flag with its proud eagle. When I look at it, it shouts at me and says, 'My son, you have become a stranger to your country.' "

Scratches on the Bedpost: Vestiges of the Lechuza

By ANN CARPENTER

IN THE TALES circulated among many West Texans of Mexican descent the *lechuza* or screech owl figures prominently. Associated with *brujas* or witches, the *lechuza* is a woman who, having sold her soul to the devil, becomes a screech owl at night. Only women—never men—become *lechuzas.* Some informants explain that women are easily influenced by the devil because of Eve's mistake.[1] Some say that even in the form of birds *lechuzas* retain the faces of hideous women. Ugly to behold, they make horrifying screeches, screams, scratches, and flappings.[2] Their screeches foretell calamity, sickness, and death, while prayer is usually the only effective means of vanquishing them. Some believe that the *lechuza* cannot actually be killed, as one man said that he shot one in the head with a deer rifle, but the bullet merely bounced off.[3] The basic pattern of the *lechuza* story in West Texas consists of a hideous woman in the form of an owl who threatens another person—usually male. In many cases she leaves behind concrete evidence of her presence.

The sign left by the *lechuza* may be as harmless as a marred place on a piece of furniture. In a typical tale one man met a *lechuza* in his own bedroom. Naturally the setting was at night, since the evil woman can take the form of the owl only at night. One hot summer night he arrived home about 2 a.m. and went to bed. His parents were away visiting relatives. The night being hot, he opened the window near his bed. Suddenly he heard a whistling and flapping noise. Opening his eyes, he saw a huge bird perched on top of his bedpost. After closing his eyes and praying for about fifteen minutes, he looked at the bed post again. The bird was gone, but deep ugly scratches covered the post.[4] Scratches are among the most common physical evidence left behind by the *lechuza.* In another story the scratches are left on living things, rather than on inanimate objects. A young man was riding a mule at night on his way home from a neighboring farm. He chanced to pass near a tree where a man had committed suicide many years before. Suddenly a large bird attacked him and began scratching him. Crying out in pain, he started praying out loud. The bird seemed to shrink into a ball and suddenly fly away. Both the man and the mule were covered with deep scratches.[5]

In some tales the evidence of the *lechuza's* presence is ominous and destructive. Some informants tell of a lady who died suddenly in 1945 near Ozona, Texas. At the time a neighbor woman bragged that she had bewitched the dead woman by making a doll of her and burning it. No one believed her tale. But on the second night of the dead woman's wake, the neighbor was going to attend it. She walked under an elm tree and was startled when the branches suddenly shook above her. A *lechuza* was on her face, scratching and clawing her. She screamed for help, and some men came just in time to see a bird fly away. She was dead and her cheeks and the entire right side of her head were torn apart.[6] Most of the time physical damage and death to a person occurs when one fails to pray when confronted with a *lechuza.* Sometimes a person who has done evil is killed by a *lechuza.* A number of warnings about one's behavior in the presence of a *lechuza* accompany the tales. If one looks back at a *lechuza,* he will have bad luck. If he angers the *lechuza*, she will put a curse on him or take away that person or thing he loves best. Correct procedures include holding up a cross, praying, or making nine knots in a rope and praying after each knot is made.[7]

The concrete evidence left behind by the *lechuza* is occasionally indicative of the womanly part of the owl's nature. In one story a man was walking home from a dance late one night. About halfway home he heard a whistling sound coming from a tall tree. On top of the tree was perched a huge bird which was whistling a high piercing cry. It seemed to be staring at him. Suddenly it came at him, flapping and scratching. He prayed, and the bird was gone. At first he thought it was merely a huge bird, but under the tree he found a woman's shawl.[8] In a similar tale an elderly man met some *lechuzas* one night outside a migrant workers' camp. He had arrived in camp for some sleep after a long day of picking cotton, but he had been unable to sleep when he saw some lights flying and diving on top of a grove of trees. When he went to investigate, the lights suddenly stopped. As he hesitated, a chill went through his body. Suddenly the lights were flying around him in a circle. The lights came from the eyes of the *lechuzas.* He prayed aloud and shut his eyes. Later he found that the lights were gone, but that a woman's shawl lay on the ground before him.[9]

Scratches on the bedpost and shawls under a tree are typical evidence of confrontation with *lechuzas.* The tellers of *lechuza* stories at times point out the likenesses of their tales with the lore of other countries, especially the Harpy of Greek mythology. Even within Texas, members of other ethnic backgrounds share similar beliefs about owls as harbingers of bad luck. Some Polish Texans retain stories from their homeland about the devil living in the form of a screech owl in a rotted willow tree and signaling to death with a cry.[10] One woman of German background is said to have died after shooting an owl near Arden in 1925.[11] Over Europe, Asia, and indeed, most of the world, the owl has long been considered a bird of witchcraft, doom, and death.[12] The *lechuza* tales of Mexican-Americans in Texas are of special interest, however, because they are among the most widespread and lively versions of bird lore in the state.

[1]Interview with David Ornelas, San Angelo, Texas, November 4, 1972. Compare attitude reported in Frank Goodwyn, "Folk-lore of the King Ranch Mexi-

cans," *Southwestern Lore,* ed. J. Frank Dobie (Dallas: SMU Press, 1931), p. 52.

[2]Interview with Aida Morales, Mason, Texas, April 15, 1973. Also see Humberto Garza, "Owl-Bewitchment in the Lower Rio Grande Valley," *Singers and Storytellers,* ed. Mody C. Boatright, Wilson M. Hudson, and Allen Maxwell (Dallas: SMU Press, 1961), pp. 218-225.

[3]Interview with Ramon Escobedo, San Angelo, Texas, December 20, 1972. The only example found of killing a *lechuza* is in Ruth Barker, "New Mexico Witch Tales," *Tone the Bell Easy,* ed. J. Frank Dobie (Dallas: SMU Press, 1932), pp. 64-66.

[4]Interview with Sammy Vaquera, Del Rio, Texas, November 1, 1972.

[5]Interview with Ben Lopez, El Paso, Texas, November 20, 1972.

[6]Interview with Pete Perez, Ozona, Texas, June 14, 1973.

[7]Interview with John Flores, San Angelo, Texas, November 4, 1972. Interview with Elo Martinez, Kerrville, Texas, April 30, 1973. Interview with Martha Campos, San Angelo, Texas, May 5, 1973.

[8]Interview with Joe Garcia, Garden City, Texas, October 30, 1972.

[9]Interview with Eliseo Lopez, Del Rio, Texas, October 28, 1972.

[10]Interview with Alyx Straach, San Angelo, Texas, June 10, 1973.

[11]Interview with Nancy Bolen, Lubbock, Texas, June 21, 1972.

[12]See Edward Armstrong, *The Folklore of Birds* (Cambridge, Mass.: Houghton-Mifflin, 1958). Also see John Strecker, "Folklore Relating to Texas Birds," *Follow de Drinkin' Gourd,* ed. J. Frank Dobie (Dallas: SMU Press, 1928), pp. 25-37.

Violeta and the Owls

By ALONZO M. PERALES

THE PEOPLE from the *barrio* swore that the old lady who lived in the house on the corner turned into a *lechuza* (owl) during the night. No one had actually seen her do this, but everyone believed it. For this reason, no one from the barrio ever wanted to walk by that house. They felt that since she was a *bruja* (witch), certainly some harm would come to them. So as evening approached, the children of the barrio, playing on the corner as was customary, would head for home so as to be indoors when darkness came. Those who had to walk past the lady's house to get home made it a point to go two or three blocks out of the way to avoid her.

One night while the children were playing, an owl flew over them several times and finally landed on the branch of a nearby tree. Its penetrating eyes fixed on the children, the owl began to screech. Upon seeing the owl, the children became frightened and ran for their homes. Violeta, who not only was slightly ugly but also mentally slow, didn't think about running home. Instead, she stayed behind, alone, playing.

The old woman looked out of the window of her house and saw Violeta playing alone. She walked out of her home and approached Violeta. She looked at the owl and waved her away.

"What are you doing here my child?" asked the old lady.

"I'm not your child and can't you see I'm playing," answered Violeta.

"I know, I can see that," said the old woman, "I'm not as dumb as you are."

Violeta ignored the old lady and continued playing.

"Tell me, Violeta, aren't you afraid of me?" asked the old woman.

"Why should I be afraid of you?" answered Violeta. "Can't you see I'm just as ugly as you are?"

The old lady finally talked Violeta into sitting down. They began to talk. Time went by. Violeta was an orphan so that no one was out looking for her. The people she lived with really didn't care for her so that she could pretty much do as she pleased. She never worried about the time.

"Tell me, Violeta, how would you like to be beautiful, rich, and intelligent?"

"What for?" responded Violeta.

"Well! If you are pretty and intelligent you can be rich and powerful."

Violeta thought for a while. It was true. If she were pretty and rich, she could be powerful and have maids waiting on her at home. Besides, she could travel throughout the world and not have to depend on anyone, particularly her guardians who made her life miserable.

"O.K. my good woman! Make me beautiful and intelligent," said Violeta.

"Now wait just one minute, my dear. It isn't that easy," said the old woman.

"Oh! Oh!" thought Violeta, "here comes the catch."

"In order to obtain all these things, it is necessary that you give me your *alma* (soul)."

"My soul? Why do you want my ugly soul?" asked Violeta.

"I need it, my child, I need it," answered the old woman.

"Yes, but what for?"

"Well, that isn't any of your business."

"Well! How am I going to be beautiful and rich without my soul?"

"My, my, what a dumb child. Well! Let me explain it to you. When you have enjoyed your beauty and richness for some time, an owl will visit you. The visit will come just before your death. The owl will suck blood from you and with it, your soul. The owl will then bring me both."

Violeta thought for a while. Then blinded by her desire to be beautiful and rich, agreed on the contract with the old woman.

Time passed and there was no doubt but that Violeta was the most beautiful girl in the barrio. "Look how beautiful she looks," commented the men of the barrio. "Look how intelligent she has become," said the women.

It was noted, however, that since Violeta had made the contract with the old woman, an owl began to visit her more frequently. The owl would fly over and around Violeta and land on a tree close to her. This caused many wild rumors and vicious gossip in the barrio. Her old friends began to ignore her to the point that no one would play with her anymore.

After several months enjoying her new fortune Violeta began to miss her friends. She became very lonely, almost depressed. She began to think that maybe it wasn't such a good idea after all to exchange one's soul for such material things as beauty and intelligence.

One night, Violeta told the woman, "Look! I want you to break the contract. I've changed my mind."

"Impossible," said the old woman. "A contract is a contract. There is no way in which to break it."

Violeta became very angry and the old woman noted this. Seeing that Violeta was angry, the owl attacked her. The first thing it did was to grab and pull her hair and attempt to suck blood from her neck. Violeta fought back. She attempted to ward off the attack but to no avail. The old woman watching the owl laughed and screamed at the same time. Her eyes flashed as if she had fire in her eyes. Then Violeta asked God for help. *"Perdoname, Dios, por ser tan vanidosa y ayudame con estos diablos."* ("Forgive me, God, for being so vain and help me with these devils.") Having said this, she noticed a big stick lying on the ground. She picked it up and began hitting the owl with it. She gave it one, two, three blows until the owl died. Then the old woman attacked her. She grabbed Violeta's hair and tried to bite her neck to draw blood. Violeta tore away from her and with the stick gave her two good blows. The old woman fell to the ground. Violeta, between gasps of air because she was very tired, saw the old woman lying there and slowly turning into an owl. Violeta ran home to tell the neighbors from the barrio what had happened. They all went to that house to see. They looked all over the place for the old woman but all they could find were two dead owls.

Taken from *La Lechuza, Cuentos de mi Barrio,* published by The Naylor Co., San Antonio. Mr. Perales is the author of the book and translated this portion for publication herein.

Violeta y Las Lechuzas, drawing by Barbara Brigham. Courtesy Naylor Company.

Mal Ojo

By JOHN O. WEST

THE EVIL EYE, or *Mal Ojo* as it is called among the Spanish-speaking *paisanos* of Texas, is quite well known all over the Mediterranean area, from Greece to the straits of Gibraltar. In fact, throughout the world the eyes are thought to have the power to cause sickness or other problems. Particularly suspect is an eye that is especially lustrous, protuberant, or unblinking.

But among the *paisanos, mal ojo* has its own peculiarities. Envy can cause the illness to be transferred, usually to the person envied. A particularly lucky person may be stricken, or a handsome or beautiful child—and the malady may even be given without intent, according to many informants.

Some children naturally attract praise, and a particularly alert and good-looking baby or youngster is especially the object of attention. But in the Mexican culture, one who praises a child must show his own absence of envy or malice by touching the child with his hand. This action, it is believed, keeps away the possibility of harming the child. The idea may be related to knocking on wood, to distract evil-wishing spirits while one speaks of his success or good fortune. One informant has reported to Marie-Ines Kaeo, a U.T. El Paso folklore student, that those in the south of Mexico who wish to keep from giving *mal ojo* to a child *avoid* any physical contact with him. There has to be body contact, she says, for the "charm" to take.

Mal ojo usually takes the form of listlessness or lethargy, although high fever and vomiting are also associated with it. The key to the diagnosis seems to be that the illness is unexpected and unexplained. Then the ritual most often found is tried: a whole egg is passed over the body, sometimes *barriendo*—sweeping—the entire body top to bottom and left to right; other techniques involve using the egg to make the sign of the cross three times over the child's body. One method involves a darkened room, with only three candles lit. Others may be present besides the diagnostician and patient, but they must be silent. Three *credos* are often recited as the crosses with the egg are made. Then the egg is broken into a saucer, with crosses of broom-straws or twigs on either side, and the saucer is placed beneath the patient's bed. After an interval the egg is examined, and if an eye has formed on the yolk, the suspicion is confirmed: *mal ojo*. The tendency of the egg to dry in a series of concentric circles makes this "diagnosis" almost always positive. But some recipes demand the appearance of bloody spots, curious shapes, etc., before the diagnosis is confirmed.

Simple inquiry usually helps determine who has "given the eye" to the ailing one, but some *curanderas*—healers—go one step farther. A special stone is heated, either in a fire or on top of a stove. Then it is examined: the face of the giver of *mal ojo* has appeared on the stone, the *curandera* says, and she arranges to have the giver spray or spit water into the face of the ailing one, and the cure is complete.

But just as each doctor is likely to have his favorite techniques and remedies, the believers and curers of *mal ojo* have many widely varying notions about the disease, its cause and cure. One event recalled by Rose Lee Smetsers, another U.T. El Paso student, is unusually direct: ". . . when I was five years old the lady who worked at the cleaners *'me hizo el ojo'* [gave me the eye]. My grandmother was in charge of taking care of me at that time and noticed how feverish I was becoming. Soon I vomited. When that happened she was sure of my illness. She put an egg under the bed and then got the lady from the cleaners to come see me. When she saw me she pinched me; I immediately started getting better." The pinching, like the ritualized spitting on the child, is apparently a reversal of praise and therefore takes away the cause of the illness. Slapping the child is sometimes used, as well as calling the child derogatory names.

Some *paisanos* believe that not all persons can cause *mal ojo,* but those who can are also able to cast spells, cause serious illness, take away love or riches, cause the blood to stop flowing within the body, or even strike people dead. But according to Judith John of U.T. El Paso, even the one with the power suffers from it: "My brother at the age of two was inflicted with *mal de ojo.* He had chills and a very high fever, therefore my mother suspected the dreaded condition. The woman suspected of being the cause was brought to cure the boy. The woman claimed that she had involuntarily inflicted evil eye on a young child before. She knew that she had done it again because she had a severe headache. She did not know though to whom she had done the harm. [Then]. the woman proceeded to cure the boy in the traditional manner using the egg."

Although belief in *mal ojo* is likely to have come over with the *Conquistadores,* there is reason to believe that the basic idea was already present in the New World. The Mayas often imagined that some enemy had placed his evil eye on a child. The medicine man was summoned. He passed an egg in front of the child's face many times, broke it, and looked at the yolk as though it were the evil eye itself. He hurriedly buried the yolk in a secret place and from then on the child was believed saved.*

Mal ojo—fact or fancy? As long as there is strong belief in it, *mal ojo* will persist in people's minds. Even those who protest most strongly that it is all nonsense can give detailed accounts of the ailment, its cause and cure. And anyone with any sensitivity to the beliefs of others will always remember to touch a child when praising him.

*Claudia de Lys, *Treasury of American Superstitions* (New York: Philosophical Library), p. 213.

Don José and Don Pedrito

By H. C. ARBUCKLE, III

IN THE LATTER PART of the Nineteenth Century in South Texas there were few medical doctors; those that were in that part of the United States were usually quite busy and did not always have time to minister to the Mexican people. Hence, the *paisanos,* as the Mexican-Texans were usually called, had to resort to folk healers, miracle workers, and the like, called in Spanish *curanderos.* The *curandero* relied hugely upon his knowledge of which roots, barks, and *yerbas* could be used for *remedios,* which blossoms of certain plants would make certain teas for cures, and the like. The largest commodity that they recommended, however, was faith, pure and simple. They would prescribe certain *yerbas* to be taken in a certain manner and, with arm outstretched and index finger extended, would proclaim, *"Con fe!"* meaning "With faith!" It mattered not how wonderful the *remedio* was if one did not have the faith, for that was the all-powerful part of the *remedio* itself.

Don Pedrito Jaramillo was one of the most significant *curanderos* of the turn of this century. His practice lasted for at least twenty-five years, and his cures can still be found in certain drug stores from San Antonio to Brownsville, from Laredo to San Antonio again, by looking at the labels of bottles and other containers. This miracle worker lost patients, surely, but his cures were and still are the talk of South Texas, not only among the *paisanos* now but also among the *americanos*, as the Anglo-Americans are known in the brush country of South Texas.

One of the persons that Don Pedrito cured was the uncle of José C. Lozano, long-time postmaster at Concepcion, a small ranching community in Duval County, right in the heart of the South Texas brush country. Don José is still living and is now a patriarch in his own right, being above eighty years of age and retired for many years. However, Don José is still quite active and walks the three miles (one-way) to the post office every day, to check his mail and make sure the post office is being run properly, i. e., subject to his approval, not Uncle Sam's.

Don José tells the following two stories about Don Pedrito, one about the cure of his uncle, the other about two men, one *con fe* and the other *sin fe,* who were seeking a *remedio* for a sick horse.

"*Mi tío,*" said Don José, "was the mail carrier from Los Olmos to Concepcion, and made the route daily. He rode a horse part of the time and walked part of the time, for it was sandy land and very hard on both horse and man to make the long, long trip. It is *muy lejos* from Los Olmos over to Concepcion, very far, maybe even five or six miles.

"*Bueno, pues,* my uncle was such a drunkard that one day he was so *borrachon con mescal y tequila* that he fell off his horse and left the mail right there in the middle of the road, made it back on the horse, and finally came home to sleep it off. *Mi tío* knew that if he kept this up he would surely lose his job and he decided to see Don Pedrito for a *remedio* to cure him of his *borracho.*

"*Entonces, se va por Los Olmos, muy lejos,* maybe even five or six miles away. The great man was at home and, when *mi tío* went to his house, hat in hand, to consult, Don Pedrito greeted him with these words: *'Hijo,* you are the *borracho* that carries the mail from Los Olmos to Concepcion and you want a *remedio* to cure you of this problem. Is this not why you have come?'

"My uncle fell to his knees, for how could Don Pedrito know this? Did he not live in Concepcion and Don Pedrito in Los Olmos, at least five miles away? Surely, *sin duda,* Don Pedrito was annointed of God and a truly wise man, if not a *mágico* himself.

"This then is what the wise Don Pedrito said: *'Acerquita a su casa, hay una laguna.'* My uncle thought, 'How does Don Pedrito know of that little lake near my house? I live *muy lejos,* maybe even five or six miles away!' The great man continued, *'En la mañana, traiga un baño en la laguna; en el tercer día, traiga otro baño; y el tercer día más, el tercer baño. CON FE! Sin fe,* nothing will help you, but *con fe, serás curó!'* Don Pedrito said no more but went into his house.

"The very next morning, *mi tío* took the first bath, clothes and all, in the *laguna;* the third morning after that, he took the second bath; and the final third morning, the third bath. All this he did *CON FE,* knowing that he would be cured.

"And, as sure as I am sitting right here and now in my house, *mi tío* never, to his dying day thenceforth, took anything stronger than coffee or tea, not touching a drop of any *pulque, mescal, tequila,* wine, or even beer. I know this to be a fact, for I was there and I know what I know. And I know that it was the faith, in Don Pedrito, in *El Señor Dios,* and in their combined powers, that cured my uncle."

Don José continued, "One day two *hombres* came to Don Pedrito, petitioning the great man for a *remedio* for a sick horse. One of them was *un buen hombre, con fe en su corazón,* but the other was *un mal hombre, sin fe todavía en su corazón.* Don Pedrito knew what they wanted—how? *¿Quién sabe?* Nobody knows how he knew, he just always did—and prescribed whatever the *remedio* was. The man with no faith and the evil heart asked if Don Pedrito's *remedio* was worth a damn or not and Don Pedrito replied: 'It will work as sure as you will be *muerto* when you return to your house!'

"Pues, the good man crossed himself, thanked Don Pedrito, said a prayer or two, and the two then left, after giving Don Pedrito something for his help. The evil-hearted man did not even thank Don Pedrito; *de veras,* he spat upon Don Pedrito's house as they left. *¡O, que mal hombre era!*

"As they walked down the road, they sang a marching song of Pancho Villa's army, and at one place they had to pull their *pistolas* and fire them three times in the air. *El buen hombre* pulled his *pistola, y lo tiró, y lo tiró, y lo tiró,* and then he put his pistol away. *El mal hombre* pulled his pistol, *y lo tiró,* but *válgame Dios!* the gun exploded and killed him dead! *¡Muerto!* And thus, without doubt, Don Pedrito's prediction came true, for the man was dead when he reached his house, and the horse, when given the *remedio*, became well and whole again."

Don José continued, "This, too, *nieto*, I know to be fact, for I was living here and working here in Concepcion, and knew both men involved. It was the faith that saved the good man and the lack of it that put the other in his grave."

Don José C. Lozano, rancher, postmaster, *gente de razón*, believer in Don Pedrito, is still alive and well, making his daily trek to the post office and back. He still welcomes visitors and is a courtly gentleman, nay, more, he is *muy caballero* to all and sundry.

When asked his secret for longevity, he replies that to have life, one must live life, and that in living life, one must live it *"sinceramente con fe!"*

THE WHITE ANGLO-SAXON PROTESTANTS

Mr. and Mrs. Ed Vance, 1882.

Thrashing crew, 1910.

Dan Waggoner's cowboys, around 1890.

The Ed Vance family in 1911.

Texas Folklife Festival.

Life and Leisure at Lucky Ridge

By W. SILAS VANCE

NEAR THE SOUTHERN BORDER of Wise County, thirty-five miles northwest of Fort Worth, on an isolated dirt road in rolling wooded country, was located the one-teacher school called Lucky Ridge. The nearest village, seven miles southwest in Parker County, was Springtown (once notorious as the base of operations of the outlaw known as Al). In opposite directions, eight miles northeast was Boyd, and nine miles northwest, Paradise, the post office for the community. For nearly half a century after 1882 Lucky Ridge was the educational center for a large cotton-farming and stock-raising community. It was also a community center for a great variety of other things: preaching, Sunday schools, singing schools, religious associations, spelling bees, song fests, ball games, Christmas parties, box suppers, and now and then for speeches advocating sundry causes. Sometimes certain citizens were known even to find it a refuge from the hubbub of home life, where one could smoke his pipe or compose a love letter in peace and seclusion. The two doors of its building were never locked.

The community was WASP from A to Z. During the more than twenty-five years that I lived there in the first decades of this century, I never knew of a single Catholic or Jew or Negro or Latin resident. I still clearly remember when, at the age of eleven, I first saw a Negro while on a visit to Decatur twenty miles away. When our five-year-old daughter first saw a Negro (a high school boy brought in for yard work) she became very excited about the color of his hands and face, so was warned not to ask him about it, that he might feel bad if she did. But her curiosity got the better of her discretion. "Ma Gay," she said triumphantly to her grandmother a few minutes later, "Oliver didn't feel bad when I asked him why his face was black." In my case there was no opportunity to question the Negro, but when my older sister pointed him out on the sidewalk as we drove down Main Street, I stared at the man with the curiosity of a boy at his first circus. Though we used occasionally to find Indian arrowheads on and around our farm, and often imagined there might be Indian treasures under some of the huge boulders on our hills, it was still later and far from Lucky Ridge and again with sharp interest and excitement that I first saw an Indian.

Soon after his arrival in Texas in January, 1883, my Scotch-Irish father moved into the Lucky Ridge community. He had grown up in Mississippi, a state which, along with other old Southern states, had been the spawning ground of practically all the settlers. Though strictly Southern and Protestant in background, Lucky Ridge never became much of a church-going community, the nearest church, with services only once a month, being three miles away. Nearly all the settlers started out as tenant farmers. A considerable minority remained tenants always, but most, like my father, managed in time to acquire farms of their own.

Farming then and there was done in the old style. A man walked behind his mule drawn plow, and his working day was from dawn to sundown, the chores being done in the gathering darkness. The immutable law of life was that one got on in the world only by the relentless sweat of the brow. Poor workers became the "ne'er-do-wells." Farming, at that time totally unregulated, unsupported, and mostly unscientific, was not a very profitable endeavor, rarely grossing as much as a thousand dollars a year.

I cannot think of my father, an unusually strong, muscular man of about 160 pounds, without thinking of his Gargantuan labors. For him, as for another Scotchman, Thomas Carlyle, there was "a perennial nobleness in work." He had a contempt for sluggards second only to his contempt for charlatans. Life was labor. His dogged pursuit of work, for all its grimness, was sometimes awesome. I have seen him hundreds of times come in at noon and again at the end of the day with every thread of his clothing saturated with sweat, yet with great reserves of vitality to discipline in thunderous tones his huge, rambunctious family, and then to carry on lively talk or help with school work far into the night.

Farming meant total involvement. Every member of the family from age six or seven had his duties either in the house or in the fields. Though Dad never exacted anything like as much from others as he himself did, he rarely left us boys idle, and we used to marvel at what seemed to us his genius for inventing work. In slack seasons, after crops were laid by, he would have us roaming over the broad pasture land cutting bull nettles, or up and down fence rows and drainage ditches cutting sunflowers and cockleburs. One of the joys of the school term was respite from physical labor.

Not that all work ended with the beginning of school. After school we had to chop and tote in firewood for the next day, find the "milk" cows in the pasture, separate them from the "dry" cows and other stock, drive them to the cow pen and milk them. Shorter tasks included shucking corn for the mules, shelling corn for the chickens, drawing water for the household, and fetching eggs from miscellaneous places where our roving hens might lay them—in the corn crib, buggy shed, hay loft, horse stall, cottonseed bin, smoke house, store room, blackberry patch, and sometimes even in our improvised chicken house. Occasionally we would fail entirely to find a laying nest, and later the hen would be discovered hatching, undisturbed, a brood of chicks. All in all, our chickens led a happy life.

In the mornings, in addition to sundry household chores (grinding coffee and slicing bacon among them), we had to get the calves from the pasture and turn them into the pen to prime their mothers for milking; then again we milked the cows and turned them out to pasture, leaving the calves penned up by day. And after breakfast, before we left for school at eight-thirty, we boys had to "run" our traps, for through the winter we trapped—for opossums, wild cats, small one-striped skunks (also called "civet cats" in the community), and best of all, two-striped skunks—and sold their furs to Funsten Brothers. When we caught something we had, of course, to skin the animal and stretch the hide before leaving for school. If the catch was a skunk, all the school had day-long evidence of our triumph.

Our farm family was about ninety percent self-sufficient. Dad built our house on a foundation of rocks gathered from our hills. We made our carpets and quilts and a part of our furniture. All the fuel used for cooking and heating we cut on our farm. We drew our water from a sixty-foot well under our back porch, and for the farm animals we built mud tanks, which we stocked with catfish. From trees on the farm we split the logs for our fence posts and rail fences. We raised our livestock feed as well as the livestock, slaughtered our own meat, and grew all our vegetables and fruit except a few luxuries—apples, oranges, bananas—at Christmas. We knew nothing of store-bought beef or pork or lamb or fish or fowl or bread or milk or butter or eggs or vegetables—canned or fresh. Preserves, jellies, pickles, sauces, and all such relishes were homemade from home-grown products. We rendered our own lard and made all our laundry soap. From our own corn we made hominy and ground our own corn meal. We put up our canned goods of every kind, dried our own fruit, and stored in the cellar for winter preservable fresh foods. We made most of our clothing and cobbled our own shoes, which we younger ones never wore except when they were needed for warmth. Dad was his own carpenter, housepainter, wallpaperer, plumber, tool-sharpener, "horsedoctor," butcher, and general repairman.

He sired fourteen children, all born at home. Our entrance into the world was not entirely without professional help and, in some instances, cost our parents as much as five dollars, though most of us made it for two or three. Thirteen of the children survived childhood, and twelve survived our parents.

Lucky Ridge School offered seven grades and ran sometimes five, sometimes six months, drawing twenty to thirty pupils, all afoot, from about two miles around it. Girls (whom we addressed only by their first names: "Miss Rose," "Miss Nannie," and so on) and young men with six to ten grades of education taught spelling, arithmetic, some history, geography, and physiology, and the rudiments of reading and writing. Few who went to the school completed what it had to offer, and virtually no one had the remotest dream of pursuing his education beyond it.

We were taught in a forty-foot-long, rectangular room, heated by a single wood stove. On cold days everybody huddled to the center of the room to recite, sometimes in a class of one, but generally in groups of about three to eight, the larger classes being formed by throwing pupils from two or more grades together to study subjects like spelling, geography, or physiology. For blackboard erasers we had only rags, and the balls and bats we played with were all homemade. A straight oak limb or sapling or a willow tree, barked, made a satisfactory bat; and we made balls by winding any kind of yarn or thread or twine around a rubber center until the ball had suitable size, and then sewing it thoroughly so that it wouldn't unwind. A woman's worn-out stocking was the usual source for our yarn.

Most of us at Lucky Ridge never saw a basketball or football or volleyball or tennis ball or golf ball or a store-bought baseball. Our game was townball. We indulged in other sports briefly: leap frog, tag, base, crack-the-whip, rope jumping, mumblety-peg, horseshoe pitching, but our constant game, in and out of school, was townball.

Often considered the forerunner of baseball, townball was a less rigidly regulated and more individualized game. Historians have suggested that baseball replaced it before the end of the nineteenth century, but we were playing townball at Lucky Ridge down to at least 1920. For us it had certain distinct advantages. First, any number could play, from teams of four or five up to fifteen or more. Second, it didn't require any equipment except a ball and a bat, and we didn't have any, not even a catcher's mitt. Third, the poorest player could take part with some success and enjoyment, since the pitcher had to deliver the ball with an underhanded pitch and usually served it as gently as possible to smaller boys and girls. Fourth, since a team remained "in bats" or "in town" (as we said, "at bat" being used only for an individual player) until every member was put out, the inept player was not the serious handicap he would be to a team in baseball.

Townball differed from baseball in several other ways. A batter could be caught out on either the first bounce or fly, and a runner was put out by throwing the ball between him and the base he was running to. A runner after once leaving a base could not return to it. The only fixed positions were those of the pitcher and catcher, and sometimes a "pigtail," as the boy was called who was put behind the catcher to stop any balls the catcher failed to stop. The rest of the players on the team in the field took positions wherever they chose. Fielders would commonly shift about, right and left, up close and back, according to the quality of the batter. The better players did practically all the ball handling. And when batting, they survived and went on scoring for their team after the poor players were liquidated.

Drinking water at Lucky Ridge school had to be fetched by pupils from the nearest farmhouse almost a half mile away. Boys did not like to go for water during recess, when, after playing hard, we frequently ran out and needed it badly. But once the bell rang for "books," boys were anxious to fetch water. When it finally arrived, there would be a general rush for the water bucket, and a line would form for use of the one dipper available for everybody.

For the girls there was a privy; for the boys, nothing except a nearby woods. But in 1917, after the boys had been "going to the woods" for more than a third of a century, some progressive trustees had a privy built for them also. It was a mistake. Immediately after the structure was set up, the boys surreptitiously turned it bottom side up. When citizens set it upright again and nailed the back of it firmly against a tree, the boys ripped it loose—everything except the one sturdy board by which it was nailed—and this time left it back side up, its two round holes, like monstrous eyes, staring grotesquely at passersby on the road.

Discipline was a major concern at Lucky Ridge. For more than seven hours each day, the teachers had in charge a heterogeneous group of raw youngsters from age seven to sixteen or more, and often their days were full of troubles. (While I was at Lucky Ridge, two of my seven teachers gave up in midyear and left, and a third spent her last day continually weeping in remorse for the chaos she had wrought.) We fought; we teased and tormented the girls; on cold days we crowded around the stove and trifled and flirted; on rainy days, confined in the one room from nine to four o'clock, we wrecked all peace and order; on fair days we roamed through the thick woods nearby and might be far away when the bell rang for "books." The teacher's special habits and weaknesses we exploited, sometimes maliciously, but more often merely to enliven a dreary day. For one teacher, having learned his ways in such crises, we would fabricate extravagant love notes, deliberately get caught passing them, and then gleefully listen to him read them aloud to the school. Once, during after-school hours, we rigged up a cowbell in the attic. By extending a rope from the bell down between the two partitions of the wall, we could ring it undetected by reaching up through large holes that boys over the years had idly whittled with their knives in the inside partition. The orderly routine of school would be suddenly interrupted by the dingdong of the cowbell—it sounded like the very animal was in the attic.

Such grotesque comedy was merely perplexing to the teacher, but sometimes the problem of discipline took a much more serious turn. Once a hefty youth brought to school a couple of iron tub handles, which he proposed to use as brass knucks on the teacher. Fortunately, the teacher found out about the knucks, confiscated them from the boy's coat pocket at recess, displayed them before the school, and then tactfully managed to conciliate the boy. On another occasion a sixteen-year-old-bully, when summoned with two other boys for punishment, bluntly declared to the teacher, "You're not going to whip me." The rest of us pupils watched in stunned silence to see what would happen. Since the idea of suspending from school an unruly youngster was unheard of at Lucky Ridge, we assumed and the teacher knew that he must solve his problem *at school.* But defied by one so nearly his equal in strength, he chose to make a total retreat. Fortunately the school term was over in two weeks, for with that confrontation his teaching career at Lucky Ridge completely collapsed. On still another occasion, a strong, combative youngster named Carl put up a vicious scrap when his teacher attempted to paddle him. The latter was pommeled and wrestled on almost equal terms before he could get the boy under control, prone on the floor, and administer some sort of punishment.

One teacher named Crockett Alexander, hired to finish the term of a girl who had left after two months, completely mastered the problem of discipline. Crockett Alexander was really an anomaly at Lucky Ridge. Unlike all the rest, he was not a young teacher, but an imposing elderly gentleman around sixty, with a long white beard. And, according to my father and others who had known him for many years (he had once been county treasurer), he had not completed six grades in his formal education. "But," they always added, "he is a good disciplinarian." In the school room all day long he carried in his right hand a sturdy yardstick, which he used for two purposes: as a pointer and as a shillelagh. Actually, he seldom found it necessary to strike a pupil. We learned from the start that he meant business, and no doubt his age, his handsome bearing and white beard commanded a great deal of respect. Whether he taught us much is a moot question, but he ran an orderly school, and at the end of his short session, he left a community highly satisfied with his performance.

Despite everything, education went forward at Lucky Ridge. We became first-rate spellers and good mathematicians. Acquirements in writing or language were very poor, and nobody really discovered the pleasure of reading, for there was nothing to read. Except for textbooks and maybe a Bible, I doubt that one family in five had a single book in the home; certainly there was not one in the school. And the fine arts had no existence there.

Occasionally, a really effective teacher showed up. I remember especially Miss Eunice, who was certainly worth to the community every penny of the $240 she was paid for her six-months service. Unlike most of the others, she must have had, I think, one or two years of teaching experience before she came to us, she was so sure of herself. An outgoing person, she took a lively interest in people and their varied concerns. She was the only woman teacher I ever knew who participated in our ball games, and she did so with joy and vigor and could wield a bat effectively. "She bats like a boy," we would say admiringly. She was also the only teacher there, of either sex, who took a keen interest in our language. Apparently she had been well grounded in the rules of English grammar, and took every opportunity, in class and out, to enforce them. She did it with good humor, and, far from resisting, we found it fun to try to please her. After more than half a century I remember the afternoon that a twelve-year-old fifth-grader lifted his hand and asked: "Miss Eunice, can me an' Frank go get some water?"

"Why, Jack!" she replied, "Why do you call Frank mean?"

Jack was puzzled, but quickly received whispered help from older and wiser pupils around him, and soon made a second try, "Can Frank and I go get some water?"

"*Can* you!" Miss Eunice said. "I just don't know. How strong are you?"

Again puzzlement, again whispered help, and finally Jack came up with the clincher: "May Frank and I go get some water?"

"Why, yes, of course, we need some fresh water." And Jack and Frank were on their way, free of "books" for a quarter of an hour.

Once school got under way at Lucky Ridge, usually the first part of November, it ran without a break, except for one week at Christmas. The community paid little or no attention to special days or holidays. We knew nothing of Hallowe'en, and paid no attention to Thanksgiving, or Washington's birthday, or anybody else's birthday, not even Lee's or Davis's. We had egg hunts on Easter Sunday afternoon, but no Easter holidays.

During the school term there were few other activities. Parties were for warmer months. Snap was the one form of entertainment, and it is a running, swinging game that belongs outdoors. Simple and unsophisticated, it is a thoroughly good mixer. Within a very short time a lively boy playing snap may meet and hold hands with practically every girl at a party. To start it a boy and girl stand facing each other holding hands. A second boy then snaps a girl to catch him as he runs around the standing couple. When caught, he takes the place of the first boy, and the girl who caught him snaps a boy to catch her. When she is caught, she takes the place of the first girl, and the boy who caught her snaps a girl to catch him. And thus the game continues. The chase is usually brief, but a spirited boy or girl may make a determined race of it, and as they speed around, they swing to the standing couple as a kind of anchor, all but throwing them off their feet. Sometimes a boy, chasing a fleet girl, by suddenly reversing his direction, may maneuver her into plunging violently into his arms. Parties were frequent in the summer, and always it was understood that everybody was invited. Youngsters might come from miles around, and when the crowd grew large, they would spread out over the yard and beyond, and as many as a dozen snap games would be going simultaneously.

Revival meetings also were summer affairs. Many of our parents did not believe in revivals, but we youngsters often went to the meetings and made a kind of party of it. We would go in the farm wagon and would fill it with boys and girls and have quite a gay time during the hour's drive to and from the meetings.

A box supper at the schoolhouse was a frequent affair. Each girl

Lucky Ridge school house, 1920.

would prepare and decorate a box of choice food, to be auctioned off at a night meeting. The boxes were not identified, but we boys never failed to find out the owner of the ones we were interested in, and sometimes a popular girl's box would bring as much as three dollars, though most of the boxes went for fifty cents to a dollar.

"Singings" were frequent in the community, sometimes held at the schoolhouse on Sunday afternoons and sometimes in private homes in the afternoon or at night. At the schoolhouse we sang a great variety of religious songs, usually the more lively ones: "Shall We Gather at the River?" "Bound for the Promised Land," "Little Brown Church in the Vale," "Stand Up, Stand Up, for Jesus." In homes we included our favorite secular songs: "Oh, Susanna," "My Old Kentucky Home," "Dixie," "Yankee Doodle," "Tramp, Tramp, Tramp," "The Old Folks at Home." But the songs most familiar to me from my boyhood were those we sang without music at home and in our daily lives, notably, "Darling Nellie Gray," "Old Dan Tucker," and among us boys, "Casey Jones." We sang only isolated verses from the last, and we boys added to its naughty turn in the fourth stanza by substituting "women" for "roads." For the most part we sang only *our version* of the chorus of "Nelly Gray":

> Oh, my darling Nelly Gray,
> They have taken her away,
> And I'll never see my darling any more.
> They have taken her to Georgia,
> There to wear her life away,
> While I'm weeping on the old Kentucky shore.

I don't think any of us related it in any way to slavery. To me it was only a song about separated lovers, why separated I had no idea. We were all as familiar with the second stanza of "Old Dan Tucker" as with the ABC's, and sometimes, since the wealthy wildcat rancher had lived in our county, we substituted "Waggoner" for "Tucker" and always substituted "funny" for "mighty" and took certain other liberties:

> Old Dan Waggoner was a funny man,
> Washed his face in a frying pan,
> Combed his hair with a wagon wheel,
> And died with a toothache in his heel.

My father never attended any of the public "singings," and I don't recall that he ever sang with others in the family. But he had a good voice, and when in an especially good humor he would break forth in a songfest of his own. His choices were more sedate than ours. While he prepared for his Sunday morning shave or "wash," his strong voice would sometimes be heard throughout the house echoing the melodies of "The Old Time Religion," "Rock of Ages," "Amazing Grace," and "How Firm a Foundation."

In my boyhood home and at school we were fond of riddles. We were constantly on the lookout for new ones, and our specialty was rhyming riddles. Among those I clearly remember is this one:

> As I was going to St. Ives,
> I met a man with seven wives.
> Each wife had seven sacks,
> Each sack had seven cats,
> Each cat had seven kits.
> Kits, cats, sacks, and wives,
> How many were going to St. Ives?

And this one, which we challenged every newcomer with:

> A man without eyes
> Saw plums on a tree.
> He neither took plums
> Nor left plums.
> Pray how can that be?

Almost no one ever got the answer: A man with one eye (not *eyes)* saw two plums, and took one and left one. This one was even more incomprehensible:

> When it was one month old,
> Adam was no more;
> Before it was two months old,
> Adam was four score.

The moon, of course, never achieves an age beyond a month, after which we have a "new moon." And finally, we liked this couplet about the speaker's own offspring:

Brothers and sisters have I none,
But this man's father was my father's son.

Occasionally the dull routine of school at Lucky Ridge was broken by something exciting. Once we had an afternoon of pure drama when the flue of the stove started a fire in the roof. Boys rushed off into the cold for water, the community was alerted, and soon we had a bucket brigade of citizens descending on us. I remember watching my fifty-eight-year-old uncle, his large coat flapping in the north wind, as he headed toward the school in huge strides across his field, bearing a ten-quart bucket of water. The fire was extinguished. (It was a later day, long after my time, that the old stove finally burnt the building to the ground.) At other times, we would experience a brief thrill when a two-horse carriage drove by the school. Three or four families in the community had one-horse buggies, but no one had a two-horse carriage, and when one came along, it was something to see. Even more exciting, after about 1913, was a Ford chugging along the dirt road. It happened maybe "once in a month of Sundays," and always someone spotted it far up the road and conveyed the message, "Automobile," and we peered through every window as it moved by us. Then there was the visit of the county superintendent, once each year. Immaculately dressed, he was a suave, soft-spoken gentleman, pleasant to listen to and look at. He always made a speech with some jokes, and told us what a superior school ours was. But the most memorable excitement of all happened unexpectedly a few days before the Christmas holidays in 1910. A man appeared from nowhere with a quaint-looking instrument, and got permission from "Miss Ruth" to display it to the pupils. He set it up, pointed its huge horn-like projection toward us, wound it up, and made it talk like a man, yes, before the afternoon's entertainment was over, a variety of men—and women. We listened in unbelieving awe. When he made human speech come from that machine, our astonishment could not have been greater had the man performed a miracle.

On rare occasions a teacher would have a Christmas program, with a Christmas tree and gift giving, at the schoolhouse. When this happened, it was the only time that we saw a Christmas tree. We never saw a Santa Claus. Indeed, we were warned that if we stayed awake and tried to see him on his nocturnal rounds, he would go away and leave no presents. We believed in him implicitly until we were about eight or nine, and after that pretended for a while to believe in him to keep the presents coming, which we always found in our long stockings on Christmas mornings.

But the big affair of the school year was the "exhibition" at the end of the session. This was an outdoor entertainment on Friday night after the last day of school. We boys would gather old lumber and build a platform just outside and joining the two doors of the schoolhouse. The "exhibition" on this makeshift stage was a varied performance—speeches, readings, clowning, jokes, dramatic dialogues, and short plays—exhibiting all the talents we had, and then some. Though I once heard a young lady of the community read Poe's "The Raven" in the most bizarre and lugubrious rendition that masterpiece perhaps ever had, the emphasis was always on comedy, and almost always Negro characters were in the acts. Most of us youngsters had never seen a Negro. He was to us some far-away creature, who spoke a funny dialect and held comical religious meetings; and nothing delighted us more than to blacken our faces with burnt cork and to clown around on the stage as Negroes.

In the Lucky Ridge community, parental authority was absolute. In our family Dad had his own methods with his large brood, and he certainly did violence to the tenets of today's specialists in child care, but if his methods developed any problem children we didn't know it. We didn't even know that children could become special problems.

I do not remember when I first heard the edict at our dining table: "Eat what is set before you." It forestalled criticism or quibbling and seemed to end all dietetic problems. When rations were put on the table, we reckoned them good for eating and went after our share. I am still a little surprised as I encounter so many children today, and also adults, who dislike so many things. In our family no one questioned the delectableness of hog liver, sauerkraut, turnips, cornbread, okra, poke salad, lamb's-quarters, buttermilk, clabber, and black-eyed peas.

Parents, fathers in particular, were especially hard on what they called "foolishness." In Dad's view, whimpering, grumbling, squabbling were definitely in the class of foolishness," and we children indulged ourselves only when he wasn't around. Worse forms of "foolishness" were petty gossip and scandal-mongering, and his contempt for these was so withering that we avoided them like a scourge. Worst of all was any form of pretense, fraud, or deceit, and Dad's scorn for such "damn foolishness" seemed always at volcanic heat, ready to consume anyone who came within its reach; so we learned to play it straight with Dad, and for me it would have been all but impossible to face him with deception.

There was not much moral instruction and only a smattering of religious indoctrination in the Lucky Ridge community. As for explaining about the birds and bees, no one came close to that. But most of us learned freely from everyday life. I was no more than ten or eleven when I began riding mares some four miles to be bred, and on the farm we saw much of birds and bees, as well as bulls and boars and billy goats; and I hardly remember a time when I had any doubt about the method God uses to bring babies into the world.

In our community were three or four "Campbellite" families, and they did indoctrinate. For a few years, beginning about 1900, there was a small "Campbellite" church in Cottondale three miles away, and the Lucky Ridge families frequently attended its services on Sunday and its revival meetings in the summer. The "Campbellites" believed intensely in the doctrinal rightness of their church. They were strict fundamentalists, and in some of their beliefs they went beyond the fundamentalists. They rejected instrumental music in their worship services as worldly. In their revivals, when one made a "confession" he was rushed off in the dead of night to a pond and immersed before anything fatal could happen to him, for they believed that his "confession" would not avail to save him unless it was consummated by the cleansing waters of baptism.

The most active religious group in the community was a sect called Primitive Baptists or "Hardshell" Baptists or just "Hardshells." There was no "Hardshell" church anywhere around, but just before and after the turn of the century they used to hold monthly "meetings" in the Lucky Ridge schoolhouse, importing a preacher who came up on the Rock Island railroad from Fort Worth. My mother was a life-long member of this sect, and about ten years after marriage my father also joined it, but later withdrew, and the last twenty-eight years of his life he was affiliated with no church at all.

The "Hardshells" believed their preachers spoke directly from God, hence rejected any special education of them; they liked to refer to theological seminaries as "preacher factories." "I am an unlearnt Hardshell Baptist preacher," one proudly declared. The "Hardshells" were suspicious of education generally. They rejected Sunday schools, believing that only preachers "called" of God were qualified to teach us about him, and that any other arrangement would mean "the blind leading the blind." They were non-evangelistic and anti-missionary—so *anti* that other Baptists than themselves were called "Missionary Baptists." They held strictly to the Calvinistic doctrine of "election"; hence there was never the slightest pressure on us children to become "Hardshells"—or to become anything religiously. They, like the "Campbellites," rejected all instrumental music in their meetings. They never took up a collection, but after the sermon, whoever among the brethren wished to contribute would walk down and put his dollar or half dollar or quarter on the table or pulpit in front of the preacher. As a symbol of humility they practiced foot-washing at their meetings.

"Hardshell" preaching was a kind of rhythmic oratory, not unpleasant to the ear, but completely devoid of practical concerns. Unlike many other Protestants, "Hardshells" did not preach about current sins or the need for repentance or the horrors of hell. Their preaching was for the comfort and delectation of the elect. At their associations, when meetings lasting two or three days with dinner on the ground were held under a brush arbor, the chosen would journey from many miles away, and preaching would go on, with intermissions, all day long. On short notice, they would preach anywhere at any time. Once, my mother, being indisposed and unable to go to the regular Sunday morning meeting at the schoolhouse but feeling a need to hear a sermon, asked my father to request the preacher to come to our house that night and preach again. He came and the people came in their wagons and buggies, bringing along chairs and lanterns, and we had another sermon as the brethren with their families sat about on the large open porch and in the yard. That was about the last "Hardshell" sermon I ever heard, now sixty years ago, and I had supposed that the sect had perhaps disappeared from the world, as it long ago disappeared from Lucky Ridge. But not so. At the funeral of the late Speaker Sam Rayburn, with the President of the United States, two ex-Presidents, and one future President among his audience, the "Hardshell" preacher who had, as the New York *Times* put it, "baptized Mr. Rayburn in the 'feet-washing Baptist' faith," delivered a "eulogy as homely as the covered sidewalks that pass through Bonham's business district."

In our family and in our community the Sabbath was strictly observed, but for the most part, only as a day of complete abstinence from farm work. We youngsters were as free as the wind. Little or no religious duty was required, and no kind of fun or diversion was forbidden on our rest day. On Sunday one could run wild as a colt. We hastened to finish our morning chores, then hit the road.

Dad usually spent Sundays playing games, visiting, and reading. Though rarely at church, he was never irreligious and on rare occasions, when a guest at dinner, he was asked to return thanks. Not gracefully but unfailingly he would respond, always abruptly and so loud that God must have been startled: "Almighty God! We are thankful for this food. And for these good people who have set it before us. Give us grace, and help us to be worthy of those who brought us into the world. Amen."

Hospitality, even to strangers, was a basic instinct in the community. Politicians and preachers and tradesmen were freely entertained, with little or no regard to their politics or their religion or no-religion. Candidates that my father did not support frequently stayed over night with us, and Jewish peddlers sometimes spent entire weekends at our house. Once our guest was a speaker for prohibition. When he spoke at the schoolhouse that night, his audience, like the community, was about ninety percent anti-prohibitionist.

Philanthropies and charities were wholly restricted to community needs. If a man's house or barn burned, or any other disaster struck, the only insurance he was likely to have was the help of his neighbors. Some man was informally delegated to canvass the community to collect whatever each wished to give. If one became sick, neighbors would visit to help; if he was critically ill, they would sit up all night with him. Wherever there was dire need someone was sure to respond to it. My father frequently became involved. I remember especially Mr. Camp, a "drunk" who had brought his large lovable family virtually to ruin. Every other Saturday morning through winter and spring Mr. Camp would stop for a note from my father addressed to a merchant in Boyd, which read: "Mr. Neel, Please let John Camp have about $15 worth of home supplies on my account." This went on for years. ("I gave it in a way he couldn't drink it," Dad said later.) Each fall Mr. Camp would pay part of it back.

About all the community knew of civil law had to do with the activities of the local constable and justice of the peace. These two officials, known by all and feared by some, were even used sometimes to frighten children into being good. To us young boys the constable especially, often seen wearing a pistol, was a fearsome character. I must have been about five when someone began warning me that if I didn't behave the constable would come and take me away. Sure enough, one day Constable Clark, with his thick black mustache, came. I was so terrified as I observed him talking in the yard with my father, certainly about me I thought, that I trailed behind my mother from room to room, clinging to her skirt, during all the time he was on the premises. Many years later my father became a justice of the peace, and by then having outgrown my fear of law men, I took a great deal of interest and pride in his official activities. Periodically he would go on horseback or in the buggy to Cottondale, a small hamlet three miles away, to hold justice court. At other times a man would come to the field where we were working and pay a fine, usually for fighting, a very expensive indulgence, costing, as I remember, $8.75 when the offender came voluntarily, more if the matter went to court. More often people would come merely seeking free legal advice. On rare occasions a couple drove up to our front yard gate on a Sunday afternoon to be married. It was Dad's most pleasant and, by all odds, his most profitable duty. Standing beside the buggy in which the couple remained seated, he completed the ceremony and shook hands with the newly married husband and wife within ten minutes. His fee was one dollar. People sometimes would ask what the job as J.P. paid. Dad loved to reply, "About $1150 a year." "Really?" the inquirer was apt to say, "I had no idea it paid so much." "Yes," Dad would add, "It's worth about $150 in cash and one gets at least a thousand dollars' worth of cussing."

Though my father and other men of the community used profanity freely, boys generally were not permitted to do so. Among ourselves, yes, we used everything, but around adults we watched our language. In our home even "heck" and "darn" were frowned upon. Our language was so immaculate that we had euphemisms for the male animal among horses and cattle and hogs. Our bull was "Old Surly." "Boars" were simply "hogs," any sex distinction being made by calling the females "sows," which was not objected to. "Jack," "ass," and "Jackass" were all out of bounds; we used only "donkey" for the male and "jenny" for the female. "Studhorse" was out of the question; the only names we used were "horse" and "mare." We sometimes may have heard the word "stallion," but seldom, some people never, saw the creature himself, and the word merely connoted to us "a very fine horse." Inconsistently, no one objected to "rooster" or "gobbler" or "billygoat" or "buck" or "tomcat," though "pussy cat" was not in good repute, and "bitch" was in very bad repute. "Cock" we never used for the fowl, no doubt because of its slang use as an obscentiy.

The old saw about talkative women and silent husbands had no meaning with us. The men did more talking. In our family Dad did all the talking—well, almost. His talk was full of anecdote, humor, mimicry, and earthy phrase. He loved to tell stories and people loved to listen to them. His supply seemed inexhaustible, but even so, his love of story-telling outran his supply, and he often repeated his favorites. His stories were as clean as any Victorian could have wished. Even among men I never once heard him tell an off-color story. Many of his stories I have heard or read in later years, and no doubt most of them were old when he told them. Some years ago I heard a lecturer tell one of Dad's favorite yarns—about a half-deaf man who bought some medicine, and when told the price was $3.08 (in Dad's version $1.08), put 8¢ on the counter and walked out. After calling unsuccessfully to stop him, the clerk wryly remarked, "Oh, well, made a nickel on it anyway."

He liked to tell of the surgeon who, having operated, agreed with his associates that the extracted appendix was as healthy an organ as one could ever hope to see. "But," he shrugged, "no harm done," and began sewing up his patient. Or of the old-time schoolteacher who, when asked by a doctrinally-split board what theory he taught—whether the earth was flat or round—replied, "Gentlemen, I have gone deeply into that question, and I am prepared to teach it both ways." Or of the old farmer who was hauling pumpkins from his field by putting them in one end of a sack and rocks in the other, then throwing the sack across the back of a mule. Asked why he didn't put pumpkins in both ends, he replied, "This is the way my daddy did it, and what was good enough for my daddy is good enough for me." And how Dad liked to impersonate the preacher reading a Bible lesson from two pages that had got stuck together (a story, I discovered many years later, that Henry W. Grady had told in his famous address, "The New South"); "And when Noah was 180 years old he took unto himself a wife, and she was [turning the page] 260 cubits long, 50 cubits wide, made of gopher wood, and lined with pitch inside and out." Here Dad would mimic the preacher pausing, knitting his brow reflectively, then continuing, "Brethren, I had never before come across this in the Bible. It shows that we are, as the Psalmist says, fearfully and wonderfully made."

Dad liked to do things on a large scale, and the many miles to trade centers made large-scale planning prudent and a large household made it necessary. He brought home sugar in 210-pound barrels, cheese in 32-pound wheels, cane syrup in 24-gallon kegs, flour in 192-pound lots, honey by the gallon, and apples by the bushel. He slaughtered a half dozen hogs in the winter and a steer in the summer, yet meat was our shortest ration. Our diet was largely vegetables and fruit, and most of what we ate we brought from our fields—in half-bushel containers, or fresh corn and melons in cotton sacks. Forty-pound watermelons we sometimes sliced three at a time, which we never ate at meal time, but midway in the long afternoon between twelve-o'clock dinner and eight-o'clock supper. (But the best of all watermelon eating was in the fields. In later afternoon we would pluck a melon from the shade of fall grass and feast upon its cool, succulent sweetness as we rested on our sacks from the backaching labor of cotton picking; as soon as it was halved, we boys would go with our knives for the luscious heart of it, but, strangely and inexplicably to us, Dad would begin at the edge and eat cleanly toward the middle.) Berries and plums and grapes abounded far beyond our power to use, and once, though in a dry country, we filled barrels for wine making. Peaches we hauled from the orchard in uncounted bushels. We canned them; we dried them; we pickled them; we preserved them; we gave them away; we fed them to the pigs, and ourselves ate them like pigs from June to October, yet the ground under the trees was often covered with fallen fruit. Eggs were superabundant, and butter we produced not by the pound but by a huge bowlful twice a week. Milk came not "frozen home in pail," but steaming with warmth in two- and three-gallon buckets both morning and evening. For winter's supply we filled the cellar and storehouse with sweet potatoes, Irish potatoes, pumpkins, cushaws, citron melons, onions, dried peas, peanuts, popcorn, pecans, and home-canned goods of many varieties. For these products there was virtually no available market—except the weekly peddler who came in a covered wagon to pick up any butter or eggs or chickens that farmers' wives might have to sell. What we couldn't use rotted in the fields.

And now the final word about Lucky Ridge: it is no more. The school was abolished in 1927, the pupils being bussed to Springtown. About the same time any community solidarity ceased to exist. The sloping farm lands, worn out and ruined by erosion, have been largely abandoned, the population being only a fraction of what it once was. The flourishing orchards and vegetable gardens and cotton and grain fields are gone. Many of the surrounding hamlets and villages have disappeared. Paradise, once a proud village of several hundred people, a dozen or more stores, a bank, a high school, a railroad, a cotton market, and many churches, today has left only a single country store. Hamlets, all within three miles of Lucky Ridge—Cottondale, Garvin, Keeter—each with one or more stores, a church, a two-teacher school, a gin, a blacksmith, maybe a barber, have completely disappeared. Only the roads through the area have improved. Once, after much planning, one counted on about two hours for a trip over dirt roads to Fort Worth in a model T Ford. Today one needs hardly more than thirty minutes for the trip. And many have taken it—and didn't come back.

Some of the above material first appeared in *Forum,* The Univeristy of Houston, 1972.

THE NEGROES

U. S. Representative Barbara Jordan.

Negro cowboys, Bonham, ca. 1909. Courtesy Mary Alice White Pettis.

Escort wagons of the 10th Cavalry, 1916. Courtesy U. S. War Department.

Professor J. Mason Brewer.

Dick the Drummer at San Jacinto, by Kermit Oliver, while he was an art student at Texas Southern University.

Texas Folklife Festival.

Cotton pickers.

Tales from *Juneteenth*

By J. MASON BREWER

I began consciously collecting these tales six or seven years ago [around 1925]. Some of them were told to me by ex-slaves themselves; others were told by the sons and daughters of slaves; still others by grandchildren of slaves going to college. Not all of them came from Negroes, though all of them are Negroid, for aged white men, once slaveholders, contributed to my stock. A country store on Saturday afternoon, a wagonload of cotton on its way to the gin, the bank of a fishing hole, the tenement district of a Texas city where the shotgun style of house prevails, the seats for loafers in second- and third-class barber shops, the grounds of rural schools and churches, the setting for a Saturday night supper and platform dance—such have been the places where I garnered. Truck drivers, business men, and school teachers belonging to the racial group have told me tales, but the best of tale-tellers has been some ex-slave bouyed up by the spirit of a Nineteenth of June celebration—the "Juneteenth"—the day on which all colored people in the South commemorate the freedom of their race from slavery. The significance of the day is so great and the tales I have collected are so bound up with the legalized slavery which, in 1865, this day put an end to, that I have used *Juneteenth* as a title. Nobody who does not understand a Juneteenth celebration can ever understand the Negro or his songs and tales.

'Possum in the Pot

Silas Jones was the shrewdest slave on the Crockett plantation. Not only that, he was the best 'possum cook on the plantation, and 'possum dinners and 'possum suppers at his cabin were regular fare. Silas' reputation as a 'possum cook spread so far that it reached the ears of the master. So one evening the master decided to go down and taste some of Silas' 'possum.

"Good evening, Silas," said Master John. "What are you cooking that smells so good?"

" 'Possum, Massa John," answered Silas.

"It certainly smells good," repeated the master. "I have been hearing about your reputation as a 'possum baker; so I thought I would come down and try a piece."

"Sho', Massa, sho'," said Silas. "Yuh's mighty welcome. I jes' put 'im on. We'll have to wait fo' 'im to cook."

The master sat there about an hour and waited, but Silas did not take the lid off the pot.

"Isn't that 'possum done yet?" finally asked the master.

"No, sah, not yit, Massa," said Silas. "Takes 'im uh long time to git done."

The master waited another hour; still Silas did not take the 'possum off.

"Silas," said the master, "it certainly takes that 'possum a long time to cook. I believe I'll take a look at him myself. I think it ought to be done." The master walked over and took the lid off the pan. He found two chickens instead of a 'possum. "These are chickens, Silas," said the master. "I thought you said they were 'possums."

"Sez dey is, Massa! Wal, dey wuz 'possums when Ah put 'em in dar. Ef dey's chickens now, Ah's gwine th'ow 'em away."

Elijah's Leaving Time

Master Dan Waller was a very sympathetic master. He visited all the cabins on his plantation every night to see how the slaves were getting along, and to find out whether anyone was sick. The slaves all liked Master Dan and generally left his chickens and hogs alone.

One Saturday evening, however, Elijah, one of the slaves who had a family, decided he would like to have some pork chops for Sunday. About nine o'clock that night Elijah went down to the master's hog pen and stole a pig. Just about the time he got back inside his cabin, the master, on his customary round of evening visits, knocked at the door. Elijah, the pig still under his arm, hurriedly put it in the baby cradle and covered it over with a quilt. He was rocking the cradle backwards and forwards when the master entered.

"What's the matter?" asked the master as he entered.

"My po' baby's sick," answered Elijah, "an' Ah's tryin' to rock 'im to sleep."

"Well, I'm sorry," said the master, starting over to the cradle. "Let me see him. He may need some medicine."

"No, sah, no, sah. Ef you pulls de kivver offen 'im, he gonna die, Massa."

"Well," answered the master, "I am not going to let him suffer. I am going to pull the cover off him and see what the trouble is."

"Aw right, Massa, aw right," answered Elijah, sidling towards the door. "You kin pull de kivver offen 'im ef yuh wants ter, but Ah ain't gwine stay hyeah and see 'im die."

Swapping Dreams

Master Jim Turner, an unusually good-natured master, had a fondness for telling long stories woven out of what he claimed to be his dreams, and especially did he like to "swap" dreams with Ike, a witty slave who was a house servant. Every morning he would set Ike to telling about what he had dreamed the night before. It always seemed, however, that the master could tell the best dream tale, and Ike had to admit that he was beaten most of the time.

One morning, when Ike entered the master's room to clean it, he found the master just preparing to get out of bed. "Ike," he said. "I certainly did have a strange dream last night."

"Sez yuh did, Massa, sez yuh did?" answered Ike. "Lemme hyeah it."

"All right," replied the master. "It was like this: I dreamed I went to Nigger Heaven last night, and saw there a lot of garbage, some old torn-down houses, a few old broken-down, rotten fences, the muddiest, sloppiest streets I ever saw, and a big bunch of ragged, dirty niggers walking around."

"Umph, umph, Massa," said Ike, "yuh sho' musta et de same t'ing

Ah did las' night, 'cause Ah dreamed Ah went up ter de white man's paradise, an' de streets wuz all ob gol' an' silvah, and dey wuz lots o' milk an' honey dere, an' putty pearly gates, but dey wuzn't uh soul in de whole place."

The Juneteenth stories were taken from *Tone the Bell Easy* (PTFS X, 1932), J. Frank Dobie, ed.

Country Black

By LORECE P. WILLIAMS

A FLOCK of wild geese flying south, appearing almost out of no place, wings in motion—movement like a symphony—gliding in the heavens, announcing an end—summer—and a beginning—winter.

So it is with rural events and life styles among many Texan Blacks. They appear to have many points of entry—seasons, beginnings, renewals—movements in life. Ceremonies are many. They are special and expected.

School Closing ceremonies marked the beginning of summertime in our country community. In some areas it was a three-day affair. One can remember looking forward to participating on that day, and many rural areas coordinated their Closings in an effort to attract people from other communities. This, indeed, provided some very special times. The competition spirit, the need to meet new people, to share talents, and to travel motivated an untold number of people.

The first-night program at Closing was usually for the elementary grades. For months now rehearsals had been of prime importance. Since they had all been together at all rehearsals, everyone learned every song, everyone's speech, including his own, and was almost beside himself with so much new knowledge and awareness. Perhaps the beauty of the total black experience is in the solo expression of its existence. For even in a group performance of those elementary grades, there were individualized movements and styles.

Seven miles southeast of Luling, Texas, by the railroad track, there was a small community called Sand Hills. There wasn't much sand in the true sense of the word, but the hills were there. They were rolling hills, stretching to a distance that gave the appearance of hills touching the sky. Mesquite trees, big stately oak trees, even pecan trees were among the foliage. The fence rows were covered with wild grape vine and sometimes honeysuckle which seemed to scent the whole universe. Blacks, Browns, Whites, Baptists, Methodists, farmers (some owners, some share croppers), teachers, preachers, friends, cousins, old, young—lived one among the others, sometimes in separate worlds, but somehow sharing a common bond of belonging to each other in this point in time.

The black rural school had grades one through twelve. For its rural location and for its time in the 1930's Sand Hills had a large school compared to other black rural schools in neighboring communities. There was a house on the campus for the principal and his wife, with enough rooms for two other teachers. There was a separate building for the home economics class, a section for the agriculture class and the extended education shop, and in later years a lunch room was added. There was a well on campus in the early years and later a pump was built which supplied water for a fountain. Of course there were the three outhouses—one for teachers, one for the boys and one for the girls. Benches were built around some of the trees on both the girls' and boys' side. There were swings and see-saws on each side. The basketball court seemed to have been the largest in the whole world for the students and participants. Rarely did Sand Hills lose a game. Many trophies were won in the district and state meetings.

Some of the children who lived more than six miles from school came on horses or in small wagon-like carts. In later years two or three families allowed their older sons to drive the family car to school. Those who lived less than six miles walked to school. Students were tardy only on very severe winter days, for the day had begun long before 8:30 a.m. for these rural families. Many had started the walk to school shortly after sun-up.

The school day started with the principal ringing the first bell at 8:25, which started the race for the front of the building. At 8:30 a.m. the second and final bell sounded. Then the lines were formed in front of that high porch which had some ten or twelve wide steps. There were four lines. The first through eighth grade girls formed one line. The ninth through twelfth grade girls formed another line, with this pattern repeated by the boys. If this happened not to be a chapel day—which was once a week, usually on Fridays—announcements were made to the group by the principal. The announcement about Pearl Harbor was made to such a grouping. For the first time those without radios heard that our country was at war. Some who had brothers or favorite cousins in the military cried. Even some of the big boys wept openly. Many of those boys in this line went to war. One never came home, lost in action. A brother and favorite cousin of others in line came home and was laid to rest with military honors.

The music at School Closing was well chosen. The National Anthem ushered in the Closing programs. Then came the Negro National Anthem. Standing in a dimly lit auditorium, shoulders erect, heads held high, bodies with the regal poise of antiquity, old faces, all hues—ebony, bronze—some by the artist of Creation, some by the journey; young faces—for some a beginning, for some an ending. They all lifted their voices in harmony singing, humming James Weldon Johnson's "Lift Every Voice and Sing":

> Lift every voice and sing, till earth and heaven ring,
> Ring with the harmonies of Liberty;
> Let our rejoicing rise, high as the listening skies,
> Let it resound loud as the rolling sea.
>
> *Refrain:*
>
> Sing a song full of the faith that the dark past has taught us,
> Sing a song full of the hope that the present has brought us;
> Facing the rising sun of our new day begun
> Let us march on till victory is won.
>
> Stony the road we trod, bitter the chastening rod,
> Felt in the days when hope unborn has died;
> Yet with a steady beat, have not our weary feet
> Come to the place for which our fathers sighed?

Lift Every Voice and Sing

James Weldon Johnson

J. Rosamund Johnson

Lift ev'-ry voice and sing, till earth and heav- en ring, ring with the har- mon- ies of lib- er- ty; Let our re- joic- ing rise, high as the list- 'ning - skies, let it re- sound loud as the roll- ing sea. Sing a song full of the faith that the dark past has taught us; sing a song full of the hope that the pres-ent has brought us Fac-ing the ris- ing sun of our new day be - gun, let us march on till vic- to- ry is won.

Refrain:

We have come over a way that with tears has been watered;
We have come, treading our path through the blood of the
  slaughtered;
Out from the gloomy past, till now we stand at last
Where the white gleam of our bright star is cast.

God of our weary years, God of our silent tears,
Thou who has brought us this far on the way;
Thou who has by Thy might, led us into the light,
Keep us forever in the path, we pray.

The Negroes 121

Refrain:

> Lest our feet stray from the places, our God, where we met Thee,
> Lest our hearts, drunk with the wine of the world, we forget
>   Thee;
> Shadowed beneath Thy hand, may we forever stand,
> True to our God, true to our native land.

School Closing was on the way. On the second night the junior high and high school students presented a three-act play.

On Friday, Commencement Day, there was dinner on the grounds. Mothers prepared boxes of food. Long tables were set and long lines formed to be served from the many boxes. Games were played, friends chatted, reminisced and enjoyed the day. Graduation exercises were held that night. Gifts were exchanged, congratulations, advice, hugs, and kisses were generously given. For some it was an ending—to others a beginning—for many it was a parting of the ways. Many left for college and usually became teachers. Others left to take jobs in the city. Among many black rural families, parents placed great value on getting a good education. They wanted for their children things that had not been available for them. Sometimes this meant sending the oldest daughter away to college while the younger children, especially the brothers, helped with the expenses. Somehow the parents and families were disappointed if the chosen fields were other than teaching. The boys who went away and became ministers were equally respected and admired. Families were usually large. This meant that older children had completed their education by the time the youngest ones entered college and were now expected to help their brothers and sisters.

The children had very special places in their families and usually had nick-names which were fondly used by most people in the community. One of the best ways to determine a loss of favorable acceptance was to be greeted by one's real name in a very detached, uninvolved manner. This was a coldness no one ever wished to experience.

Rural life among Blacks in that area seemed to revolve around the school and the two black churches—one for the Methodists and one for the Baptists. Distance was often defined by the number of miles one lived from the school or one of the churches. Some of the families who sent their children to the school lived in a small adjoining community of Mt. Pleasant, where there was a Baptist church. Down the road west of the school about five miles was the weather-beaten, yet beautiful in its agelessness, Black Methodist Church. A few yards away stood the parsonage, where during the earlier years the minister and his family lived. In later years the supply minister lived in one of the neighboring cities of San Antonio or Austin and did not use the parsonage. On second and fourth Sundays there were services. Sunday School was held every week. Sometimes the ministers and congregations had special programs at the white church in the community. The spirit of worship prevailed even among the racially separated groups.

Then there was the "tracting" meeting (from "protracting") and also the Association. Both were versions of modern day revivals. The meeting usually lasted a week, culminating on Sunday. This was a time to bring the lost to the fold and time for the saved to testify to the wonders of the Creator. Many saved souls in the years to come would refer back to these meetings and the time when they gave up the things of the world. This was really a homecoming event for many relatives and friends who had moved away. They usually came for the Sunday services unless during one of the week nights a very well known minister was preaching.

There was one such minister who across the years preached at the Association. Even the young gathered around the tabernacle to hear him. The way he walked, talked, preached, prayed, sang, and grasped the pulpit seemed electrifying. It seemed as if some of the shouters began shouting from anticipation as soon as he stood to walk to the pulpit. There he stood—well into a song, amens ringing out, the music and choir softly humming or faintly singing the song in the background—his head leaning back, his eyes fixed toward the heavens, hands outstretched, sometimes clenching them, sometimes as if carressing himself—voice ringing out in startling beauty—

> If when you've tried and failed in your trying,
> Hands sore and scarred from the work you've begun,
> Take up your cross, run quickly to meet Him,
> He'll Understand and say "Well Done."

At both the "tracting" meeting and the Association there were stands for selling soft drinks, ices (called glass-ade), homemade ice creams, candy, chili, and pastries. The crowds were large. People from other rural areas and communities also came.

No one was a stranger there at the meeting, even though this might be his first time with these people. Sometimes the young ones laughed among themselves about the shouting habits of the elders but never about the need to shout. Services began with the group assembled, few in number to begin with, someone in a clear moving voice giving out words to an old spiritual, songs such as "Nobody Knows the Trouble I've Seen," "Amazing Grace," "Precious Lord Take My Hand," "Steal A Way to Jesus," "I'm on the Battlefield for My Lord," "Take Your Burdens to the Lord," "I Shall Not Be Moved."

The person giving out the hymn always prayed. These prayers were filled with thanksgiving, praise, helplessness but never hopelessness, faith, and most of all, love. The prayers were usually in three parts. As the person prayed, the congregation during the first part hummed in unison the beginning:

Father I stretch my hands to Thee—for no other help I know. Oh my Rose of Sharon, my Shelter in the time of storm. My Prince of Peace, My Hope in this weary Land. You've Blessed me when I was too mean to live and unfit to die.

This morning You touched me and brought me out of the land of slumber, gave me another day—Thank You, Jesus.

The shift to the second part of the prayer was on the way. The humming became quieter, some softly singing. All seemed to be praying separately. This was indeed a personal petition. One heard, but did not intrude by listening too carefully to the second part of the prayer, for that was an invasion of one's Divine Privacy.

Almost as if timed, the praying voice became inclusive, collective, louder; then the humming and soft singing began. In unison once again, the congregation began the third part of the prayer:

When I've come to the end of my journey, time for me shall be no more; when these knees have bowed for the last time, when I too, like all others must come in off the battlefield of life, when I'm through being 'buked and scorned, when the troubles of this world will be no more, when I too must cross Chilly Jordan—meet me over there in My Home with Thee. Over there where a thousand years is but a day in eternity, where I'll meet with loved ones and where I can sing praises to Thee throughout eternity for Christ's sake—Amen.

After several of these hymns and prayers the main program commenced. A few speeches from youngsters, a few solos, and then the preaching. The sermon was usually long, the minister moving rhythmically and with emotion in his motions—frequently looking to the heavens—and begging for strength to bring God's message to His children. Amens rang out, shouts. The minister, usually renowned for both his preaching and singing, ended his sermon and moved into song—almost as if possessed, he sang. All who were not moved by his preaching were inevitably moved by his singing. By this time "that church rocked." Testifying and church joining came, then collection and adjournment. Friends, acquaintances, and relatives visited and made plans for the next night or the next year or whenever the next meeting was scheduled.

Other special events could bring these people together again. Weddings were expected to be held at the church. Most often the girls who had gone away to larger cities came back home to the church of their childhood days to be married. Everybody who wished to attend was automatically invited to attend the family's home for the reception—usually quite a feast—after the wedding ceremony. Written invitations were seldom sent. You somehow heard about it and were expected to attend. Not attending was to insult the families of the couple, for if both bride and groom were from the area, one had to know some of the relatives.

Funerals were homecoming occasions. Regardless of distance or financial condition, families felt it an obligation to bring the deceased to his respective community, church, family, and friends to be a part of a final farewell. These were emotional experiences for all involved. The final rites were usually long. The eulogies were directly concerned with preparing the living for this day more than for eulogizing the deceased, yet the services seemed especially designed for the deceased. The deceased's favorite song was sung, and sometimes a special poem was read or recited. Sometimes they sang "By and By When the Morning Comes," and "All the Saints of God Gather in Home," "We Will Tell the Story of How We Overcome," and "We'll Understand It Better By and By." They always sang "God Be with You 'til We Meet Again" and "Nearer My God to Thee."

Some of the family traditions were well known to others in the community. It was expected that some families would have Sunday dinner with the father's parents every Sunday, especially if this was the oldest or youngest son in that family. In other families the Sunday dinner was always eaten at the mother's parents' home. Rarely were there exceptions. The children ate at separate tables or later. On holidays, especially Christmas, the day was shared between both sets of parents and with many friends and relatives. Sometimes families paid short visits from home to home. At each stop cakes, cookies, and sometimes "spirits" would be served. Weeks of preparation had gone into this. The safes were filled with cakes and pastries.

The rural life styles that existed in each family could be witnessed on a day-to-day basis. Such things as a ritualistic heritage, ceremonies, prophetic signs, superstitions, and legends of a people were proudly shared and accepted as a way of life. There was a saying for most things about life and living. Prophesies, superstitions, and signs were shared by elders and told to the young, generation after generation. Even to this day one remembers, and as the intellect attempts to reject, intellectualize, or explain these many beliefs, one most often silently but firmly accepts the old beliefs and "takes care—just in case." An itching nose—company is coming; walk under a ladder— bad luck; a crowing hen—a death; right hand itch—receive money; left hand itch—a letter; right eye jumping—happiness; left eye jumping—anger; wearing of the asafetida bag—to ward off colds; the rabbit foot—good luck.

Two well known midwives lived in the community. They "waited on" everyone, Whites, Blacks and Browns alike. They were sometimes paid with canned goods, quilts, eggs, chickens, hogs and many other things besides money. This seemed to be expected and accepted from some families. These two women were older women and boasted of having been midwives for more than forty years. They lived quite a distance from each other, each one having her own area to serve. Counsel was given to the troubled, inspiration to the young, medicine to the ill (herb teas, homemade salves, and other home remedies) and many other services remembered by many in times of need. These two women spoke fondly of each other and took pride in having been friends since childhood. It was difficult for the young to imagine that either of these women had ever been a child. One belonged to the Methodist Church and the other one to the Baptist Church. Many were the times one of them hugged an adult tenderly and added, "I brought you into this world—by the help of God and your mamma."

It was common among rural families to start the day before the crack of dawn and to end it long after sunset. Cows had to be milked, and the milk had to be strained and put away in crocks. Animals had to be fed and all this before breakfast. The girls took turns churning and helping to prepare breakfast, most often a breakfast consisting of home-cured sausage or bacon, rice or other hot cereal, sometimes potatoes, eggs, biscuits, home-made preserves or jelly, milk, and coffee for the adults. In some families the Sunday breakfast might include fried chicken, steak, or chili, as well as the regular breakfast foods. In the lean years all three meals included the same foods, all of which were home grown. There was no money for the extras then. After breakfast was prepared and eaten during the school year, the children dressed for school and began the walk, for most a walk of three to five miles to arrive before 8:30 a.m. In the evenings there were eggs to gather, turkeys to be brought home, cows to be milked, animals to be fed, chips, wood, and kindling to be gathered, the supper dishes to be washed, lessons to be studied, and time to get ready for bed, prayers to be said, and then at last to sleep.

Most families took their children and went to town on Saturdays. There they bought groceries for the next week or month, walked the streets, visited with friends and window shopped. Most of them ate lunch at the market, usually a meal of barbecued sausage, beef, crackers or bread, and a cola. Sometimes the children were given spending change with a warning to save for a rainy day. After returning home from town there were the evening chores and getting ready for the Sabbath. It was expected that all would work during the week. Children were constantly told that work made them healthy in body and mind. Saturday night meant ending the major tasks. Only the necessary chores like feeding the animals and cooking occurred on Sundays, for the Sabbath was to be kept Holy. Most families went to church.

Juneteenth (the 19th of June) was another festive occasion. New garments were purchased, plans were excitedly made, and everybody was happy. The day began early, as all were up and getting prepared for the big day. It was a known and expected fact that certain locations were responsible for certain activities. People from the Sand Hill community went to the Hoods Point community about thirty miles away some years and to the Nash Creek community about twenty miles away on other years. At either place a big dinner was served—barbecued beef and mutton, vegetables, desserts, beverages, watermelon, and canned foods galore, all served with a festive attitude and enjoyed by all. Sometimes the food for the affair was provided by local campaigning politicians. They donated the beef and mutton and the soft drinks. The barbecue pit was a deep hole dug in the earth and covered with garden wire. The cooks (always men) started on the day before, preparing the barbecue. Many times some of the neighbors who were not black attended these festivities and looked forward to the coming event each year.

Baseball games were played by organized teams. Evening came and everyone tripped off to the outhouses, cars, or anywhere possible and dressed for the night at the park in town. At one time the pavilion for dancing seemed unbelievably huge. In recent visits it seemed to have diminished in size. A band played. The instruments were usually the guitar, piano, and drum. Good dancers, poor dancers—each couple doing the in-vogue dance for that time. Usually the "city people" were the best dancers. Some were wonders to behold. Other dancers even stopped to watch.

Most families began leaving around midnight or shortly before, some even earlier, especially those from the rural areas. To stay up until midnight even on the Juneteenth was too much! Goodbyes, hugs, and kisses were shared as a great day of celebration came to a close. Youngsters and some of the women would discuss these events for months to come, either comparing it with the last Juneteenth as being not as good, or better, or the best one yet.

The rest of the summer would be filled with work. Cotton was forever there to be planted, chopped, thinned, picked, weighed, hauled, and sold. Between those times there was the cane to be stripped and taken to the molasses mill, and molasses to be made. The corn was chopped, roasting ears gathered and canned, tops cut and tied. There were peas to be picked, shelled, orchards, watermelons and gardens to be cared for, fruits and vegetables to be canned, potatoes and peanuts to be harvested. There was wood to be hauled, and for some, water had to be hauled. Rarely, if ever, was there an idle moment during the summer months. Neighbors shared in the field work and helped each other to lay the crops by. Some families hired out. Help was automatically given to families who had experienced illness or some misfortune during the year. Not only was help given but also some of the farm products. This was accepted in the true spirit of sharing for it was known that "it could be my family next time."

Some of the adults belonged to benevolent societies or fraternal organizations; the women were Heroines of Jericho and the men belonged to the Masons. The meetings were usually held on different Saturdays at the lodge hall in town. Once a year they had a special day on Palm Sunday and would "turn out," the women dressed in white and the men in white aprons and white gloves. This attire was also worn to the funerals of a deceased member, as these organizations usually presided over part of the ceremonies. Circles and Guilds were church oriented. These were also very active organizations and the members took great pride in their membership and performed accordingly.

Beginnings and endings, ceremonies and seasons seem to be monumental features in the essence of Black rural living. They gave date to time, described today, and held tomorrow's dreams.

Seasons of the year came and went—slowly. Each brought and left some distinguishing event, etched forever in the memory. Each summer was always the "longest, hottest summer we've ever had"—the fall so different—the winter "the coldest ever." Spring always ushered in a newness. The wild flowers grew in an incredible abundance, scented the universe, filled the eyes with spectacular wonder and inspired the imagination of the inquisitive child. He was told about "all these things" and about a Creator Who lives "even in the flowers as well as in the birds soaring through the sky."

Even the wildest imagination wouldn't have dreamt that one day would witness a super highway rising above, cutting across, going around, adding new dimensions to some areas and abolishing some. Many had left forever; some had only come back to remember; a few stayed—all seeing a totally new way of life.

For everything under the sun—there is a season.

Waco Jive

By ALFREDA IGLEHART

ONE OF THE FIRST TASKS that I undertook in preparing to write about the urban Negro was to review literature on the subject. I quickly, however, became discouraged with the results of the literary review. I agree wholeheartedly with Charles Keil's view as stated in *Urban Blues* (1966) that today's urban Negro can be found only in a set of sociological statistics on crime, unemployment, illegitimacy, desertion, and welfare payments.

Because I was up to my ears in cultural deprivation, community disorganization, social pathology, social impoverishment, and statistics, I abandoned efforts at surveying literature on the urban black. Granted, the literature is plentiful, the authors numerous, but none seem to speak of *my* experiences, *my* encounters, and *my* situations. Consequently, I will speak for myself. The "Urban Negro" concept will be dropped and substituted in its place will be "An Urban Black," because, for the next few pages, I will offer some personal glimpses of my life as a black in Waco, Texas.

Waco could be considered a medium-sized Texas city with a population of over 100,000, located about a hundred miles north of Austin and approximately ninety miles south of Dallas. To the people of Houston or Dallas, Waco is probably regarded as a small place, but to the residents of Marlin, West, Hillsboro, McGregor, Moody, Eddy, Mart, and similar surrounding towns, it is the hub of activity. Waco has been described as Baptist country because the Southern Baptists are quite numerous and because of the presence of Baylor University.

My father was born in Onalaska, Texas, and lived in several other country places before moving to Waco. My mother represents the first city-living generation in her family.

I am reminded of Joseph Douglass' article in *The American Negro Reference Book* (1966) which notes that, in emigrating, Negro families had to give up old patterns of behavior and leave old associates behind. Apparently, my father never read Douglass' article because old patterns and old associates have lingered on in his life. Perhaps the giving up of these patterns is more applicable to later generations.

As children, my two older brothers and I endured the "I remember when" syndrome experienced by Daddy. The "I remember when" syndrome followed a pattern similar to this: "I remember when I used to walk eight miles to school in the rain," or "I remember when I used to pick cotton for 50¢ a pound." I found it awfully difficult to identify with such experiences. After all, our school was no more than seven blocks away and the only cotton field I had seen was from a car while riding to Dallas. Besides, most of the time my mother took us to school.

Sometimes, if I insisted long enough, I would get to walk home in good weather. Walking from school was some adventure, especially when you live on a street like Clifton Street. One section was outlined with respectable businesses and residences. Three or four blocks from there the street was shadowed with dilapidated buildings where winos and loafers hung out. That part of the street still remains the same with the addition of a few more falling down buildings and a few more winos. I have often wondered why the city has not condemned those rotting structures.

When walking from school, I knew to step off the sidewalk as I passed "the corner." That was really a scary feeling. Beer bottles and wine bottles littered the area. The buildings were so old and dirty looking. Guys hung in doorways shooting the breeze. Some sat in front of the lounges watching cars pass. Sometimes I would stretch my neck to get a glimpse of the inside of one of the hang-outs. On several occasions I saw a smoke filled room where men stood around a pool table over which dangled a dim light. Just like in the movies.

Some days I was more afraid and would take an alternate route from school, completely by-passing the corner. Other days found me more curious and so brave that I would not even bother to step off the sidewalk. Still, the minute anybody spoke to me or even looked my way, I started walking so fast that any onlooker would have sworn I was running.

At one time the blacks down on the corner gathered at "the square," which was just across the Brazos on First Street. The tornado of '53, however, put an end to that by wiping out many of the lounges and cafes there. Some of the places rebuilt, but the square was never the same after that. Clifton Street took over as the stomping ground.

Eventually, urban renewal bought out the square, put bulldozers to work, and now Waco has its very own Convention Center as an attraction for tourists and businesses.

If urban renewal took over some sections of Clifton Street, the dudes down on the corner would find another place to congregate.

As can be readily observed, my walk from school was considerably different from my dad's jog from the school in the country. Sometimes Daddy would bring the country closer to the city by asking my mother to cook coon or oxtail stew or crackling bread. Believe me, I have nothing against any of these dishes. For the people of Onalaska, they served a purpose. But I concluded that crackling bread was much better without the crackling, chicken could run circles around coon, and ox could use a bit more meat on its tail. Dad's favorite dishes were novelties and I would try them out just to get an idea of the taste. I always preferred all the neat things my mom could do with ground meat—meatballs with gravy, macaroni with ground meat, okra gumbo. Let the coon stay in the woods and out of the pot!

Daddy visited Onalaska once in a while for homecoming. Once, I went with him and that was an experience I will never forget. Small shacks dotted the dirt road and some of them seemed to stand on a hope and a prayer. Clothes were flung over wooden fences, drying in the sun. No clothesline in the back yard? No washaterias? It was unbelievable. Many of the houses seemed to be void of electricity. No television? No Captain Kangaroo? No Popeye? It was becoming even more unbelievable. The highlight of the trip was seeing my first, real-live, authentic one-room school house. No cafeteria? No library? What about the bathrooms? I really felt that I had one up on the kids in Onalaska. After all, we had television, Alpha Theater, plumbing, a giant-sized school, paved streets, and television. When I returned home, one of the first things I did was make sure the television was still intact.

Sometime later, I had an opportunity to accompany my mother when she visited relatives living about ten miles outside Tyler. The only things I remember about that trip are cornfields and a watermelon patch. I guess when you have seen Onalaska, you have seen just about everything.

Certainly Waco offered all the advantages of city living, but it did offer a great deal more. In most places, railroad tracks serve as the dividing line, separating them from us. In Waco, however, the Brazos River had that honor. Most of the blacks lived on one side of the river in East Waco. Very few, if any, whites lived in our part of town. Whites came, did their business, and left. More than likely, they did not feel too secure about running around East Waco at night. Some of them were even a little anxious about being there in the daytime. I remember the elderly white couple who parked in front of our fish market. The little old man came into the store to buy some fish. As soon as he got out of the car, his wife rolled up all the windows and locked the doors. I wanted to go out and sit on the hood of the car just to give her a little scare. My mother, however, convinced me to refrain from doing so.

As Waco's residential sections were segregated, the same held true for the schools. Andrew Jackson Moore High School. My high school. The only black high school in the Waco Independent School District. Now it exists as only a memory.

On the left side of the school was a lower-class Mexican-American community. To the right was a cemetery. The murky water of the Brazos River flowed behind the school. Railroad tracks ran in front of the school. How many schools could boast of such outstanding boundaries?

Books received from the central office were not in the best of shape. We theorized that white schools received the pick of the litter. We did not have microscopes in our science class until I was in the tenth grade and our band uniforms were not too groovy. We had enough spirit and togetherness though to make up for all the things missing and the band wore those faded maroon and white uniforms proudly. In that one school, blacks from all social classes, from various backgrounds, united under one school song. With a black faculty and a black student body, all shared a common black experience.

The unequal treatment our school received was seen as something that was a reality to be lived through. Faculty members were instrumental in helping us see that the injustices were not a reflection of any ignorance on our part. The ignorance rested with those responsible for the injustices.

During the late 1960's, a bond election was scheduled that called for the building of two high schools. One of the schools would replace Moore High if the bond passed. My high school journalism class was extremely active in campaigning for the passage of the bond. We spoke at black churches, urging members to support the bond. After all, Moore was built sometime in the late 1800's and a new school was indeed in order. I would end my announcement by telling congregations, "Moore High was built to be a school, not a monument."

This experience represented my first taste of political involvement. Through the bond election I could see some action finally being taken to change a situation that had been crying for years to be changed.

My younger brother was in the second class to graduate from the new Jefferson-Moore High School—a school with structure and equipment geared to meet the needs of the 'seventies.

The old Moore High? At first, it stood vacant, desolate, dying. Finally, the buildings were torn down and the land cleared. Picnic areas and camping sites are on the old football field, shading the banks of what is now Lake Brazos.

I have no bitterness or anger about what happened. Progress was made. I do have some mixed feelings about the entire situation. My old school died—a death that was long overdue. When I think about it, I feel empty, sick inside, and a sad feeling comes over me.

Is the new school a black one? Some efforts are currently being made to see that it is racially mixed. During the summer of 1973, the Waco Independent School District drafted an integration plan. The black community opposed the plan from the beginning because it called for the bussing of black students. The bussing plan did more to rally forces among the blacks than anything I know. A school boycott was planned and executed. Steps are being taken to appeal the decision.

Waco is relatively conservative. The blacks in Waco are likewise relatively conservative. For them to unite, organize, plan, and act, the cause would definitely have to be bigger than average. The integration plan touched a nerve that sparked the whole thing. Schools and children have to be handled with care in almost any community.

In our community, churches as well as schools ranked high in importance. If you were new in town, you could meet people and become involved through the church. There was a church to fit your need. Many churches had numerous activities ranging from Youth Day to Women's Day. Revivals, district meetings, and state meetings were usually heavily attended.

Often political leaders emerged from the pulpit. Ministers were held in high regard and offered political direction to their congregations. In the Waco bussing dispute, several ministers were influential in the organizing.

My family is Holiness, which means that we have a great deal of group participation in our church. Tambourines, piano, organ, hand-clapping, and singing keep the services moving. The only lag in the service occurs around offering time.

Our church services were enough to keep me on the edge of my seat. Shouting, speaking in tongues, and music were integral parts.

To me, the music was the heart of the service—the choir singing, a solo, testimony service, or congregational hymns. A soloist's rendition of "Precious Lord" was enough to still the church. I would close my eyes and let the music fill me as I tried to choke back the tears. Rare was the person who remained untouched. A joyful noise resounded from the walls when the choir sang such songs as "I'm a Soldier in the Army of the Lord." Feet patting. Hands clapping. Voices lifting in song. The entire church swayed in time with the music.

Many of our members were as old as the church itself. They were active in church activities and were on the church steps every time the doors opened. I remember trying to guess the ages of some of the oldsters, but the agelessness and the timelessness of their faces suggested that the task be given up. They were simply amazing—still creeping around, taking care of themselves or living with their kids. During this time, the nursing home concept had not caught on in our community. Anyway, most of the nursing homes were still segregated. Now, however, nursing homes in Waco are becoming more populated by blacks. This is one trend that has come about during my generation.

In a sociology class at McLennan Community College, the professor ranked religious denominations according to their economic level. Holiness fell in dead last. The professor then gave an extremely negative description of the "Holy Rollers." I was utterly speechless. He was not talking about *any* religion; he was talking about *my* church. I was deeply hurt. I kept reminding myself that the value of a religion does not lie in economics. The hurt, confusion, and anger fused somewhere around my stomach and sought to escape through my lips. With all the control I could muster, I tried to keep from lashing out at the professor. In a predominantly white class containing only three blacks, I knew I would receive no understanding, no sympathy. That class ceased to be my favorite.

Occasionally, a big name entertainer would perform a concert at the Heart O'Texas Coliseum. James Brown must have made the scene at least three or four times. Concerts at the coliseum were colorful, gala, fashionable affairs. Usually every conceivable style could be seen, from the most coordinated to the most brazen. Heads turning. Necks craning. Eyes surveying. Every once in a while I even found time to watch the performer. The black clubs also managed to book name entertainers. Tyrone Davis or B. B. King posters hugged telephone poles on the East Side. The goings on at the clubs provided another arena for a display of the latest style or hair-do.

For the black youths desiring to remain in Waco, various possibilities awaited them. Paul Quinn College, McLennan Community College, Texas State Technical Institute, Baylor University, business schools, and limited jobs greeted eager young blacks with open, half-open, and not-so-open arms, depending on the leanings of the institutions. Joseph Douglass, in the book cited earlier, sees the slowness of the rate of progress of Negroes in urban society as due in large degree to the special handicap of race imposed upon them by the majority group. The special handicap of race was a key factor in determining opportunities available to blacks in Waco.

("The special handicap of race": For some reason that phrase bothers me. "The special handicap of prejudice, as possessed by the majority group, hindered the rate of progress of Negroes in urban society," sounds more appropriate.)

The special handicap of prejudice colored the type of treatment blacks received at the hands of law enforcement officers. Needless to say, much information is already available concerning the relationship, or rather the lack of relationship, between blacks and policemen. Policemen have seldom been seen as protectors of black freedom. In Waco, policemen had a reputation of "knocking heads and kicking butts." An unwritten code of ethics governed behavior and attitude when approached by a law officer. Summarized, it included some of the following advice:

> DON'T RUN.
> DON'T MOUTH OFF.
> DON'T CURSE.
> DON'T FIGHT.
> DO WHAT HE TELLS YOU TO DO.
> KEEP BOTH HANDS VISIBLE.

Of course, my upbringing included learning to "respect" the servants of the people. This "respect" seemed to be necessary in order to survive. When a policeman was involved, a chip on the shoulder or arrogance could only lead to trouble. As children, we devised cute little ditties that somehow revealed our true sentiment toward policemen. "I saw a car with a cherry on top. Nothing in it but a bald-headed cop."

Efforts have been made to change the image of the policemen in Waco. The police department has set up a community relations office to help bridge the lack of communication that has separated them from us. Blacks are being recruited to join the force. The gap was a long time in forming, so an abundance of community relations is needed to close it.

As some gaps widen, others close. For years we celebrated the June-teenth (Negro Independence Day) on the 19th of June. Our family, along with other black Waco families, celebrated the day on a park ground outside of Mexia. This annual celebration was an old-time one with singing, dancing, games, food, and thousands of people.

With the passage of time, the Juneteenth phased out—at least for numerous black families in Waco. I do not know if people still gather at the grounds. The Fourth of July is the big celebration day now. Daddy even closes the store for half a day to barbecue chicken or sausage.

I recall one white customer asking Daddy about his plans for the 19th of June. A distinct sneer was present in his voice. Without looking from the fish he was cutting up, Daddy replied, "I plan to celebrate the Fourth like you." Another trend changed before my eyes.

Our wit and ingenuity shone forth in many of our activities. I am reminded of the importance of rhythm in achieving the bouncy, light beat of our simple nonsense verse which represented a combination of catchy, rhyming syllables and sounds. An old favorite started with:

> Eenie, meenie
> Haja, keenie
> Oo-bop!
> Thumba-leenie
> Hotchi-totchi
> Liber-rachi
> I love you!

The verse usually ran on and on with additions, repetitions, modifications, and variations of the syllables. Of course, the one who could repeat the entire verse without error in syllabication was considered "with it." Timing as well as proper use of voice inflection seemed to be the key to success.

As we grew older, our rhythm experiences grew more sophisticated. Nonsense verse became kid-stuff with the emergence of "Hand Jive." "Hand Jive" involved a sequence of movements following a rhythmic pattern. Directions for the basic jive included:

> Pat knees with palms twice.
> Clap hands twice.
> Snap fingers twice—right hand.
> Snap fingers twice—left hand.
> Point right thumb over right shoulder twice.
> Point right thumb over left shoulder twice.

Variations of the jive existed calling into play various actions and movements. The trick was not to lose time and not to get the motions out of sequence.

Obviously, rhythm played an important role in our fun activities. We were usually up with the latest popular dances, adding our own individual touches. Everyone offered a different interpretation so that an individual was not *doing* a dance; he *was* the dance—moving, feeling, sensing. In a time when the controversy over the definition of "soul" was yet to come, we were too busy living soul to define it.

During the era of sit-ins and boycotts, blunt little sayings which originated elsewhere were being recited in the community. I say that they originated elsewhere because I knew we were not quite sophisticated enough to come up with:

> If you're white, you're all right.
> If you're brown, stick around.
> If you're black, get back.

We used this one so much that we were almost convinced that it originated in Waco. Besides, several kids stood ready and willing to accept the credit for devising it.

One-upmanship weighed heavily in determining the winner of verbal battles. Quick wit and a fast tongue led to having the last, undisputed word. Smart was the person who had a gem of wisdom to fit every occasion. An individual who thought he was smart and sly could be put in his place with, "You think you're smart, but you can't slide on a barb wire fence." Trying to impress a sweetheart? Her ear could be turned with, "I love you so-o-o much that I would walk into a lion's den wearing a pork chop jacket." Such maneuvers kept us sharp, alert, and always formulating. Creativity and imagination flourished through our daily fun and saturated our experiences.

Many of the experiences related may bear some resemblance to those in other cities. Rural ties, religious affiliations, political involvement, restricted housing, integration hassles, urban renewal, black-white tension, poor police-black relations, racial distrust, and changing trends are surely not uncommon in most urban areas. In the midst of all this, blacks and whites in Waco remained distant—The distance was both physical and psychological. With frustration mounting and pressure building, our black community provided the warmth and security needed to keep our heads together. Cultural deprivation? Social impoverishment? With a background rich in cultural heritage and overflowing with black experience, I hardly think of myself as culturally deprived.

Folk Anecdote Survives in Black Fiction

By JAMES W. BYRD

NEGRO SHORT STORY WRITER Arna Bontemps writes about an old wornout share cropper in "A Summer Tragedy." The feeble black man prepares for his joint suicide in the river with his frail and aged blind wife:

"I reckon you'll have to he'p me wid this heah bow tie, baby," he said meekly. "Dog if I can hitch it up. . . . My fingers is gone democrat on me."[1]

The last sentence was meaningless to me until Texas' leading Negro folklorist J. Mason Brewer identified it as being from a Negro folk anecdote after the Civil War, when Negroes were Republicans, of course. The anecdote was also told by numerous Anglo after-dinner speakers, according to ninety-five-year-old A. C. Ferguson, President of East Texas State University in 1946. The version he tells is the obviously "white" version below.

"Uncle Charley, an humble old darkey who was born in slavery, continued to live near the home of his former master, a distinguished Southern educator. Politically, Charley was a staunch Republican. He earned his living by driving a one-mule express wagon about town.

"One day as he drove on the railroad tracks, his mule and wagon were struck by a northbound train, killing the mule, demolishing the wagon, and throwing the old Negro upon the embankment where he was badly stunned. When his former master hurried to the scene of the accident, he found Charley sitting on the ground, with his hands clasped about his knees, in deep meditation.

" 'Why, Charley, what in the world has happened?' exclaimed his white friend.

"Scanning his eyes over the wreckage, Charley said very earnestly: 'Mistah Randolph, de whole damn thing have done gone Democratic!' "[2]

[1]Arna Bontemps, "A Summer Tragedy," in Martin Mirer, ed., *Modern Black Stories*. New York: Barrons Educational Series, 1971, pp. 175-76. Bontemps told me in 1954 that he heard the expression in his native Louisiana.

[2]E. V. White, compiler. *Chocolate Drops of the South*. Austin: E. L. Steck, 1932, pp. 4-5.

THE GERMANS

Karl Sachtleben.

A German barbecue. Courtesy Dr. M. W. Sharp.

Tschirhart family. Courtesy Dr. M. W. Sharp.

A. L. Cornisinger, ca. 1917. Courtesy Dr. M. W. Sharp.

August Haller. Courtesy Dr. M. W. Sharp.

Texas Folklife Festival.

Customs Among the German Descendants of Gillespie County (in 1923)

By JULIA ESTILL

NO ONE BORN AND REARED among the hills of Gillespie County, the unusual features of Fredericksburg, its county seat, and the peculiarities of its native population are taken as a matter of course until the exclamations of an observing visitor call attention to the fact that a really unique condition exists in the mountain community. To the observant stranger within the gates, the bright splashes of local color, evident to him at every turn, and the community life, totally unlike that to which he has been accustomed, are of rare interest.

Approached from any direction, the town appears like a dream village suspended among the hills. Truly the German pioneers who selected the site in May, 1846, chose wisely when they laid out Fredericksburg between the branches of a swift-flowing stream tributary to the Pedernales River, and surrounded by flat-topped mesas which yielded a good quality of limestone for houses and fences. The stately live oaks still to be found along the streets of Fredericksburg testify to the majesty of the virgin forest trees in the fertile valley where the little village sprang up.

Only a few reminders of old colony days remain, however, to attract the casual observer. The old rock mill, built on the banks of Baron's Creek, and turned by its turbulent waters, has gone to decay and the stream itself is almost dry. Twenty-five years ago (c. 1900) the march of progress swept down Main Street and tore from its foundations the majestic old church, which in early days served as town-hall, fortress, school, and sanctuary. The queer octagon-shaped structure blocked traffic and was unsightly, besides! Thus have many of the original buildings been torn away to give place to more modern structures far less picturesque, leaving Fredericksburg still a unique village, however, in which the old and the new are quaintly blended.

Among the most interesting buildings still to be seen, a picturesque reminder of earlier days, is the Nimitz Hotel on lower Main Street, standing at the crossroads, a most convenient place for travelers to stop for a substantial meal served in the same old dining-room where Generals Lee and Longstreet, and, perhaps, Sidney Porter refreshed themselves in days gone by. If you desire, you may drive your car into the back yard where the old stage coach used to stand behind the substantial wall of stone twelve feet high. For the asking, you may have a "cabin" opening out upon the "upper deck" of the old ship-shaped hostelry. The queer fourposter bed, once the property of General Lee, is yours for the night, should you care to sleep in it. In the parlor, below stairs, you will find paintings of the infant Fredericksburg, of the old mill at Barton Springs, Travis County, and a representation of the tragic death of Isolde.

A drive over the town will show you the quaint log-and-stone huts of unique architecture and careful workmanship basking stolidly in the sun on the by-streets, and the little brown Catholic church with its old-world belfry, where you expect to find a monk in his cowl telling his beads. Beside it stands protectingly the handsome stone edifice built in recent years.

But queerest of all to you will be the Sunday houses. Nowhere else in the world do they exist. They may be found almost anywhere in Fredericksburg: on Main Street nestling comfortably against the village smithy, in the fashionable suburbs beside a modern bungalow.

The custom of building Sunday houses originated with the farmer of Gillespie County, who, being of an independent nature, chose to buy a town lot and build, under his own vine and oak tree, a box-like structure of lumber, sometimes with only one room on the ground floor and a second surmounting it, with stairs leading up on the outside.

To this city home the farmer comes on Sunday morning when his family is religiously inclined; or on Second Christmas, Easter Monday, or Pentecost Monday when the young folks want to attend the public balls that begin promptly at 2 p.m. in the various halls. When shopping is to be done, or a sick member of the family needs medical attention, in comes the farmer to his Sunday house, where he is independent and safe from disturbance.

Of necessity, then, these temporary homes are furnished, one room often serving as kitchen, pantry, dining room, bedroom, and living room. But, at any rate, the relative or good friend in town is not thrown into a panic by the unexpected descent of a family of more or less dimensions to eat dinner and remain over night. And the thrifty farmer goes home with money in his pocket, for he has not been forced to partake of boarding-house fare. Besides, he has the satisfaction of knowing that he is under obligations to no man.

Later, when the farmer is weary of labor in the fields, and has a plump little bank account all his own, he and his faithful wife, who has helped him accumulate this wealth by practicing thrift and economy, leave the old home to their son, and come to town to spend a peaceful old age in the Sunday house to which, perhaps, a room or two and a little front porch have been added.

For the convenience of out-of-town members owning no Sunday houses, several Protestant churches in Fredericksburg have built houses in the church yards, where the members gather at noon to eat the lunches prepared at country homes the day previous. These combination kitchens and dining-rooms are provided with oil-cloth covered tables, home-made benches, and a cook-stove where food may be warmed and coffee boiled. Young and old remain for Sunday school, which is held at two in the afternoon.

A beautiful custom in Fredericksburg is the ringing of *Abend-glocken* (evening bells) at sunset every Saturday. When the last chime has floated cloudward from the seven spires of the hamlet, a holy quiet seems to settle over the town; and when the twilight melts into darkness, and the stars come forth from the deepening blue, the weary laborer feels that after all "God's in his heaven; all's right with the world."

The women in town set apart certain days when their particular friends are bid to a *Kaffee-Kraenzchen* (coffee-circle), or *Kaffee-Klatsch,* as it is sometimes called, an afternoon affair at which guests sit about and chat, busying themselves meanwhile with a bit of crochet or sewing, for bridge is to them unknown.

After an hour or so, the hostess announces that coffee is served, whereupon the guests betake themselves to the dining-room, where a wholesome meal is spread: *Schmierkaese* with thick yellow cream; wild plum jelly and watermelon jam; homemade bread and sweet, fresh butter; and occasionally, in season, a small plate of thinly-sliced, home-cured raw sausage. Then there is always a whole family of cakes: *Mandel-brot* (almond-bread), *Pfeffer-kuchen* (pepper nuts),

Zimmitsterne (cinnamon stars), *Lebkuchen* (ginger-bread) and *Kaffee-kuchen* (coffee cake). And all the while savory brown coffee flows freely. It seems, in fact, that the cookie jar in Fredericksburg homes is never empty, for an afternoon guest in the parlor will invariably be offered a plate of small cakes, and, in the old days, *ein Glaeszchen Wein* (a small glass of wine).

Kaffee-Kraenzchen pale into insignificance, however, when compared with weddings, confirmation fests, and birthday celebrations. On these high days and holidays, all the relatives (and they are legion!) are bid to the feast, which, in the language of Irving Russel, is "a 'ticlar sarcumstance." The fatted porker has been slaughtered, and, besides the immense roast, there are quantities of sausages, great and small, of the beef-pork, venison-pork, liver, and blood varieties. Several turkeys and perhaps a goose have been sacrificed. Besides these meats, the long hospitable board groans with eatables of all kinds: homemade noodles, Irish and sweet potato salads, rice with a "topping" of cinnamon and sugar, bean salad, and occasionally a salad of fruit prepared by a member of the younger generation. The herring salad is never missing from the feast of this kind. It is made by mixing diced boiled smoked herring with beets, hard-boiled eggs, pickles, apples, Irish potatoes, and vinegar, all properly seasoned. Everyone drinks coffee. But the cake is saved for "four o-clock coffee," when the table is reset, with fifteen or twenty cakes accompanied by a wonderful variety of cookies. The invariable first course, however, consists of sliced sausage, bread, butter, and several kinds of "home-grown" cheese: *Schmierkaese* (cream cheese), *Koch Kaese* (cooked cheese), and *Hand Kaese* (ball cheese). Occasionally, too, there are cream cheese pies made of cheese, cream, butter, eggs, and raisins. Oh, there is always food in abundance.

The hill folk of Gillespie County have more "feasts" than people of other sections, it seems. Besides Thanksgiving, Christmas, and New Year's Day, there are "Second Christmas" (the 26th), "Second Easter" (Monday), and "Second Pentecost" (Monday), "when young and old come forth to play." The first of these holidays is for sacred observances; the second for festivities. Then there are merry-makings everywhere; and nothing can dampen the holiday spirit of the crowd.

These customs were, no doubt, brought by the original settlers from the Fatherland, as were also the customs of St. Nicholas' visits, the Christmas tree in the home, and the coming of the Easter Rabbit.

St. Nicholas first visits the homes in Fredericksburg on the night of December 6th and occasionally thereafter until Christmas Eve, surreptitiously leaving candy and fruit in little stockings hung from the bedposts and often peering through the casement to see whether or not the children of the household are obedient to their parents.

But the day of all days for children as well as for grown-ups is the 24th of December, for it is then that at least *one* Santa Claus comes to the homes. He enters about the time the candles on the cedar tree are lighted and the home circle is gathered in the "best room." Every child is then asked to pray. This is the little petition the children lisp: *Ich bin klein, mein Herz ist rein; soll niemand drin wohnen als Jesus allein* (I am small; my heart is pure; no one shall abide there save Jesus alone).

Santa, being satisfied, then leaves an apple or an orange with each child and repairs to the neighboring house—if the children have all responded with the prayer. But woe to the unruly youngster who refuses to pray! He is soundly rapped with the huge stick Santa carries concealed under his mantle. Sometimes two or three of these Santa Clauses visit the same house in a single evening; and the program is usually repeated each time. On Christmas night all the churches have enormous trees for the children. Each child repeats a few verses in a lively monotone and, after the program, receives a bag of candy, fruits, and nuts, and often a small present.

The next holiday the children look forward to is Easter. By this time bluebonnets and *Osterblumen* (Easter blossoms: "butter-and-eggs") are out, and Saturday afternoon, the wee tots, accompanied by an older sister or friend, go forth with baskets to gather wild flowers for the Easter nest to be made in the garden in the evening.

That night great bonfires burn on the hills east and west of town: the members of the Easter Rabbit Family are gathered around the boiling cauldron, busy with brush and dye, preparing rainbow-hued eggs to delight the human children on Easter morning. That night, when the little folks are abed, the Rabbit Family members distribute the eggs, leaving in each nest at least eight brightly colored eggs.

The *Kindermaskenball* (children's masquerade ball), too, is a great event. Then practically all the children in town gather at one of the public halls for a frolic. Nymphs, fairies, butterflies, brownies, gnomes, witches, peasant maids, flower girls, and clowns skip about merrily until 10 o'clock when they are either whisked off home by their elders, or (in case the elders, themselves, want to enjoy an hour or two of dancing) put to bed in the dressing room, which is provided with a bed or two and numerous quilts for pallets.

Besides these holidays and merrymakings that delight the children especially, are the various "fests" for grown-ups. Chief among these are the *Schützenfests* (shooting fests) and the *Saengerfests* (singer fests). The country people take special delight in the former, for the festivities are held in some sylvan grove far from the city's dust and heat. The band, composed of country boys and men who blow lustily (and often discordantly!) on the wind instruments so dear to their hearts, entertains the multitude at intervals all day long. Between times, the crowd surges down to the rifle range, where boys and men try their skill at shooting the bull's eye. There is a bounteous feast spread at noonday, of course, and the usual cake and coffee at four o'clock. The festivities wind up with a dance at night.

The *Saengerfests* are great events, too. Nearly every community in Gillespie County has its choral club composed of men who sing the old German melodies taught to them by their fathers. Every spring or autumn there is a big gathering of all the singing clubs for a song festival. Then the "hills re-echo the mighty sound."

The Casino "Sylvester," or New Year's Eve ball, was one of the crowning events of the winter season. This, too, was held at the Nimitz Hotel. Then all the girls came out in new evening dresses, and the men wore their best Sunday suits. The leader of the grand march, one of Fredericksburg's "von's," invariably wore conventional evening dress; but he was the only man present who was thus attired.

At midnight when the church bells "rang out the old, rang in the new," the lights in the ballroom were extinguished and everywhere excited voices could be heard wishing everybody a happy new year, while above the din, resounding smacks came distinctly to the ear—for the Casino was all one big family, you know! When the greetings were over, the entire company marched into the dining room for a midnight supper. Needless to say, the merrymaking continued until the clarion call of the cocks "awakened the slumbering morn."

Truly, if Peter Hildesmueller and his neighbor, Hugo Hefflebauer, were to return to the village in the valley they left seventy years ago, they would find that time had wrought many changes. The days of skat and pinochle are over; *Beer-suppe, Hasenpfeffer* and *Wiener-schnitzel* are delicacies of the past; the young people no longer talk proudly of *Der alte Kaiser Wilhelm* and *unser Vaterland* in the pure German language of their fore-fathers. No doubt the visitors would shake their puzzled heads in disappointment, puffing thoughtfully meanwhile on their long-stemmed Meerschaum pipes, and pass back through the neglected vineyards to the recesses of the Bear Mountain caves, there to await for another seventy years the return of *Die guten alten Zeiten* (the good old times).

Following him into their retreat would go the defiant shriek of the sturdy little locomotive which, since 1913, has been ushering progress from the big outside world into Fredericksburg. As the clouds of gray smoke filled the valley and settled lightly over field and town, the colors, once so bright in the local scheme of things, would blur and fade away at length, leaving only a prosaic gray town among the hills where once stood the unique little "Dorf" of Fredericksburg.

Taken from *Coffee in the Gourd* (PTFS II, 1923), J. Frank Dobie, ed.

The Old World Antecedent of the Fredericksburg Easter Fires

By TERRY G. JORDAN

WHILE many Texas-German folkways have yielded to the forces of assimilation, the Teutonic custom of annual Easter Fires at Fredericksburg has survived for over a century and a quarter. In recent times the Fires have become somewhat of a tourist attraction, complete with a pageant. The celebration centers on the lighting of bonfires atop as many as 22 specified hills flanking Fredericksburg on the Saturday evening preceding Easter. At the appointed time, the church bells of the German town toll; all lights are extinguished, and the hilltops burst into flame.

The present paper is an inquiry into the beginnings of this lovely custom, a subject surrounded by confusion. The folklorist Julia Estill, one of the first to mention the Easter Fires, was silent on the subject of their origin,[1] but local tradition provides the generally accepted answer. According to this tradition, the beginnings go back to 1847 when the colony of Fredericksburg was less than one year old, at a time when a treaty was being negotiated between the Adelsverein leader John O. Meusebach and the Comanche Indians. While Meusebach and several chiefs conferred at a camp many miles from town, Indians keeping watch on the settlers supposedly lit signal fires at night on hills around Fredericksburg. These fires, reportedly used to communicate messages to the gathered chiefs, terrified some of the children of the German settlement, prompting one imaginative mother to tell her offspring that the Easter Rabbit and his helpers had lit the fires to cook eggs, prior to decorating and distributing them among the children on Easter morning.

So widespread is this story concerning the origins of the Easter Fires that it has found its way into various publications, including those of the Institute of Texan Cultures.[2] It is the explanation offered to visitors attending the pageant. This is unfortunate, since the traditional explanation is at best incomplete and possibly altogether erroneous. In this respect, several points should be made. First, Easter Fires occur widely in the Old World, including parts of Germany. While this fact is apparently known to some of the Fredericksburgers and has been pointed out by several scholars, it has not been given adequate attention. Myrtle Murray, in a 1951 article on the Easter Fires, spoke briefly in passing of "similar fires of the Fatherland";[3] I made reference to the German antecedent in my 1961 Master's thesis;[4] and Irene Marshall King raised the same point in her 1967 biography of Meusebach;[5] but our findings do not seem to have gained much attention.

The German antecedent is widespread and occurs in certain provinces which contributed large numbers of emigrants to the Hill Country German colonies in Texas, including Fredericksburg. The German folklorist Richard Beitl wrote in 1933 that "in wide areas of northwestern Germany, particularly in Westphalia, Hannover, and Oldenburg, the custom of Easter Fires is still in active practice. . . ."[6] The custom extended to the borders of Denmark in the north, to the Dutch border area in the west, and into the provinces of Hesse and Thuringia in the south and southeast. These Easter Fires of north-

western Germany, like their counterpart in Texas, were lit on specified hilltops, known in Germany as "Easter Mountains" (*Osterbergen*
or *Paskebergen*).[7] From certain vantage points on Easter Eve, a great
many bonfires could be seen dotting the German countryside with
bright points of flame. The practice originated in prehistoric pagan
times. In some districts, it was the practice until recently to throw
squirrels, horses' heads, or goats' horns into the fire, and in other
districts livestock were driven through the flames, thereby gaining
protection from illness or other harm. The fires also guaranteed
fertile fields and protection from lightning bolts.

Many if not most of the Fredericksburg colonists were from provinces and states where Easter Fires were common, especially Hannover, Westphalia, Brunswick, and Thuringia. These provinces and
others in the Easter Fire area contained 387 or almost half of the
868 identified villages which contributed *Adelsverein* emigrants to
the Texas Hill Country.[8] A contemporary account, written in the
1840's, noted that Hannoveraners constituted one of the two largest
groups in Fredericksburg.[9]

Thus we find Easter Fires on specially designated high points both
in Fredericksburg and in certain German source regions of the Fredericksburg colonists. Surely this cannot be coincidence. There can be
little doubt that we are dealing with a cultural transplantment and
that the Fredericksburg pageant is descended from an ancient, honored German custom. This view is reinforced by the fact that the rabbit and egg are also associated with the Easter celebration in Germany.
It seems likely that the Fredericksburg immigrants from Hannover,
of whom my great-grandfather was one, were the ones instrumental
in transplanting the custom.

A second major point which tends to detract from the Indian signal fires thesis is that the Meusebach-Comanche negotiations, which
tradition places on Easter Eve, occurred instead on March 1st and
2nd, 1847, long before Easter, which could not have occurred earlier
than March 28 in that year.[10] Meusebach's party returned to Fredericksburg several days later, still well in advance of Easter. Nor am I
convinced that Comanches were in the custom of using nocturnal
signal fires. It would be interesting to hear from some experts on
Comanche culture concerning this point.

The question remains as to how the Indian story became associated
with the Easter celebration. In all probability this occurred some

years later, perhaps in the period of renewed Indian hostilities in the 1850's. The two events of the spring of 1847, the Indian negotiations and the first Easter celebration in the new home, blurred and merged in the memories of those who had experienced them. It is also possible that the original incident of frightened children occurred at the Easter celebration fires in 1847, rather than being based on Indian signal fires. The children, perhaps of families not derived from the Easter Fires area in Germany and therefore unaccustomed to the practice, could have misunderstood the meaning of the celebration flames and mistaken them for Indian fires, prompting the mother to tell the Easter rabbit tale. A child from Nassau or Württemberg, who knew nothing of Easter Fires and was already terrified of Indians and insecure in his new homeland, could well have reacted in this manner. In any case, while the Indian story adds an air of frontier adventure to the celebration, the European antecedent seems the more important ingredient.

[1]Julia Estill, "Customs Among the German Descendants of Gillespie County," *Publications of the Texas Folk-Lore Society*, No. 2 (1923), pp. 71-72.

[2]William Petmecky, *Legendary Tales—Easter Fires of Fredericksburg* (Fredericksburg, 3rd ed., 1962), pp. 2, 10-12; "German Texans Perpetuate Heritage, Add to Mainstream," *People*, Vol. 1, No. 3 (May-June, 1971), p. 7; (Institute of Texan Cultures), *The German Texans* (San Antonio, 1970), unp.; Myrtle Murray, "Easter Fires," *Texas Parade*, Vol. 11 (1951), p. 4.

[3]Murray, *op. cit.*, p. 4.

[4]Terry G. Jordan, "The German Element of Gillespie County, Texas," Master of Arts Thesis (Geography), University of Texas (Austin, 1961), pp. 159, 162.

[5]Irene Marshall King, *John O. Meusebach: German Colonizer in Texas* (Austin, 1967), pp. 119-120.

[6]Richard Beitl, *Deutsche Volkskunde* (Berlin, 1933), p. 251.

[7]"Ostergebrauche," *Meyers Konversations-Lexikon*, (Leipzig & Vienna, 1897), Vol. 13, p. 281.

[8]See Terry G. Jordan, "The Pattern of Origin of the Adelsverein German Colonists," *Texana*, Vol. 6 (1968), pp. 245-257.

[9]Wilhelm Hermes, "Erlebnisse eines deutschen Einwanderers in Texas," *Kalendar der Neu-Braunfelser Zeitung fuer 1922* (New Braunfels, 1922), p. 24.

[10]King, *op. cit.*, pp. 115, 120, gives the correct dates, but errs in stating that they fell on Easter.

THE IRISH

E. S. Emmons and Henry.

Irish Catholic Sisters. Courtesy Sister Aloysius.

Texas Folklife Festival.

Green Flags Over Texas

By MARTHA EMMONS

IN THE DAYS of silent movies Richard Dix appeared in a film which showed him on the eve of some fantastic venture urged upon him by his father. His faithful friend and man Friday, a raw Irishman, proposed to go with him, stoutly declaring, "Ye'd be worth nawthin' without me, at all." As one reads the history of Texas, with all its drama, all its glamour, he must conclude, if unbiased, that surely the whole story of Texas "would be worth nawthin'," without the Irish contribution. Irishmen trod Texas soil even before the filibusters, and were liberally represented in that group of adventurers. The whole Gulf Coast Plain would have gone begging for settlement had not Mexico allowed staunch Irish Catholics Mc-Mullen and McGloin, Power and Hewetson to colonize there. Shutting off that inviting part of Texas to Anglo-American settlement, the leaders in Mexico saw an advantage in having the region opened up to "wealthy Irish families." Just in case the other newcomers, most of them Protestants, should give trouble, these Catholics could be depended upon to stand true to Catholic Mexico, and to be a buffer between that country and any dissident elements among its colonists.

If the Mexican government counted on the Irish to keep peace while others fought, they overlooked a few facets of Irish character. Irishmen have always loved liberty. Born for freemen they gave England more trouble than any or all of her other possessions. No Irishman would miss a good fight. And so it was in Texas. Twenty-five of them signed the Goliad Declaration in 1835; four, the Texas Declaration of Independence on March 2, 1836; eleven died in defense of the Alamo; fourteen, with Fannin; and the Irish comprised over a seventh of Sam Houston's army at San Jacinto. The first Texas flag was made by an Irishman, Captain Dimmit. Made of white domestic, it pictured a red arm and a hand grasping a sword.[1] Mexico made a sad mistake on these sons of freedom. That is certain.

Undoubtedly Sam Houston's army at San Jacinto would have been worth "nawthin' " without that one of every seven men. Who knows what Irish wit, what Irish gaiety, what songs in camp may have lightened hearts and spurred men on to follow their leader in that dark situation? The army's marching song, "Will You Come to My Bower," was written by Irish Thomas Moore. Fit and proper it was that even that battle which in so few minutes changed the history of the world should have romantic overtones.

More practical was the overtone voiced by Mrs. McCormick, owner of the land on which the battle was fought. She was less impressed by the romantic and patriotic aura than by the stench of dead bodies left on her land by fleeing Mexicans. To the great general himself she made her complaint. Linn in his *Reminiscences* reported General Houston as addressing the lady: 'Madam, your land will be famed in history as the classic spot upon which the glorious battle of San Jacinto was gained."

"To the divil with your glorious history!" retorted the lady. "Take off your Mexicans." They did.[2]

In the drab story of the Civil War one bright episode is that of dashing Dick Dowling and his 42 Irish dock workers from Houston and Galveston who in less than one hour crippled the Union fleet, sank one vessel, captured two, killed of the enemy a number equal to almost half their own, and took 315 prisoners, and all this with "positively nobody hurt."

The Irish have been well represented in any wars of the state or nation. They have made their impact on other fronts as well as those in battle. In a privately published paper for the Society of the Sons of Erin, J. M. Woods declares,

The Irish have fought, sung, laughed, shouted, prayed, and served their way across the pages of Texas history, and they have carried the burden of others' woes, they have dispensed charity . . . and have striven for stability in society and government.

In education the Irish took the lead. Miss McHenry taught children in Austin's colony. Austin College, first in Huntsville, now in Sherman, had on its staff M. B. Brown, widely known as "a well-educated Irishman," and had another Irishman, Samuel McKinney, as president for a dozen years. William Mallet had the distinction of being the first departmental chairman in the University of Texas. All over Texas, in the bleak days of Reconstruction and even later, Irish school masters single-handedly staffed one-room schools. Such a person was one called "Uncle Joe" Nugent, a well-educated Irish Canadian, well known throughout a wide area of central Texas. Somehow he managed to stick to his principle, "Don't come to me with what your mas and das say." From all accounts, parents as well as "scholars" accepted the dictum.[3] Dr. Francis Moore, lawyer, surveyor in the Republic of Texas, was editor of Texas' leading newspaper, *Telegraph and Texas Register,* and author of *Maps and Description of Texas* (published in Philadelphia), and was also a member of Texas Congress, and was for a time state geologist. Irish churchmen were and are well out in front in establishing hospitals in Texas. In politics and government, echoes of Erin sound all down the years in names of our public servants: "Pegleg" Ward, land officer, architect and builder, mayor; and in names like Collingsworth, Bryan, Thomason, Lindsey, Dan Moody. One governor bore the name Ireland.

The Irish led in good neighbor policy with Mexico. In 1832 Irish colonists at San Patricio inspired Mexican Governor of Tamaulipas to a magnificent gesture of over-the-border friendship between Irish businessmen of Matamoros and those of Irish colonies in Texas. The colonists participated in the festivities called "El Banquete."[4]

Contrary to the caricature of Irish immigrants as lazy and shiftless, much business enterprise in Texas has had and still does have Irish entrepreneurs. In very early days William Barr and associates formed a substantial trading company in Nacogdoches; and as for railroads in Texas, how could the rails ever have been laid without Irish laborers?

On the agricultural front, many Irish immigrants have made history in Texas: Dunn at Corpus Christi with his cabbage culture; Thomas O'Connor with his half million fenced acres in south Texas, with cattle enough to range those acres; Peter Gallagher, with his activated vision of irrigation on land near present Fort Stockton; John Adair who with Charles Goodnight developed the JA Ranch in the Panhandle.

But agriculture was not the particular forte of most Irish. Many of those in the coastal settlements were unable to cope with such entirely new conditions as drouth and wide acreage, gave up farming and drifted into one town or another, to find employment as day laborers. A number of such families found their way into San Antonio. A little cluster of oddly assorted houses north of the present Post Office became known as the "Irish Flats." Most of the residents were poor and lived on uncertain income. But from all accounts, even in their poverty, they gave refuge and often wise counsel to many a friendless drifter.[5]

Irish immigrants' ignorance of Texas farm methods is proverbial. From a rural economy themselves, they met conditions too dissimilar from those in "the ould counthry" to make necessary adjustment. They have never seemed to hit it off with our agricultural ideas and procedure. Many are the tales of the ineptness of the raw Irish farm hand. Baylor professor T. H. Claypool, who lived some years near Burleson, used to tell of a farm family in that community who gave employment to one of the Irish "foot paddies," often seen in those days. They showed him around over the place, explained such things as they supposed needed explaining; then one day the whole family went to Fort Worth for the day and left the new man to pick cotton. When they returned that evening, had the family evening meal, and sat around the fireplace for a while, talking over the experiences of the day, someone asked the Irishman how he had fared picking cotton.

"Well, I think I got about as much br-reshed out today as I can gether-r up tomorrow," he proudly announced.

It is often said that "More lies have been told about the Irish than about any other ethnic group—and more than half of them are true." Most of the tales, factual or non-factual, are in a measure true, and they do reveal certain traits or facets of character attributed to the Irish. Some of them they tell on each other, others are told on them by "outsiders," as they call non-Irish. Chief among these traits is a tendency to vociferous boasting, bragging about one's physical prowess, as one young Irish lad in the employ of Mr. C. M. Gossett, of Taylor, said of himself one day: "You know, I've just been taking stock of myself lately. Educationally, I'm nothing much; morally, not too hot; but physically, I am hell!"

Especially do Irishmen glory in their Irish blood. At a patriotic gathering in New Braunfels one day, the talk was growing more and more fervent extolling Texas and her brave sons. An Irishman in the crowd began reminding those present of the large part which he and his fellow countrymen had had in the cause of Texas' greatness. His monologue, no doubt helped along by the "wee drap" he had taken, became a bit boring. One young lad, with a slight German accent, rather sarcastically inquired whether he were "really an Irishman." That set him going. Loudly and yet more loudly he began to proclaim his ancestry.

"Yes, I'm an Irishman! Indade I'm an Irishman. Me father before me was an Irishman. His father before him was an Irishman. I'm an Irishman now; I was an Irishman born; and when I die I'll be an Irishman, dead, and so I will!"

"Vell, ain't you got no ambition at all?" came casually from a Jewish passerby.

Justly or unjustly common report has it that most Irishmen are pretty well gifted with profanity. One thing to remember is that most of our Irish immigrants in the nineteenth and first quarter of the twentieth centuries found employment in the very hardest, roughest work, building railroads, digging ditches, and hauling heavy loads.

In course of an irrigation project in the rice country of Texas, many Irish were employed. One day the superintendent of the project was showing a Houston priest around, explaining the great effect all that would have on the economy of south Texas. As they watched the dirt fly from the shovels of the great, broad hands, they could not but hear profanity flying just about as far and as fast as was the dirt. The superintendent was embarrassed; the priest was grieved. At last the reverend father spoke. "Oh, my good men, where did you learn such language?"

"Lord save your riv'rence," exclaimed one of his faithful parishioners, doffing his cap, "you couldn't learn it, Father; 'tis a gift."

Quick wit of the Irish is a trait which none would gainsay. It flashes in conversation; it flames in action. In the great booming days of railroads, Fort Worth was an important center, and Irish laborers were an important factor. One depot in the city served both the Santa Fe and a line then called the H&TC, a branch of the Southern Pacific. A crusty station master there commanded the respect of those under his power. The story used to be told of an Irish workman who one day burst unceremoniously into "the Old Man's" office and demanded a pass to Houston or Galveston, to visit his "wife an' childer." Stunned by such boldness, the great one replied, "I don't know whether I'm going to grant the request or not, Pat. But certain decorum should be observed. What time does your train leave?"

"Six o'clock."

"Well, then, suppose you do this. About four this afternoon, you come to the door and knock; when invited come in, take off your cap, take the pipe out of your mouth, introduce yourself; and when asked to state your business, do so. Could you do that?"

The Irish   161

"Sure."

Promptly at four came a heavy knock at the door. In answer to "Come in," entered the Irishman, deferentially removing both cap and pipe. Guilelessly he inquired, "Is this Misther _____?"

"It is."

"I'm Pat Casey, a workman in the yards here."

"All right, Mr. Casey. What can I do for you?"

"Sor, yez kin go to hell. I've got me pass over the S.P."

But the icing of the cake is the supernatural, the highly imaginative. Nowhere in all Texas are there more tales of buried treasure than in that part most tinctured by Irish influence, as for instance the counties of Atascosa, McMullen, Live Oak and Bee. Let him who doubts see accounts by J. Frank Dobie in *Legends of Texas* (Texas Folklore Society's *Publication* Number III, 1924; 1964). Most of that treasure is there yet. Either the settlers failed to bring along enough leprechauns or else the little rascals refused to cooperate in unearthing it. Nevertheless, the real treasure, that of the tales, is with us today, such as the one of the strange creature, who roamed the Navidad, known as the Wild Woman—who turned out to be a man!

Even Irish fairies have been more active in mundane affairs in Texas than some persons may admit. According to Mike Welch, who ought to know, his home near Thorndale stood on the very site of an Irish castle transported thither by fairies. How did he know? Didn't he hear the songs and shouts of merriment emanating from revelers in the castle now sunk in Texas soil? Why, he had with his own eyes seen the pair of lovers for whom the castle was intended.[6]

The Irish, on their own soil or transplanted in a new, habitually move in a saffron glow of the supernatural. It was so with the colonists; it is so with many to this day. The old story of McGloin's warning of McMullen's death has been so oft repeated that except for the rankest unbelievers it is now taken as fact.

In the early morning of January 21, 1853, McGloin in his home down near the Coast was awakened by cries of "Help! Help me, James!" He recognized the voice as surely that of McMullen, his partner in colonizing and now his father-in-law. In his vision he saw the victim in bed, all bloody from knife wounds in his neck and chest. The cry persisted: "Help me!"

McGloin sprang out of bed, began to dress, saying, "I've got to go to McMullen. He's in trouble. He needs me."

Knowing his overwrought condition and ascribing the nightmare to his recent worries, a member of his family persuaded him to wait until daylight to start on his long horseback ride to San Antonio. As soon as he could see the ground before him, McGloin was on his way.

Arriving at the home of McMullen he saw people standing around the house, all of them "extremely sober." He asked what was going on, and someone answered, "Why, didn't you know? McMullen was killed and robbed by someone in the night." On inquiry McGloin learned that the time of the murder was exactly that of his dream.

Even yet, down along the Gulf Coast, at least one ghost claims attention. Many are the travelers who give an account of being stopped by a nun and asked to give her a ride to some point on down the road, later to find the seat empty. Accounts vary. One tells of two young soldiers going from Sinton to Corpus Christi, in 1942. At her solicitation they opened the door and assisted the nun into the back seat. Soon the conversation turned on war. She told them it would end that year. At Corpus Christi she asked to be taken to the cemetery and left there. Just as they were driving away she handed them a note and asked them to convey it to the priest at Sinton. The priest read the note, then brought a large book of pictures of nuns and asked the men to select the one that most resembled their passenger. The two quickly identified the nun they had left in the cemetery. The picture selected was of a nun who had been dead for several years—and lay buried in the cemetery at Corpus Christi.[7]

Irish traditions are far from forgotten in Texas. Their number, variety and intensity vary, but in one degree or another they are still with us, and they forge a green link between the Emerald Isle and her children here in Texas. Dallas sometimes makes much of St. Patrick's Day. The year 1962 was one of the high-point occasions. The festivities began at 8 a.m. with Mass at Sacred Heart Cathedral, included elaborate pageantry all day, and ended with a grand ball at the Statler Hilton that night.[8] Shamrock has a notable celebration on that great day.

St. Patrick's Day celebrations go all the way from the wearing of green ties and a shamrock here and there to the likes of Pioneer Day combined with St. Patrick's Day, in Dublin, Texas. There the whole town goes all out to honor the good saint. The parade, sometimes in the morning, sometimes after work hours, features high school bands from neighboring towns, all a-wearin of the green; the Riding Club, resplendent in green breeches and green felt hats, with appropriate trappings for the horses. Men on the streets wear green derbies; women, pioneer costumes; and everybody sports green. Festivities close with an Irish stew supper at the high school cafeteria and a talent show after that, or along with it. Honor students guided by Mrs. Betty Culpepper (currently the president of the Historical Club and curator of Lyons Museum), by Coy Wall and other Irish citizens of the town, and with the overall help of the school faculty, present a skit. Committees judge costumes for uniqueness and appropriateness, and usually on the basis of costumes choose a Miss St. Patrick and a Mr. St. Patrick, two or more leprechauns, and sometimes a queen of the festivities. Willard Mann is lord high chef for the Irish stew. The very Irish Mrs. Mann when asked the recipe answered, in words and accents of old Erin: "Would ye believe it, Miss, there is no recipe? And even if there was one, we wouldn't be following it at all."

Yes, that is believable entirely. No true Irishman ever follows a recipe exactly. By and large an Irish stew recipe is about like this: Dice about a pound or so of lamb or mutton; combine with an agreeable amount of not-too-large potatoes, onions according to taste, several carrots diced, by all means one yellow turnip, salt and pepper to one's liking, and always some sprigs of parsley. Cook all that until meat and vegetables are tender; thicken with flour-in-water and "simmer a bit more"—and nobody knows how much or how long the "bit" is. Enjoy it in an atmosphere of Irish conversation and gaiety.

Though Dublin claims no connection with Ireland for its name, it does feature the Irish motif in many ways; street names such as Grafton and Patrick, and even a section set aside called Belfast. With such names as Ross, Raley, Shehan, and Galloway among its citizens, the visitor need not be surprised at the Irish twinkle in the eyes, and the radiant smiles he sees everywhere, any day in the year, in Dublin.[9]

Even as on St. Patrick's Day shamrocks, leprechauns, and clay pipes prevail from Houston to Shamrock, and many besides the Irish do be a-wearin' of the green, so it is that the history of Texas is romantically frosted over with lively Irish green, an Irish imagination, Irish wit, Irish courage, and Irish tradition, without which the whole story would be "worth nawthin' at all."

[1]*People,* published by the Institute of Texan Cultures, San Antonio, March-April, 1971.

[2]Bernadine Rice, "The Irish in Texas," in *Journal of American Historical Society*, XXX (1932), 66, quoted from *Gulf Coast Line Magazine*, Summer, 1906.

[3]My chief source was my father, E. S. Emmons, and some of his friends of Mansfield and Cedar Hill.

[4]Edna Mae Tubbs, "When Erin and Mexico Frolicked Together," *Dallas Morning News*, June 26, 1932.

[5]Marie Fitzgerald, *Irish Flats* (San Antonio: Naylor, 1972); and a painting in Witte Museum, San Antonio.

[6]Louise von Blittersdorf Moses, "Irish Fairies in Texas," J. Frank Dobie and Mody C. Boatright, eds., *Straight Texas* (Austin: Steck, 1937), pp. 185-89.

[7]Ruth Dodson, "The Ghost Nun," Mody C. Boatright, Wilson M. Hudson, Allen Maxwell, eds., *Texas Folk and Folklore* (Dallas: Southern Methodist University Press, 1954), pp. 124-26.

[8]*Dallas Morning News*, March 18, 1962.

[9]My chief informants in Dublin were Mrs. Betty Culpepper, Mrs. Loyd King, Mrs. Galloway, Mr. and Mrs. Barnes, in Barnes' store, Mr. Early Knox (present mayor) and Mrs. Willard Mann.

THE SCOTS

Bosque John McClennan.

Cameron Lumber Company. Courtesy Texas Collection, Baylor University.

Texas Folklife Festival.

Annual Texas Highland Games in Waco. Courtesy Scottish Society of Texas.

Scottish Texans
and the Highland Games

By HARRY GORDON, President Emeritus, Scottish Society of Texas

THE SCOTS came to Texas singly or as families, rarely in groups. It was an expression of their individualism. They did not establish colonies; they dispersed rapidly and were soon integrated into the society in which they took root, freely giving of whatever talents they possessed.

Texans are a people with a distinctive background, even in our very diverse United States, different markedly from folks from Kansas, Missouri, and Arkansas. Individual Scots have played a part in the development of this distinctive background, especially where the Scot has left the imprint of his character on the culture of Texas.

One of the little known stories in the life of Texas Scots in the last quarter of the 19th century is the story of Aberdeen stonecutters solicited in Scotland through newspaper ads for work on the state capitol. Some sixty-five or more were recruited in the Aberdeen area and brought over for the express purpose of fashioning the great blocks of pink granite used in construction of the capitol. These Scots were later absorbed in the Texas community, where they continued to use their special skill.

It would be remiss of anyone speaking of Scots in Texas history not to mention that Scots played their part in the Battle of the Alamo. Bowie and Crockett were among the Scots who died there. However, not until 1963 at the instigation of the Scottish Society of Texas, the Scottish Society of San Antonio, and the Daughters of the Republic of Texas did the flag of Scotland stand side by side in the Alamo with other flags of nationals who died there. It was that year in October that Lord Polworth of Edinburgh, representing the people of Scotland, came to Texas and to the Alamo to present the Scottish Standard with appropriate ceremonies covering the historic event 127 years after the battle.

To appreciate better the role of Scots in Texas history one has but to listen to the roster of Texas counties bearing Scottish family names: Anderson, Archer, Barnet, and Austin; Caldwell, Cameron, Clay, and Cochran; Bell, Bowie, Armstrong, and Brewster; Dallas, Dawson, and Denton; Edwards, Fisher, Gillespie, and Hamilton; Henderson, Houston, Hutchinson, and Jefferson; Mitchell, Montgomery, McCulloch, and Robertson; Rusk, Sterling, Stephens, and Taylor; Walker, Williamson, Wilson, and Young.

There was Thomas Drummond, noted Scottish naturalist, who explored Texas in 1833 and 1834 and produced the first major scientific collections for leading European museums. His reports to the University of Glasgow were among the first scientific reports on Texas flora and fauna.

Dr. George Cupples, who came to Texas in 1844 in search of health for his wife, was noted for his achievements in surgery and is reputedly the first Texas doctor to use anesthetics.

Thomas Affleck established one of the earliest nurseries in Texas. He traveled widely in Scotland encouraging his countrymen to come to Texas. His books and articles bore him out as an authority on Texas agriculture. When he died in 1868 he had been working on a packing plant for beef, fruit, and vegetables.

In the field of religion and education (so closely allied in Scottish history) there was John McCullough, who established the first Presbyterian Church in Galveston in 1840. Joining him the same year for the organization of the first Texas Presbytery were W. Y. Allen and Hugh Wilson. In 1846 McCullough served in San Antonio and there organized the First Presbyterian Church. He was active in early efforts to establish a Presbyterian college in Texas.

As a tiller of the soil and a herdsman, the Scot has historically always been close to stock, both cattle and sheep. Ewan Cameron, one of the earliest of Camerons to come to Texas, entered the cattle business after the Battle of San Jacinto, hiring young men to gather wild cattle from areas abandoned during the Texas Revolution. A wily Scot by the name of W. K. Bell came out to Texas in 1870, served as sheriff in lawless Palo Pinto County, later bought up cattle, fenced them in, and by 1879 had one of the finest herds in the area. William Menzies, Sr., was one of the later arrivals in Texas who established himself in what is now Menard, pioneering sheep and cattle ranches. And when one thinks in terms of cattle and their drives overland, one thinks of the Chisholm Trail founded by Jesse Chisholm running from Kansas into Oklahoma and later extended into Texas.

In the late 'seventies and 'eighties many wealthy Scottish investors became interested in profits to be made from cattle on the open range—free range—in West Texas. The Matador Cattle Company was one result, with 300,000 acres of land and 60,000 head of cattle forming assets. By 1910 the company operated ranches not only in Texas but in South Dakota and Wyoming as well.

Murdo McKenzie, in his extensive career as bank clerk and law apprentice, became manager of the Matador Land and Cattle Company. A man of considerable business acumen, he is credited with successful passage of the bill entrusting the Interstate Commerce Commission with power to fix rates on interstate freight. President Teddy Roosevelt, who called him the most influential of western cattlemen, appointed him to the National Commission for Conservation of Natural Resources.

One of the great lumber barons of Texas was William Cameron, whose activities in Denison, Dallas, and Waco centered around more than sixty lumber yards. His first lumber venture was part of the development of the MK&T Railroad for which his company supplied ties and other construction material.

Also, Neil McLennan must not be overlooked. In 1801 when he was fourteen years old his family removed from Scotland to America. Later, in 1835 he and his brothers John and Laughlin came to Texas and settled in what is now Falls County. In 1839 after the loss of Laughlin and his family in an Indian raid, Neil joined George Erath's Milam County Company to help stamp out Indian uprisings. In the period of the Mexican-American War in 1845, he bought land and settled on the south bank of the Bosque River eight miles from Waco in the area where McLennan Community College is now located in the county bearing his name and on territory he surveyed as a member of Erath's company.

The traditions of these early Scottish settlers of Texas are celebrated by the Texas Highland Games, held every May at McLennan Community College. For years Texas Scots searched for a place reminiscent of Scotland itself to hold their Highland Games. They concentrated on the Central Texas highlands, with lakes and deeply wooded glens.

The spot finally selected was the campus of McLennan Community College with its 150 acres of magnificent rolling terrain on the banks of the Bosque. After nine years in Austin in temporary locations, the

Texas Highland Games in 1972 moved permanently to the campus of the new and thriving young college.

It is fitting that these lands along the Bosque were once owned by a pioneering Scot, name of William Cameron. He landed in New York in 1852 from Blairgowrie, Perthshire, Scotland. In his "pooch" was $18; in his heart was a burning desire to find fortune and happiness in the new state of Texas. The county of McLennan appealed to him. In 1878 he arrived there, later to amass a fortune in cattle and lumber, becoming one of the great "lairds" of his day in the environs of Waco.

Things Scottish stand out at McLennan Community College: the college paper is "The Highland Herald," the school magazine is "The Clan," and the school's colors and crest are from the tartan and arms of Clan MacLennan. So it is fitting that this campus is the site for the Texas Highland Games.

Historians have documented the Greek Olympics, but the beginnings of the Highland Games is lost in antiquity. Long ago during Scottish summers, clans would hold a "tainchel," or deer drive. It was similar to a military maneuver, with all the men of each clan taking part. Such gatherings were sponsored by Scottish chieftans or kings, who found them ideally suited for recruiting the finest and strongest for vacancies in their ranks.

The custom of the gatherings grew in popularity, and it was not uncommon for *sassenachs* (Englishmen not always held in high esteem by Scots) and Lowlanders to compete. The *sassenachs* were the visiting players (so to speak), but the Scots were the usual victors in most contests.

"Modern" Highland Games date from the middle of the 18th century and were organized to preserve the colorful culture and traditions of the Scottish people. Highland societies were formed, and the first organized "Gathering" in Scotland was held in 1781 at Falkirk.

It took Texas Scots a bit longer. The Scottish Society of Texas has sponsored the Texas Highland Games since 1963.

The spectator sees the full panorama of the national pastimes of Scotland at the Texas Highland Games. These pastimes range from demonstrations of muscular prowess to exhibitions of the weightless grace of the Highland dancers. With deceptive ease, the dancers trace the intricate steps of the Fling, the Sword Dance, the Seann Triubhas (shane trews), and the Strathspey Reel of Tulloch. The artistry of solo pipers and the pomp of marching pipe bands are also there.

Events requiring muscle are tossing the caber and tossing the sheaf. The caber, which looks like a small telephone pole, has no official weight or length, but usually it's ten to sixteen feet long and weighs from 90 to 150 pounds. The caber is tossed forward from a vertical balanced position—striving not for distance, but for a 180-degree flip ending in the "12 o'clock position."

The sheaf is simply a sixteen-pound bale of hay, tossed with a pitchfork. Farmers all over the world do it, but Scots make a sport of who can pitch the bale highest over a horizontal bar. A Scot has sent the bale thirty-five feet high!

This annual celebration of the Scottish Highland Games brings into focus parts of the history and the finer nature of the Scot. The event highlights some of the qualities that have made him through the years a very satisfactory settler in Texas, with a culture one would want to see integrated into the variegated culture of Texas.

THE DUTCH

The Koelemay family at the Orange Hotel, Nederland. Courtesy Windmill Museum.

Harvesting rice at Pine Island Bayou, 1902. Courtesy Windmill Museum.

W. L. Freeman Hardware Store, Nederland, ca. 1904. Courtesy Windmill Museum.

KCS Railroad Depot, Nederland, ca. 1905. Courtesy Windmill Museum.

First school in Nederland. Courtesy Windmill Museum.

Footprints of Wooden Shoes

By ROBERT J. DUNCAN

JUST BEFORE THE TURN of the last century many settlers from Holland immigrated to Texas and founded the town of Nederland halfway between Beaumont and Port Arthur. Many of the present residents are sons and daughters of those immigrants.

Nederland was known as "the largest city in the world" for a few days in 1960, when it annexed 650 square miles comprising virtually all of the unincorporated land in Jefferson County plus a sizeable wedge of the Gulf of Mexico.[1] This colorful distinction, plus the unusual opportunity of having first generation Americans as informants, formed the basis for my decision to study the folklore of the Dutch and Dutch descendants in this city. In addition, I soon learned that Arthur Stilwell, president of the Kansas City Southern Railroad, who traveled to Holland to solicit financial assistance for his railroad and to recruit Dutch settlers for rice farming along the Texas Coast, later claimed that he was guided by ghosts or brownies in deciding the location for his railroad. Perhaps stranger still was the name he gave to this route to the sea: "the airline route," considering that this was while the Wright brothers were still fooling around with bicycles. So, everything considered, the subject of folklore in Nederland seemed like a natural.

Stilwell went to Holland in 1893 to obtain financial support to complete his railroad from Kansas City to Port Arthur. He was obsessed with the idea of providing reasonable rail rates for the transportation of inland products to the sea. Because of the Panic of 1893, Stilwell was unable to obtain financing in the United States; however, he managed to sell three million dollars worth of stock in his railroad to Dutch investors. Some people in the Netherlands still own stock in the KCS.

Later Stilwell and others formed the Port Arthur Land Company and encouraged the Hollanders to immigrate to Texas. Land company agents showed the Dutch people photographs of lush vegetation and told them that they could go barefoot at Christmas in Texas. The photographs were later found to have been taken in Florida and, ironically, that first year was the coldest that has ever been recorded in the Nederland area; the temperature got down to 2º above zero. In 1897, the first immigrant, George Rienstra, came to the low, flat prairie that was to become the town of Nederland. He bought eighty acres of land from the Port Arthur Land Company and was given four "town" lots for commercial enterprises. A commemorative book published in 1973 for the seventy-fifth anniversary of the city graphically relates the isolation of George Rienstra and the desolation of this unmarked land:

He chose the spot on which he would build his home and unloaded his stove and other supplies to mark the spot. He then went to Port Arthur to get a load of lumber to start construction. When he returned to Nederland it was dark and he could not see his stove. George spent the night on top of his load of lumber and had to shoot the wolves that came up near the horses and wagon. The next morning he located his stove about a half mile from where he had camped.[2]

Within a few months about fifty families from Holland had joined him, and the Port Arthur Land Company had built a three-story hotel to accommodate some of the immigrants while they constructed their houses. The hotel was named the Orange Hotel, in honor of the royal house of Holland which had come into power with William of Orange. Appropriately, it was painted bright orange in color. On September 6, 1898, the Coronation of Queen Wilhelmina was held in Amsterdam, Holland; in Nederland, the celebration probably rivaled that of the fatherland, for there was dancing, racing, fireworks, Dutch beer and an elaborate banquet menu including orange soup, liberty cake and something new to the Hollanders: ice cream. A dedication ceremony was held in the park across the street from the Orange Hotel and a tree was planted in honor of the occasion. A time capsule in the form of a sealed bottle containing historical documents was placed in the ground along with the tree. There is a vague but persistent rumor that Queen Wilhelmina had sent some gold to be buried along with the tree so that the Dutch in Nederland "would always have some money." The tree has been gone for as long as anyone can remember and the bottle apparently has never been dug up.

Mosquitoes were a serious problem in the early days. Smudge pots were kept burning outside the church on Sunday nights to protect the horses from mosquitoes. When girls went to dances or picnics they often had to wrap newspapers around their legs under their stockings to protect them from mosquitoes. There were also snakes and alligators; one little girl in the county was reportedly eaten alive by an alligator.[3]

There was some disillusionment on the part of the newly arrived immigrants. Some families returned to Holland, but many toughed it out. Dirk Ballast was an ordained minister and a skilled carpenter. He arrived in 1897. His first job in Texas was to dig a grave in Port Arthur. "He was so discouraged that first day that he is quoted as having said that he felt like crawling in himself."[4] Dan Rienstra was skeptical enough of the land company's promises about the climate to bring his ice skates from Holland. When the temperature got to 2° that first winter, he went skating on the Neches River, feeling that he had been hornswoggled.

A baby was born to the Westerterp family in February, 1899, during that same cold spell. The baby's two sisters had to take turns holding him in an open oven to keep him warm enough. Maarten Koelemay had ridden a horse into town for supplies before the storm hit and on his return trip home his big, full beard froze in the blizzard.[5]

The settlers had come to Nederland for a variety of reasons. Some simply wanted adventure. There was compulsory two-year military service required of all males in Holland at eighteen years of age, and some people migrated to avoid it. Holland was overcrowded and the plentiful land at ten dollars an acre sounded good. Some settled in Port Arthur, Hamshire, Winnie and other nearby places, but the majority settled in Nederland. Rice farming, cattle raising and dairy farming comprised the economic base for the community in the early years. The Dutch were old hands at cheese making and dairy farming. In 1901, Spindletop gusher came in just a few miles from Nederland. The growing oil industry provided jobs and encouraged population growth. The momentous 1915 storm and the digging of a deep canal allowed salt water to invade the fresh water and rice farming was hurt for many years.

There is very little trace of Dutch architecture left in Nederland. The Orange Hotel was torn down in 1915 or 1916. Nellie Rauwerda Fowler's house on Luling Street was built to the same plans as her family's home in Holland. In 1969, Mr. M. L. C. Lucke, Gene ("Sam")

Bass and other interested citizens proposed that a Dutch windmill be constructed in a tiny downtown park. Despite some skeptics, a three-story replica of an authentic Dutch windmill became a reality late that year. Blueprints were obtained from the Netherlands via Holland, Michigan, but all measurements had to be converted from the metric system before construction could begin. Today, the tall tourist attraction houses a gift shop where wooden shoes and other imported goods from Holland are sold at surprisingly reasonable prices. The two upper floors contain museum articles and archives recounting Nederland's rich history. Otherwise, no hint of Nederland's Dutch heritage can be found in the local architecture, at least to the unpracticed eye of this observer.

The Dutch are a very pragmatic and realistic people, possibly a result of their having to wrest their native land from the sea. Americanization was therefore a fairly rapid process. Many of the first generation Americans never learned enough of the Dutch language to speak it. Dutch was used in church services, but from the first the schools were conducted in English. Mr. M. J. Stappers told me that his father cut all ties when he left Holland; that when he came to America, he became an American. This sort of thing is admirable in a way, but it is disturbing to the folklorist. Another problem is that the Dutch, historically known for their industry, thrift and conservatism, are not a very imaginative people; their realistic view of life precludes almost all superstition. They believe in hard work and determination, not in luck. Albert Rienstra, a nephew of George and son of Dan Rienstra, another early settler, told me that he thought that these Dutch qualities had rubbed off on other residents of Nederland. A Dutch "saying" used when someone has undeserved good fortune is, "He fell with his butt in the butter."

The Dutch immigrants were a religious people. Early in 1898 they began holding Dutch Reformed Church services in the Orange Hotel. In an effort to keep them content, the land company provided them with a minister and paid his room and board at the hotel. Mrs. Marie (Rienstra) Fleming is a local historian. Her maternal grandfather and step-grandfather, Mr. and Mrs. Dirk Ballast, managed the hotel at that time. Apparently the land company made the understandable mistake of giving the rent money directly to the minister, because when Mr. Ballast tried to collect the overdue hotel bill from him, it came to light that he had spent the money for another purpose.

Prayer and the Dutch Bible made up a major part of family life in the settlement. Mrs. Fleming says that *each* of the several children in her family was required to say this simple prayer before every meal:

> *Heer, zegen deze*
> *Spys en drank. Amen.*
> (Lord, bless this food and drink. Amen.)

However, if their grandmother was visiting, only the grandmother prayed, but she constructed such lengthy prayers that the hot food would get cold on the table before she would finish. It so happened that the old lady was hard of hearing. She would sit down at the table and say, "Now ve bidden!" meaning, "Now we pray!" The Rienstra children would be sitting around the large table, and one of the five boys sitting on grandma's left would say, under his breath, "I bid 30." The next one would say, "I bid 31," and so on around the table like "42" players. The grandmother, of course, could not hear them.

Mr. John Bandsma is a first generation American whose family settled in Wisconsin and later moved to Hamshire and then to Port Arthur. His family visited Nederland often. His father worked for the Texas Company (later Texaco) for a while and the city of Port Arthur for a while, and finally went into the dairy business. He told me that for years and years, at mealtime his father would pray in Dutch; then the meal would be eaten, followed by his father's reading a chapter from the Dutch Bible, and finally by another prayer. This was the standard procedure at every meal.

One folk joke about the use of English in the Dutch Reformed Church was related to me by Mr. Bandsma. He said that the Reformed Church services were originally conducted in Dutch. As the children grew up, they did not understand much Dutch, so it was decided to begin having the services in English. One Sunday morning, the preacher got up and started praying in English. One old Dutch lady nudged another and said, "That preacher shouldn't pray in English; the Lord doesn't understand it. He can only understand Dutch."

There were a lot of humorous vignettes resulting from language problems and misunderstandings. Peter Terwey once went to the drug store and asked for "wapor rub." No one could understand him until he elaborated: "Wicks wapor rub!" He got what he went after. Some of the Dutch immigrants could never learn to pronounce "th." One Hollander went to Beaumont to apply for his citizenship papers. He was asked his and his wife's ages. He replied, "Mine vife is dirty and I am dirty too." One sharp young lad wanted to go to school with his sister, but he was too young. He told the teacher that he was five in Dutch and six in American. He got to stay.[6]

When Dena DeVries was a little girl she begged her mother for some pears that were in a bread box. Mrs. DeVries thought she might get sick if she ate any more, so she told Dena that she couldn't have them. She kept begging her mother, until finally her mother said, "Lope te de Drummel"—"Go to the Devil." Later her mother saw her eating a pear and asked her why she had disobeyed. Dena said, "You told me to lope to the trummel." The trummel was a container or box, so she had taken her mother's statement to mean, "Go to the container," a beneficial interpretation.[7]

During my first trip to Nederland I heard this joke that came from Denver, Colorado: There were two old Dutch ladies on a streetcar, and there was a lanky fellow on the streetcar whose feet stuck out into the aisle. He had on some loud colored socks and they were showing. The two old ladies started laughing up a storm and talking about his socks in the Dutch language. He did not appear to understand Dutch, or they would not have talked about him. Finally, one of them said to the other, "I wonder what he paid for those socks." The fellow leaned over toward them and said, "I paid thirty-five cents for the pair," in Dutch.

Several of the Hollanders were in the dairy business. The Dan Rienstra family delivered bottled whole milk twice daily to their customers, since the milk spoiled easily in the old fashioned ice boxes or in pantries. The Koelemays had a prosperous dairy business, also; one of their wooden sign boards is on display in the Windmill Museum. Milk cows were a source of income and were valuable. A local sharpster sold Dan Rienstra a cow one time. He said that the cow would give a lot of milk after recovering from having a calf. He guaranteed that within six weeks she would be giving six gallons of milk. Rienstra went home a happy man and told his family what a good deal he had just made. He declared that six gallons of milk a day was great. But in six weeks the cow was still giving very little milk. Rienstra went back to the man and said that she wasn't giving milk like he had been promised. The sharpster replied, "Why, Dan, surely she has given six gallons of milk during this six weeks. That's only a gallon a week. That's all I promised."

The Dutch have some unusual food favorites and some of our foods were unusual to them. Dan Rienstra and his bride returned to Holland for an extended honeymoon. When they came back to America, they were supposed to land in Galveston, but there was a bad storm in the Gulf, so the ship diverted its course to Baltimore. Later it returned to Galveston, but while they were waiting aboard ship in Baltimore, there were fresh fruit peddlers on the dock. Rienstra went ashore and bought some cantaloupes; he had never seen any before. When he cut them open and saw the pulpy, seedy center, he thought they were spoiled. He threw several of the melons overboard before realizing that they were good.

As I mentioned earlier, the Dutch were not familiar with ice cream when they came over; it was a new delicacy to them. Mrs. Fleming said that her mother always thought of tomatoes as a fruit and treated them accordingly: she always cooked them and added some sugar and cornstarch. One of the sons went off to the university and came back telling them about sliced raw tomatoes with salt. Her mother would allow the children to eat them that way, but would not eat them herself. The Hollanders often cooked *Rode Kool,* red cabbage with apples in it, seasoned with vinegar and sugar. It is supposed to be a very good dish. The Dutch were unfamiliar with cornbread at first, but soon learned to appreciate it. John Bandsma told me, "When you take potatoes and cheese away from a Dutchman he starves to death. When I go to the store I look for the biggest cheese they've got."[8]

To celebrate New Year's, the Dutch in Holland cook *Olie Koeken,* a kind of doughnut or fritter with an apple center. Then they ice skate. Some of the Dutch descendants in Nederland still cook *Olie Koeken* at New Year's. This was a specialty of the Orange Hotel. It has also been recalled that flapjacks were cooked in the hotel right on top of the wood stove, without a skillet.[9]

Many of the Dutch continued the tradition of having an afternoon tea. Tea time was usually at about 4 p.m. and included snacks as well as hot tea. The Dutch usually took their tea with milk, not lemon. A *theelichtje,* or tea pot, was kept warm all day long, much as a coffee pot is in some American homes now. For a while, tea was imported from Holland, as was cheese. Later, the Nederland Dutch began to use brands of tea that were available in America.

In 1948 Nederland had a Golden Jubilee and in 1973, a Diamond

Jubilee. In both instances a queen was crowned and young maids, in Dutch tradition, swept the streets before a street dance.

Gerrit Terwey came to America in 1892 and worked in Canada for two years. He then returned to Amsterdam. He visited in the DeJong family's house there and saw about six pairs of newly polished shoes by the fireplace. He seemed especially interested in one particular pair of the shoes and asked who was the owner. A young girl in the family said that they were her sister's but that she was away from home that day. Gerrit made an appointment to return for another visit on a day when she would be at home. At their first meeting, it was love at first sight. They were later married and migrated to Nederland.[10]

As mentioned earlier, the Dutch were thrifty. They walked almost everywhere they went and saved their horses for plowing. At the Diamond Jubilee I chanced to talk to "a hillbilly from Lovelady" who had some Dutch relatives by marriage. He said, "If one of them gets fifty cents, it belongs to him. You'll never see it any more." But he said it with a gleam in his eye. In today's economy such a description could be an expression of admiration and envy. Dan Rienstra was probably typical of the early settlers—he never bought anything on credit. If you didn't have the cash, you went without. One of Dan's sons worked for a week or two for a local man, and he was supposed to get ten dollars for the work. The man paid him in one-dollar bills. When the Rienstra boy, Dick, got home and re-counted the money, he found only eight dollars! The man had folded two of the bills over, so that each one looked like two when you just counted the ends. Rienstra did not rush back and complain that he had been cheated; he bided his time. . . . Years later, Dick went into business, and one day his former employer came in and bought something. Dick pulled the same trick when he gave the man his change. The man had not re-called the earlier episode. He was indignant and complained, "Hey, Dick, you don't know how to count!" Dick replied, "Oh, yes, I do. You taught me!" Then the man remembered the earlier incident, and they both enjoyed the joke.

Mr. C. L. Freeman is not Dutch, but he was a merchant during the very early days of Nederland and he knew the Dutch people well. Now 97 years old, he was a grown man in 1901 when the Spindletop gusher came in just a few miles from Nederland.[11] As he talked about the Dutch settlers my four-year-old son, Brad, came into his living room with a pair of wooden shoes that I had bought at Nederland's Windmill Museum that weekend. Mr. Freeman recognized them as he reminisced, "That looks like a wooden shoe. My friend Dan Rienstra used to wear them all the time. On a little gray horse. . . . I can see him now. . . ."

There are vestiges of other ethnic groups in and around Nederland. French and Cajun workers migrated from Louisiana to work in oil fields and refineries. Germans make up a portion of the populace. The bulk of the present population consists of plain old melting-pot Americans, but the many Dutch descendants still play a prominent role in the business, cultural and social life of the city.

The Dutch immigrants rapidly adjusted to the American style of life, and many of the old customs and most of the old-country language was abandoned as the people concentrated on building a town and making a living for their families. The actual footprints of wooden shoes did not last long. In recent years the city has begun to see the desirability of advertising and promoting its Dutch heritage, as symbolized by the new Windmill Museum. The Dutch are proud of their heritage and the other citizens share in their pride. The symbolic footprints—the cultural impression of the people of that area—will remain for decades to come.

[1] There are, of course, extenuating limitations that must be mentioned, such as the following: 1) The title refers to area, not population. 2) The city never actually annexed the area; it just made the first of two readings of the ordinance that would have been required to make the annexation official, so the city limits were never actually enlarged. 3) A few days later, Houston made a similar move, which covered a larger area than Nederland's intended acquisition. Nederland's action must also be put in historical perspective: in 1959 and 1960, many Texas coastal cities were competing in a land-grab race that became partly a defensive tactic to protect the option for future growth. Under Texas law the only criterion for annexation was that the property must be adjacent to the existing city limits. The courts upheld claims based upon a single reading; this gave Texas cities the benefit of a legally protected option to annex the area without burdening them with the corresponding responsibilities to the area. A second reading would bring responsibilities with it, so the surrounding area of many Texas cities was left in the limbo of being quasi-annexed for a while.

[2] Mrs. Jack M. Fleming (Marie) *et al., Nederland Diamond Jubilee* (Nederland, 1973), p. 4.

[3] Lorecia East, *History and Progress of Jefferson County* (Dallas, 1961), p. 115.

[4]Fleming, *op. cit.*, p. 8.

[5]*Ibid.*, pp. 8-9.

[6]*Ibid.*, pp. 54, 91.

[7]From a short, unpublished source paper prepared for Fleming's *Nederland Diamond Jubilee.*

[8]Interview with Mr. John Bandsma during the Diamond Jubilee.

[9]Fleming, *op. cit.*, p. 16.

[10]From a short, unpublished source paper prepared for Fleming's *Nederland Diamond Jubilee.*

[11]Mr. Freeman remembered the past vividly. He moved to Nome, Texas, west of Beaumont in the 1920's when his cattle business grew to such proportions that he had to move out of Nederland. About the Spindletop gusher, he says that Mr. Lucas had bought supplies at his store in Nederland. Freeman rode out to Spindletop right after the gusher came in. He says that he and a one-armed man built a levee to save some of the oil. That night it came a big rain and virtually all of the oil, floating on top of the water, spilled out of the temporary reservoir.

When George Rienstra died in the thirties, Mr. Freeman, Con Wagner and several other men rode to the funeral together. On the way home, they got to speculating as to which of them would be the next to die. Within a week, Con Wagner, the youngest man among them, fell dead in his own yard. Freeman says he got superstitious and wouldn't go to Wagner's funeral.

THE DANES

John Twohig. Courtesy Witte Memorial Museum.

Christian Madsen and wife Kirsten at "Dansk Farm," ca. 1900. Courtesy H. D. Madsen.

Danish group in a mule-drawn wagon. Courtesy Mrs. Ella Hansen.

Old Ansgar Lutheran Church, Danevang. Courtesy Mrs. Ella Hansen.

Danevang Confirmation Class, 1908. Courtesy Mrs. Ella Hansen.

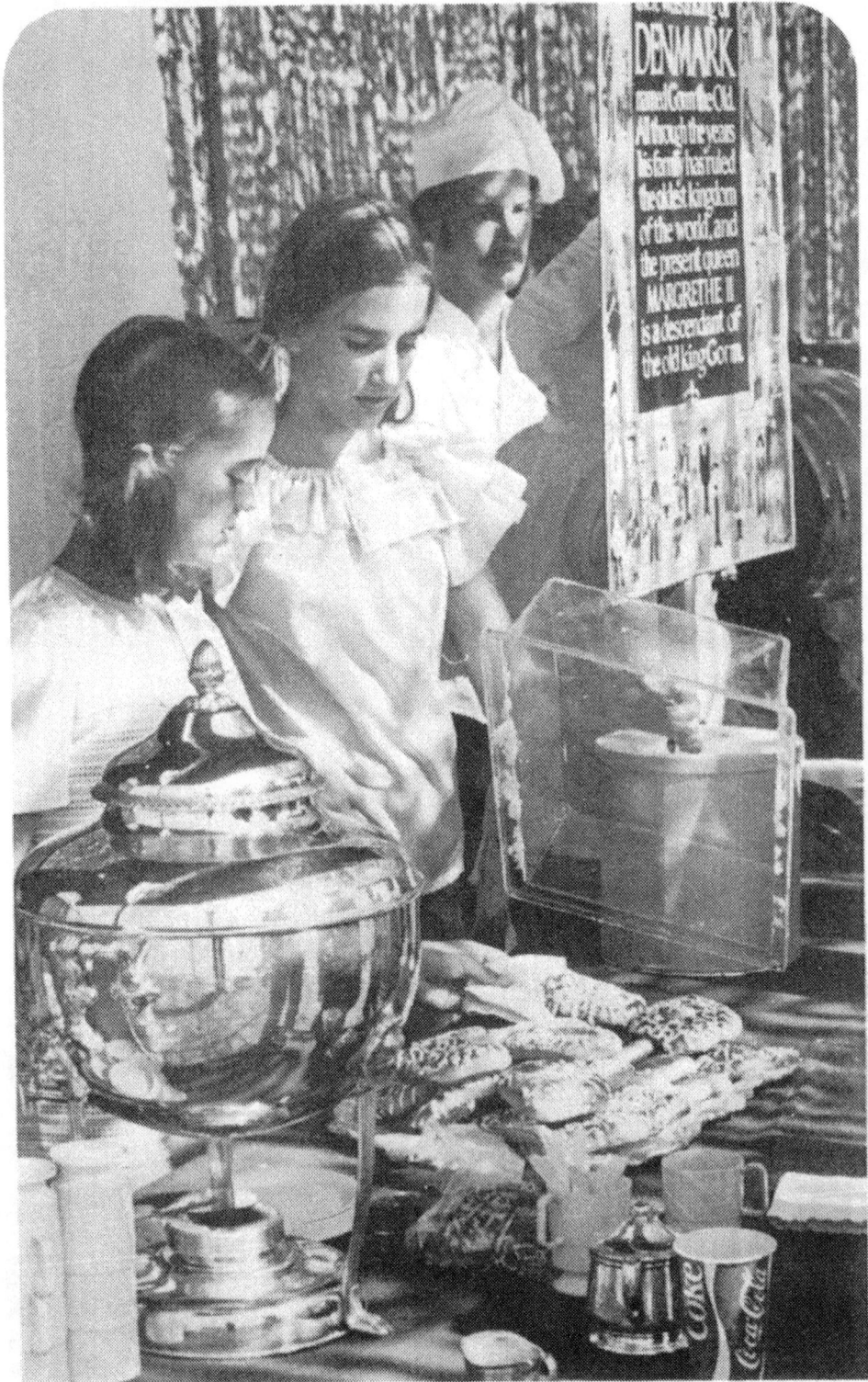

Texas Folklife Festival.

Community Celebrations in Danevang

By SUSAN LUCAS and SARA CLARK

Mrs. PETERSEN laughed when she quoted the saying in Danevang: that if you get two Danes together, at least one of them will bring a coffee pot. And anywhere that you find a Danish coffee pot, she explained, you'll find also a well-stocked pastry board: cakes, cookies, and breads of all sorts. Another saying in Danevang, according to Mrs. Roberts, is that Danes eat five meals a day! Danes do like to eat and they like best of all to eat together.

It was no surprise to us, therefore, to discover that the community-wide celebrations that took place in this tiny Wharton County town, the only Danish settlement in the Southwest, were primarily great communal feasts, though they commemorated many different special occasions in the life of the settlement and the lives of its individual inhabitants. Birthdays, gold and silver wedding anniversaries, house-warmings, church holidays, July 4 and June 5 (Danish Independence Day), even the monthly community meetings, all were excuses for elaborate festivities, the center of which was always the table loaded with rich Danish food to be shared by all.

From the time the first settlers came to the 25,000 acres eleven miles south of El Campo, which the Danish People's Society had secured for a townsite in 1894, the dedication to doing things together as a community was already developing in Danevang. From the beginning, forty-five acres were set aside for the Danevang Lutheran church, parsonage, and church farm. On this tract the community hall was built in 1895. It became the center of the life of the settlement, housing the school during the long term and the classes in Danish culture, arts, and language during the summer. The hall also provided a roof for all the other gatherings which claimed the interest of the community as a whole: social events as well as religious celebrations and civic meetings. Indeed, the settlers soon discovered that *all* occasions when the members of the community came together, for whatever purpose, provided much needed social diversion.

There were, in addition to the commonly-held lands and buildings, several other powerful factors contributing to the strong sense of the integrity of the community in Danevang. The Danish immigrants who came to this village after first settling in Iowa, Illinois, Kansas, and Nebraska, brought with them from Denmark strong ideas about the value of cooperation. They worked together to help each other and to accomplish things for the whole community which couldn't have been managed otherwise.

In 1897 the first organized cooperative business was formed, a mutual fire insurance company. A cooperative telephone company, which provided the exchange free of charge, was established in 1913. Both of these companies have now been sold, but the Danevang Farmers Cooperative Society, which was organized in 1920 for the purpose of buying cotton insecticides more cheaply in quantity, has grown into a farm supply store, cotton gin, blacksmith and welding shop, bulk gasoline station, filling station, liquid fertilizer mixing plant, and grain drier, all of which are still owned and run by the two hundred farmer members. Cooperation was a way of thinking, living, and being in Danevang.

The physical and psychological isolation of this tiny settlement provided further strong impetus to the development of a cohesive community. The nearest place where a Danish-speaking immigrant could be understood when he spoke was at a similar settlement in Mississippi. The wilderness of the English language confronted him on all sides. Until 1932 Danevang was eleven miles by dirt road (which was often impassible mud) from anywhere, which happened to be El Campo. There was no railroad, no navigable stream, only miles of black clay surrounding the community in every direction.

Given such interdependence and isolation, it was only natural that the people of Danevang, who worked together as a large Danish "family" to help each other, would want to celebrate together all festive and joyous occasions: those commemorating milestones in their personal lives as well as more public holidays, both civic and religious.

There were several kinds of events in the personal lives of the citizens of Danevang which were celebrated by the whole community; among them were birthdays, housewarmings, and golden and silver wedding anniversaries. Each of these occasions called for a different sort of party, and the customs governing each type of party were always followed.

Twenty-fifth and fiftieth wedding anniversaries were celebrated in the community hall. Sometime before the date of the anniversary, a committee of the couple's friends was formed to contact every member of the community and collect contributions for a "nice" gift which the community would present to the honorees. (A list of the names of the actual contributors, however, was kept and also presented to the couple.) The silver anniversary gifts were usually "household" type gifts, gifts addressed to the couple as a family unit: silverware or, later, stainless steel flatware, silver trays or bowls. The gifts for the golden anniversaries were usually more personal, gifts to the man and woman separately: a gold watch, for instance; a brooch, perhaps.

The community hall was lavishly decorated for these anniversary celebrations, in a gold or silver theme. There were always streamers and greenery and yellow or white flowers. Mrs. Nelsen smiled broadly as she recalled climbing the ladders to build the elaborate trellised archway which transformed the wooden-walled community hall into a "ballroom" for one of the parties many years ago. Surpassing this extravaganza, however, in Mrs. Petersen's opinion, was the time they strung the huge tractor umbrella upside down from the center of the hall. Pieces of colored glass were attached to the umbrella and streamers stretched from its ribs to the corners of the room, providing a dazzling canopy effect.

On the afternoon of the anniversary, the honored couple and family were seated at the head table, and the rest of the community at tables which filled the hall. Everybody brought food "for coffee" which they all shared: sandwiches, rich cakes, cookies, coffee breads of all sorts, and always a wedding cake, sometimes with a bride and groom on top, to recall the happy event.

Someone always played the piano while the guests ate and plotted among themselves for the surprises and revelations of the spontaneous "program" to follow, a program which afforded everyone in the community a chance to reminisce publicly about the couple and their marriage. Out came the sentimental recollections, the embarrassing tidbits, the forty-year-old grudges. The pastor or a close friend tried to emcee the hodgepodge, but often gave up in laughter when faced with stories like the one about the honeymoon trip from California that was largely spent changing thirty-five flat tires on a Dodge roadster.

In the days following the anniversary celebration, the honored couple would often show their gratitude to the community by hosting a dance at the hall or an open house at home for their friends.

The birthdays and the housewarmings were different from the anniversary celebrations in that they took place at the homes of the honorees. As a person's birthday approached, the women of his or her family began to bake. Though there was no single cake identified as *the* birthday cake, there were cakes and cookies and pies enough to feed anyone and everyone who cared to drop by on the birthday afternoon to offer congratulations. There might be "six or six dozen" visitors: you never knew, since no invitations were given. Once, for a respected grandmother's birthday, the baking went on for a week beforehand, and eighty guests in all were served. If the weather was clear, tables were often set up outside under the spreading trees which no Danish homesite would be without.

The guests, forbidden by tradition to bring gifts or food, brought only themselves and their good wishes. Since no invitations were extended, everyone was automatically expected to be there. And if you weren't, Mrs. Petersen assured us, you could expect to be stopped on the street and questioned about your absence. Mrs. Roberts nodded agreement.

The housewarmings were surprise parties celebrated whenever anyone bought or built a home in the community. Again a committee was formed beforehand, and contributions were collected for a gift. On the day of the celebration, a friend would make arrangements to be sure the honored couple would be at home, and at the appointed time, all the well-wishers would descend upon the new house, bringing food for the party and a "nice" and needed household gift.

There were other community celebrations in Danevang which commemorated occasions that were important collectively, not just personally. Each one had its own traditional form, its own customary activities and accessories. These were the religious and patriotic celebrations of the community, and, as such, they were all held at the community hall at the church, none at private homes.

For instance, there were the twin Independence Day celebrations held every summer, a month apart, on June 5 and July 4. All day long on these two days, Danish Independence Day and American Independence Day, the whole community would celebrate with games like sack races, turtle races, ring riding (in which a ring was caught from horseback or even "bicycle-back"), dollar and horseshoe pitching, and many others. There were concessions that sold soda water and ice cream from the creamery in El Campo, and huge tubs of boiled coffee to which egg was added to clear away the grounds. The Danish flag and the American flag flew side by side, "with maybe the American flag a little higher." And there were speeches and dancing to fiddle music and much high spirits far into the evenings.

Another important celebration in the Danevang community was Christmas. The festivities lasted a week and there were special foods to eat and activities for each day. The celebrating started on Christmas Eve with the traditional pumpkin pie and the exchange of simple and practical gifts. Children would receive one toy and items of clothing that they needed.

At dinner on Christmas Day the entree was usually a goose stuffed with prunes or perhaps a pork roast or spare ribs, never turkey. There were always sour cabbage and "aeblekage" (the famous Danish apple cake), and a touch of excitement in the dish of rice concealing a hidden almond. The person whose portion contained the almond followed a string which was fastened to the bowl, followed it all over the house until it led to a secret prize. There were other special dishes for the Christmas season, including a tiny spicy cookie called "pebbernodder" or "pepper nuts," flavored with almonds and white pepper. The cooks were hard-pressed to bake them fast enough to keep ahead of the little fingers which eagerly pounced on these once-a-year delicacies.

On the third day of Christmas, December 27, Danevang celebrated at the community hall with dancing around the huge community Christmas tree. This Christmas dancing was not done in couples but in huge circles, holding hands, around the Christmas tree, so that everyone could take part in this joyous occasion. Truly together, with no one left out, the people of Danevang celebrated their Christmastime happiness.

There were other collective celebrations in Danevang: the Fall Festival, a church-centered feast celebration; the Fasterlavn Party on the Friday before Lent when two barrels were filled with candy, a strong one for the adults and "a poor one" for the children, who then attacked the barrels with sticks to break them open, much as they might a piñata. There were "Monthly Meetings" held regularly at the community hall when the people got together simply to socialize with no festive excuse. Readings, square dances, polkas, humorous stories, and sing-songs were often part of these Monthly Meetings. (Sing-songs were often included in the other community celebrations as well.)

Sometimes there were plays at the community center, sometimes humorous farces like "womenless weddings," which entertained the community when there was no special occasion to celebrate, just loneliness and boredom and the longing for company, which people in this rural community knew so well and worked so hard to overcome.

Things are different now in Danevang. As we sat around Mrs. Nelsen's warm dining room, drinking hot coffee and munching Danish cakes and cookies, Mrs. Roberts explained how things are done there nowadays.

Today the anniversary celebrations are open houses at the community hall, not seated feasts as before. People still bring food to share, but the program is more formal, all planned in advance, with no room for spontaneous "tidbits" and raucous and hilarious possibilities. The decorations are less elaborate and inventive, relying much on gold and silver spray paint and often artificial flowers and greenery.

The birthday visiting is different now too: People wait to be invited instead of just dropping by. Sometimes these days they even bring their own food to the party because it's considered too much trouble for one person to do all that baking. That's what it's coming to, Mrs. Nelsen shook her head sadly, bringing their own food. They also take birthday gifts now and often there is a single "birthday cake." Things are different.

The June 5 and July 4 Independence Day Festivities are no longer celebrated at all. All the boys are veterans now and they take their families to El Campo for the July 4 patriotic gathering there, Mrs. Petersen explained.

Christmas retains more of its tradition. The dancing around the tree still occurs, though it's been changed, for convenience, to the weekend nearest to December 27, so the young people who've moved to Houston or Corpus can come home and take part.

The Fall Festival has become simply a church revival. Just this year the Danish Dinner, featuring traditional recipes, which used to accompany the revival as a part of the Fall Festival, has been discontinued. The Fasterlavn Party is no longer celebrated at all. Neither are there any longer Monthly Meetings or sing-songs or dances or plays or womenless weddings. Housewarmings are rare. People don't get together much anymore. Most of them barely remember that community-wide celebrations were once frequent in Danevang, not really so very long ago.

Mrs. Nelsen sighed and pushed her chair back from the table a little bit. Mrs. Roberts stirred her coffee.

"What happened?" we asked. "What changed it all?"

Well, the people don't know each other anymore; they aren't like family for each other any longer. They stay to themselves and associate just with their own. They all have kids and grandkids now and in-laws, not like in the old days when it was just them themselves, the Danes that came over and their kids that grew up Danish. Back then they needed each other, to help with the work, to help with the fun; just to be together they'd jump at the chance.

"For the association, you know," Mrs. Nelsen explained.

But now the young ones go off to Houston, to Corpus, and they marry non-Danish, and they bring the wives back maybe and they don't cook Danish and they don't speak Danish. "Yes," agreed Mrs. Nelsen, "Always we had the Ladies Aid meetings in Danish. Now we don't have the Danish Ladies Aid anymore, not since '71."

"They came from the Institute of Texan Cultures and recorded the last meeting with tape recorders," Mrs. Petersen explained.

But there were other things that had happened too, besides the families changing, the kids going away, the new ones coming in.

Now, you see, there's highway 71, finished in '32. Everything changed after that. That's how the kids can go get jobs in El Campo, can meet non-Danish to marry—the highway. You that've known highways all your lives, don't underestimate that highway. Before it was built sometimes no one could get out for a month when it rained. They'd have to bring food from El Campo in sleds. Wagons couldn't make it 'cause the wheels couldn't turn in the mud, so they'd hitch up tractors to sleds with runners like for snow, and they'd bring in the flour and the feed. That's the way it used to be before the highway—not very long ago—in '32.

Then they built the highway and people could go anywhere they wanted to anytime. They could go to El Campo on Saturdays to shop, to go to movies, school programs there. They could go out to dinner in a restaurant on their birthdays; they could go see the kids in Houston on their silver wedding anniversaries. That highway 71 connected

The Danes   197

Danevang with the world—They just didn't have to be so dependent on each other for association.

Then in '39, just a little over thirty years ago, poles were put up and lines were strung to bring electricity to Danevang. And so, of course, everybody had radios for entertainment. And then TV. They all watch TV now. We all involuntarily turned our glances to the blank screen on a nearby table, aimed toward the sofa.

They don't need them anymore, the celebrations, the association. And they're just too much trouble if you don't need them. It's just a few older ladies that know how to cook Danish, just a few people that can speak the language. They don't have the Danish classes anymore in the summer, you know, just Vacation Bible School now. It's too hard: everybody wants to do something else now; they're all too busy with their own things, their own families. They keep the Farmers Co-op going because they need it, but they don't need the celebrations like they used to. They got other things now.

The ladies mentioned in this article are Mrs. Joyce Petersen, Mrs. Lillian Roberts, and Mrs. Emilie Nelsen, all of whom live in Danevang.

THE POLES

The John Anderwald family, Bandera, ca. 1910. Courtesy Mrs. W. C. Allen and St. Stanislaus Museum.

Saloon, La Vernia, ca. 1915. Courtesy Mrs. Frank Katzmarek.

Parishioners in front of St. Stanislaus Catholic Church, Bandera, ca. 1915. Courtesy Mrs. Coy Ross.

A typical Silesian cottage near Płużnica in Poland (above), is similar in structure to the Gawlik House at Panna Maria, built in 1858 (below). Courtesy T. Lindsay Baker.

Abandoned stone Silesian cottage at Panna Maria. Courtesy T. Lindsay Baker.

Texas Folklife Festival.

O Ty Polshi!

By ANN CARPENTER

IN AN INSIDE JOKE told by Polish residents of Texas, it is said that a group of Polish settlers were traveling northward across Texas in oxcarts in 1854. They had suffered from extreme weather, rattlesnakes, and yellow fever. At last they were attacked by Indians. While the others took cover, one man fell on his knees out in the open and cried, *"Matka Boska bron mie* [Mother of God, save me]!" As the Indians circled closer, he pleaded again, *"Matka Boska bron mie!"* One Indian jumped down from his horse, grabbed the settler's hair, and menaced a tomahawk above the man. Again the Pole implored, *"Matka Boska bron mie!"* Dropping his tomahawk, the Indian exclaimed as he hugged the Polish man, *"O Ty Polshi* [Oh, you're Polish also]!"[1] While the joke loses some impact in translation, it does reflect the vitality of much Polish folklore in Texas. The lore of Polish Texans has been growing steadily since nineteenth century Polish immigrants arrived in the state, armed mainly with a determination to overcome hardships.

It was the determination to overcome political, economic, and social problems in the homeland that brought Poles to Texas. After the partitions of 1772, 1793, and 1795, there was no Poland, the country having been gobbled up by Russia, Prussia, and Austria. Polish revolts were brutally suppressed. Agrarian reforms aimed at abolishing the feudal system forced peasants to leave one-half of land previously held. More economic turmoil resulted from newly-instituted taxes, typhus and cholera outbreaks, and rising food prices. During a long period Poles were forbidden to use their native tongue. Traditional songs, emblems, and dress were forbidden. Therefore, accounts of Texas as a land of promise from newspapers, from emigration agents, and especially from Poles already in Texas provided the needed impetus to large-scale migration.

The one man most responsible for Polish interest in Texas is said to be the Reverend Leopold Moczygemba, a Franciscan friar from Upper Silesia (Prussian Poland), who saw in the growing prosperity of German immigrants to whom he ministered in Texas a new hope for suffering villagers in his homeland. In 1853 he wrote letters to encourage his relatives and friends to come to America, and his letters had impact. While a small number of Poles had arrived in Texas before 1854—some of them soldiers who aided in the Texas Revolution and others professionals who became leading businessmen—the first permanent group of Polish settlers arrived in the state when around one hundred families of farmers and small businessmen answered the summons of Father Leopold, left their homes in Upper Silesia, and after nine weeks at sea arrived in Galveston on December 3, 1854. Other groups were to follow, making an estimated 17,000 Poles in Texas by 1906. The settlers branched out to many Texas towns, including Bandera, San Antonio, St. Jadwiga, Meyersville, Yorktown, New Waverley, and Huntsville.

Most Polish Texans today know some part of the early settlers' hardships. Although the immigrants expected a land of plenty and tolerance, they found a wilderness where both man and nature seemed antagonistic toward them. The ocean voyage was the immigrants' first disappointment. The Poles made agreements with emigration agents to provide transportation to Texas. One traveler reported those ships were converted cattle quarters where poor emigrants were packed four to a bunk and fed musty flour, half-rotten potatoes, moldy bacon, and sugar that had grown too hard to sell to sailors. Some agents duped people by inflating prices two to three times the normal charge.[2] Those who perished at sea were wrapped in canvas, weighted with lead, and dropped into the ocean. Many settlers recalled their distress at having the fish feed upon the body. Conditions improved little throughout the nineteenth century migrations. Typical was Joseph Bartula, first Polish settler to Bremond, who lost three sons and all his possessions on the trip from Galicia to Texas in 1873.

No less bitter a hardship was travel overland in Texas. The new arrivals had little money, knew nothing about conditions on the wild frontier, and were susceptible to disease after the change in climate. Some piled their belongings on ox carts with solid wooden wheels and walked to Indianola and then along the ancient Mexican Cart Road to San Antonio. Many were struck with yellow fever. Traveling was made more miserable by a December norther, and many had no shoes. Furthermore, the Poles received little encouragement from Americans during their trip, possibly because they did not speak English and because they wore old country costumes that made them appear strange to Americans. The women wore skirts two or three inches above the ankle (very short for the time), and the Polish wooden shoes and broad-brimmed black felt hats were nothing like the clothes worn in Texas. There are stories that Poles were shunted from town to town by Americans who feared they might become burdensome charges on the community.

After finally meeting Father Leopold in San Antonio, the first settlers were directed to the land that had been secured for their purchase—land that was to be Panna Maria, the first permanent Polish colony in America. According to tradition, they arrived on the site on Christmas Eve, 1854, and celebrated mass under the largest live oak tree on the site. Panna Maria residents still point to a tree that is by legend that very shelter of the first group. To name their first settlements, the Poles used the name of the Virgin Mary, the one to whom the Polish had turned for help for hundreds of years. According to legend, Father Leopold dreamed of the Church of Panna Maria (Virgin Mary) after his arrival in Texas. The memory of that dream was so vivid that he suggested the name *Panna Maria* for that first town. The picture "Our Lady of Czestochowa," sometimes called "The Black Madonna" because of the dark skin tone, has served as an inspiration to suffering Poles for centuries. Polish love for the picture led to the naming of another early settlement—Czestochowa (Saves Often).

The early years of settlement were marked by hardships. Shelter was primitive. At first settlers dug pits and covered them with grass until they had time to build huts of mud and pickets roofed with sagebrush or dried grass. Much later came the oak or stone houses with steep roofs similar to the Silesian house in Poland. Having little equipment, the Poles raised the first crops by hand with hoes, and they fashioned wooden plows for the second year to raise corn, sweet potatoes, beans, and cotton. Settling in the new land was made more difficult by unfriendly Americans who regarded the Poles as objects of practical jokes and as dupes whose money was available for the taking. Some Poles found they had paid too much for the land, and some found that Americans refused to pay wages that they had earned. A Polish man was sometimes beaten by Americans just for the fun of it, and Polish priest Bakanowski recorded American persecution of Panna Maria, where Americans rode horses into the church and shot at parishioners as they left the service and American women waited in buggies outside to watch the excitement. Soldiers had to be brought in to restore order.[3]

Other dangers caused problems for the settlers. Tall grass concealed rattlesnakes, so that settlers had to be armed with sticks or hoes to fight them off. A usual tale focuses upon the first meeting of Polish arrivals with the snakes. In one Panna Maria anecdote Father Leopold was once entertaining new arrivals in his hut and feeding them a meal of his own making when a rattlesnake fell through the grass roof and landed on the table.

Indians were among the Poles' other troubles. Theodore Kindla, a 25-year-old Pole, was killed while herding sheep in Sabinal Canyon in 1872; the Indians "roped him, shot several arrows into his body, lanced him several times, . . . scalped him, and peeled the skin from the soles of his feet."[4] Narrow escapes, however, are the favorite tales of the Polish Texans. One man was shot with an arrow while investigating noises outside of his hut, and he survived only because his wife pulled him inside and cut out the arrow with a butcher knife. Two Poles had to hide for eight hours under a ledge after Indians stole their horses near Utopia. The unpublished journal of a Polish woman contains a typical tale of life near Boerne when her father joined the Home Scouts: "Whenever they heard of Indian raids . . . they would send the Home Scouts. That left Mother alone with the children. One day the cattle did not return home, and Mother sent my oldest brother who was 10 years old then out to look for them. While he was out he was met by some Indians. He was so frightened . . . , but they only took his horse and let him go his way. He did not lose any time getting home, and Mother would never send him out again."[5]

The bitter years of early Polish settlement were almost maddening. The colonists blamed those who encouraged them to leave their homeland for this wilderness filled with snakes, Indians, starvation, disease, and unfriendly Americans. According to some, at one time the immigrants even wanted to hang Father Leopold.[6] Many asked the question, "Why did we come here?" But they were in Texas, and having no way to return to Poland, they lived off the land and overcame seemingly insurmountable obstacles.

Without formal medical aid, Polish settlers had to meet problems of ordinary medical care as well as snakebite, wounds, and diseases of the new climate. Handed down through the generations have been the settlers' home remedies. Every Polish housewife once had to know how to set fractured limbs, dress wounds, make poultices, and relieve suffering. Most areas had individuals who specialized in helping with certain problems, as Mrs. Constantina Adamietz served for years as a midwife around Bandera and Mr. Wiatrek was the local bone-mender in Falls City.

Most home remedies in Polish Texan lore were made from herbs, roots, and bark. Numerous salves were made from combinations of ingredients. One recipe for salve called for a combination of kerosene oil, turpentine, and rendered tenderloin suet. One salve made of pecan oil, butter, and rosin reportedly once cured a man named Kaspar Adamietz of a cancer-like growth on his neck. Liniment, according to tradition, was made from egg and turpentine or from coal-oil mixed with cedar berries. An effective poultice was made by scraping the tuber of the madiera vine. Rheumatism and lumbago medicine took some time to make; the roots of the prickle ash, a thorny bush with small, shiny leaves, had to be washed and soaked in coal oil for a week before it was considered effective. Numerous teas also belonged to the lore of the Poles—sassafras tea and senna tea to purify the blood, linden-leaf tea for a sick stomach, tea made from sagebrush roots for laxative, and tea made from ice weed roots for chills and fever.

The problem of food was another challenge that the Polish settler had to meet with resourcefulness and endurance. Severe drought in 1856 as well as shortages in other years made hunger a reality for the Poles. Produce was so expensive that few could buy anything, and few supplies could be had anyway. One Polish descendant recalls that her grandmother as a child had to herd the family geese each day, and for a time she was given every morning a piece of coal that she had to use to cook her lunch of one potato. Poles around Bandera had to walk fifty miles for supplies. Nearly every family tells of mother or grandfather walking to Castroville after their first milk cow and driving her home on foot, and most tell of people who took a bushel of corn in a wheelbarrow all the way to Quihi to be ground. Settlers devised their own substitutes for coffee by parching acorns (or sweet potatoes, rye, corn, okra), and some families had to exist for a while on such simple fare as corn meal mush and molasses. The molasses was homemade, processed from sugar cane in the fall. At the local mill, a horse was used to pull the mill around and around. The juice, pressed out of the cane, was cooked for hours, turning from green to honey colored in the process.

In succeeding years, the Polish Texans raised everything they needed. They raised their own tobacco, laying the leaves flat on boards to dry. They made their own candles by melting beeswax, skimming off the comb, and pouring the wax into homemade molds. Polish wives made their own starter for yeast by boiling hops to which they added grated Irish potatoes, flour, salt, and sugar. When the mixture soured, they added flour, cornmeal, and water to fashion the starter into patties. The Poles raised their own cabbage for sauerkraut. They grated the cabbage on an old-time wooden box with iron graters and packed the grated cabbage in large crocks, alternating layers of cabbage and salt. They mashed the mixture down every day or two and covered the crock with a cloth, a large rock, and a lid. When the mixture soured, they boiled it. Sauerkraut was sometimes preserved along with Polish sausage. The meat was cured in a brine solution, seasoned with cayenne, black pepper, salt, and garlic, and packed in casings the pioneers cleaned themselves from intestines of a pig. Sausages were smoked, and any mildew was wiped off with a vinegar rag. Usually sausage was packed in jars covered with boiling grease. When the grease hardened, it sealed the top. Pioneer Poles stored green beans by boiling the beans, then boiling again in a solution of water, sugar, and vinegar before sealing in jars. The same "sweet and sour" method was used to preserve pickles, beets, and pickled peaches. Sometimes the early Poles dried peaches or pears by cutting the fruit in half and placing it on a tin roof covered by a mosquito net. The drying process took about seven days. Pioneers made their own cheese, somewhat like cottage cheese. After the cream was skimmed off, the milk was allowed to clabber. Warmed slightly, the clabber was placed in a cloth bag until all water drained; then it was placed in a pan, sprinkled with salt, and stirred periodically. When the cheese became stringy, it was considered done. Sometimes it was mixed with cream. Distinctive recipes using the cheese were developed, such as cheese dumplings. The dumplings, made from flour, water, cheese, salt, eggs, and sugar, were worked into a dough and dropped into boiling water. When they came to the top, they were done and were served with a sauce of butter, sugar, and cinnamon.

While most Polish settlers were farmers or small tradesmen, many also had to learn new skills to support their families. Some chopped cedar and made charcoal out of it to sell in neighboring towns. They put dry cedar kindling in a pit which they filled with successive layers of cedar and dirt. The pit was then burned until a certain point when barrels of water were emptied on it. When cool, the coal was sacked. Around Bandera most Poles were engaged in shingle-making, for Charles de Montel had contracted with Polish immigrants to come to Bandera to work in his mill. Some became champion shingle slicers, as they were called. Shingles were made from cypress blocks sawed into 32-inch lengths. A good shingle maker could make a thousand in a day (which brought $4.50 in San Antonio) by a process in which the cypress block was marked off to proper thickness, "split and rived with a froe knife and wooden mallet, then taken to the old shaving horse, and trimmed to a feather edge with a drawing knife."[7] After seasoning, the shingles were hauled in homemade ox wagons to market.

Peace-loving, hard-working, persistent, self-sufficient, religious—the Polish Texans tell stories about early settlers who stand as epitomes of traditional values. In the early days of Thurber, Anton Bercilli was so self-sufficient that he even dug his own grave and prepared the cross for it. Father Thomas Moczygemba, who became pastor in Yorktown in 1912, had such a magnetic effect on his parish that he became a legend. Before his time parishioners left during church with the excuse of tending their horses, but when he came to the pulpit, "even the jack-asses listened and the old grey mare was as gentle as Mary's lamb."[8] Then there is that peace-loving, persistent ghost of a Panna Maria settler who is said to be still looking for his head, lost in 1867 when the old graveyard was moved so that the site could be used for a new Polish rectory and school. Arrayed in shiny black boots and black cloak, the headless ghost of Panna Maria has appeared most often in the rectory itself. His appearances are mild, for he merely sits in a rocking chair or strolls down a moonlit path.[9]

Especially were the Polish women expected to epitomize traditional virtues. Mrs. Frances Moravietz was just sixteen when the grist mill was built in Bandera in 1856, but she is still remembered there as wielding a pick and shovel as expertly as a man to dig the mill race for a distance of about one mile. Mrs. Constantina Adamietz, the local midwife, risked her life to swim a flooded river to help deliver a baby. It is said that in youth Mrs. Adamietz had a white streak in the front of her black hair, but as her hair turned white, that white streak turned black in her old age. The tales of Polish pioneer women make clear why it is said that while there is a single Polish woman left, the cause of Poland is not lost.

Although each generation has become more Americanized in speech, dress, diet, and daily routine, even today Polish Texans value traditions and customs, some of which they practice and some of which they merely remember and talk about. Naturally customs vary from place to place, but social practices revolving around religious festivals, christenings, weddings, and similar events are known in some manner to most Poles. The activities of Polish organizations such as the Polish National Alliance and the Polish American Congress of Texas reflect a renewed interest in the traditions of the Polish people.

The Polish holiday calendar begins with Christmas time, from Christmas Eve to Three Kings Day (Dec. 24 to Jan. 6). Polish Christmas celebrations have an appealing simplicity. Having spent Advent quietly at home, the Polish family gathers on Christmas Eve to begin rejoicing with a simple supper when the first star appears in the evening sky. Before the meal that breaks their day-long fast, the head of the household breaks a small flat oblong wafer (called *oplatki* or offerings) that has been blessed by the priest and shares it with everyone present while exchanging good wishes. The *oplatki*, symbolizing love, friendship, and forgiveness, are usually stamped with a picture of the Nativity or of a religious symbol and are sometimes distributed at church. The supper that follows consists of special foods, although the meal is meatless as a remembrance that, to receive, one must first give. Dishes may include fish, *barszcz* (beet soup), mushroom patties, almond soup, and small honey or seed cakes. A typical Polish dish for the supper is the *Kucja*, which may be made by boiling a pound of shelled wheat and adding salt and vanilla before cooking. When cool, the wheat is mixed with ½ pound poppy seed (symbol of peaceful sleep), ¼ pound honey (symbol for sweetness and contentment), ½ pound crushed walnuts, and 4 tablespoons sugar. Some people have an extra place ready at the table for surprise visitors, evidence of a customary hospitality, as is indicated by the saying, "A guest in the house is God in the house."

After the Christmas Eve supper, there is much activity. First, the children receive small gifts. Usually someone plays the traditional role of the Star Man (or Santa) and questions the children over their behavior and their prayers. Even the small ones are expected to recite a prayer such as "Our Father." Children are warned during the year that if they're naughty, they will get only a piece of coal in their Christmas present. One woman remembers that her little sister, who had a habit of sticking out her tongue, once received on Christmas Eve a ball that stuck out a tongue when it was squeezed. She remembers, too, that the reminder did no good; her sister got under the table and pulled out the tongue from the ball. Also on Christmas Eve there is the singing of carols *(Koledy)*. Some have a haunting simplicity about them, such as the traditional Christmas lullaby which is translated in one version in this way:

> Hushaby, Jesus, my heart's dear treasure,
> Hushaby, Baby, sweet beyond measure,
> Hush and Your mother will stop Your sorrow,
> Baby will smile on the world tomorrow.

Later in the evening, Polish Texans attend Midnight Shepherd's Mass *(Pasrerka)*, followed perhaps by a small feast of sausage and other delicacies when they return home. Christmas Day itself is one of rest. Goose is one traditional dish for the day, and goose soup is still served in some families. It is made by draining the blood from the head of the goose into a pan containing vinegar to prevent the blood from curdling. Thickened with flour, the blood is boiled with the broth made by boiling the whole goose. When the broth is nearly done, homemade noodles, raisins, and prunes are added.

The Christmas tree *(Choinka)* in the Polish home is traditionally decorated with only handmade ornaments *(Ozdobki)*, constructed from paper, straw, eggshells, pine cones, nuts, and beads. The Nativity scene is usually present. One Polish mother explains that in her family a piece of straw is added each day to a small manger; when it is full, the children in the family know that it is Christmas Eve, time for the birth of Jesus. Ornaments for the Christmas tree usually have some symbolic value, as the paper chain indicated unity, the *jezyki* or spiked hedgehogs symbolize good luck. A principal ornament is the star, for Christmas is sometimes called *Gwiazdka*, or Little Star.

Of no less importance than the Christmas celebrations are the Easter traditions of the Polish Texans. Lent is a serious religious time to most Poles. The last Thursday before Lent is called fat Thursday *(tlusty czwartek)* because it is a time for feasting. Then Lent begins, and the Lenten fare of the Polish Texans is still rather frugal. It is said that hundreds of years ago a Bishop gained permission from the Pope so that the Poles could eat meat on Wednesdays during Lent, but no one in all of Poland could be found to use the privilege. Traditional spring cleaning usually comes the last week in Lent, and houses are sometimes decorated with plants and perhaps paper cut-outs of ancient designs. During Easter week it is traditional to greet others with the saying, "A Joyful Alleluia to you *(Wesolego Alleluya)*!" The blessing of the Easter food on Holy Saturday is still observed in some Texas towns. Traditionally a basket of Easter food is taken to church on Holy Saturday to receive from the priest a blessing.

The Easter feast is the most elaborate in the entire year. Before the meal the head of the family divides a colored Easter egg among those present. He gives one piece to each while going around the table to kiss each one and to wish happy Easter and joy at the Resurrection of Christ. The table is decorated with green leaves. The centerpiece is generally a lamb made of sugar or butter or a cake made in a lamb's mold, a symbol of Christ. The blessed Easter fare is composed of such foods as ham, sausage, roast pork, salads, Babka bread, *chrusciki* or Polish love knots, sweet cakes, made of honey and filled with nuts and fruit. Mushrooms are favorites, as are sauerkraut, noodles, dumplings, and buckwheat groats called *Kasza*.

Always present are the marvelously colored Easter eggs. Ornamented in three ways, the eggs may be painted in solid colors *(malowanki)*, may be dyed in solid colors with a design scratched on the egg with a sharp instrument *(skrobanki)*, or may be batiked with marvelous traditional designs *(pisanki)*. It is for the *pisanki* that the Poles are most famous. Decorated with complex lines, dots, and symbols, the *pisanki* are truly works of art, each one being the product of hours of work. No two alike, they may sometimes be multicolored. Some people prefer to use blown eggs for decorating; in this process, the eggs are emptied of their contents by making a pin hole at each end and blowing the contents into a dish. Many people use hardboiled eggs for dyeing, although any egg to be used should be at room temperature. For the *pisanki* the design is sketched on the egg with beeswax, which is applied with a stylus or some homemade tool such as a pin stuck in an eraser or the tip of a shoelace. Designs for the *pisanki* center around a series of symbols. The sun suggests good fortune; the rooster or hen, fulfillment of wishes; the stag or deer, good health;

flowers, love and charity. Christian symbols such as the fish or the cross are used, as well as dots, wavy lines, intersecting ribbons, and cross hatches.

It is traditional to dye the eggs with natural dyes which give subtle color effects. The natural substance is boiled in water, strained, and cooled before the egg is dipped. To give multicolor effects, one must wax and dip the egg repeatedly. Red, symbolic of the blood of Christ, is the most popular color. Each color has its own traditional source. Moss produces a light green egg; spinach leaves, green; outer skin of an onion, mottled yellow; cochineal, scarlet; saffron, yellow. An unusual effect comes from the use of sassafras bark, which produces an egg that is yellow where the wax has been applied and red on the unwaxed areas. When dry, the decorated egg is wiped with grease.

After being blessed by the priest, the eggs serve several purposes. They are central, of course, to the opening of the Easter feast. They are given away and sometimes treasured for years as good luck charms. Years ago young Polish girls would give as many as one hundred eggs to favored suitors as signs that their attentions would not be unwelcome. The eggs serve as entertainment for the young, too. In one Easter game, two children face each other, each holding a hard-boiled egg with the pointed tip up. Each tries to break the other's egg by knocking it with his own. The winner gets both eggs and good luck. Those accomplished at the game say that one should hold his egg to show as little egg as possible. Another game is the old practice of girls and boys splashing each other with water on Easter Monday. The victim who is splashed must give the other an Easter egg. An ancient game, it is sometimes called *Dyngus*. One man recalls only part of the rhyme that he said as a boy while dousing girls on Easter Monday: "Don't shriek and cry and run away, / It's good for you on *Dyngus* Day."

Various mythical stories are told to account for the presence of the *pisanki* at Easter. One is that Mary made the first *pisanki* to amuse the Infant Jesus. Another tale is that Mary Magdalen and her companions took a few boiled eggs with them when they went to the Sepulcher to anoint Christ's body. When they got ready to eat, the eggs were miraculously colored. In another version, Mary Magdalen prepared food for others on Easter morning, and every egg she had turned a glowing red. Another explanation for the *pisanki* concerns a peasant who once set down his basket of eggs to help a man who was being forced to carry a heavy wooden cross by some soldiers. He did not know that the man was Jesus Christ on His way to death. When the peasant returned to his eggs, each one had turned rosy red.

Other intricate decorations are associated with Easter, such as the paper cut-outs *(wycinanka)*. Although no longer confined to use at Easter only, the cut-outs are said to have originated in Easter season as Polish peasants cut the first designs freehand from folded paper with their sheep-shearing scissors. While the technique appears simple, the Poles have developed intricate and delicate designs. Today the designs are produced more by specialists than by ordinary folk, although they seem to be enjoying something of a revival among Polish Texans. Traditional designs include the Easter cock, tree, flowers, stars, doves, human figures, and wedding or village scenes. Sometimes the cut-outs are built up in several layers of differently shaped and colored papers. The designs may be mounted on stiff white paper, on cards, or on blown eggs.

Many other holidays belong to the traditions of the Polish Texans, including Corpus Christi Day, All Souls' Day, various harvest festivals, and many more. The sacraments, too, are surrounded with many traditional observances. For example, christenings are followed by celebrations in the parents' home where gifts (usually money) are left to help meet the needs of the baby. The child's sponsors or godparents are regarded as relatives by the interested families and are called *"potek"* or *"potka,"* as evidence of the child's deep relationship with them. It is said that the child takes on qualities of its godparents. Some believe that godparents affect a child's life by the way they hold the infant at baptism.

Not all occasions are happy. A Polish saying ironically suggests the inevitability of death by stating an impossibility: "If a man stays in the sunshine all the time, he will never die." Death is accompanied, too, by traditional observances. Traditional wakes are held in the home of the deceased, with neighbors offering help with meals and chores. The wake, it is believed, is necessary for the rest of the deceased. Some say that a crowing hen is a sign of death and must be killed to break the spell. A dog, it is believed, howls before a death because he can see the spirit leaving the body.

None of the Polish customs are more colorful than those associated with matrimony. Polish weddings last for several days. Years ago they were usually held in the fall after harvest. Typically there are many guests and a huge wedding party, ideally a maid of honor, matron of honor, best man, ten bridesmaids, ten groomsmen, two junior bridesmaids, a flower girl, and a ring bearer. Before the wedding, the bride and groom meet together in the home of the bride's parents to receive, one by one, a blessing from each parent. They walk or ride together to church, often accompanied by friends and musicians playing traditional songs.

After the church ceremony, the entire wedding party and hundreds of guests return to the home of the bride's parents for the wedding feast. The food for the feast has been in preparation for days: spicy country sausage, turkey, ham, veal, vegetables, salads, pastries, wine, and other beverages. Musicians playing the fiddle, accordion, and other instruments provide traditional Polish songs. The fiddle in particular seems to have always played the central role of setting the pace in the polkas, waltzes, mazurkas, and other traditional dances. "The Bremond Polish Wedding Waltz" and other traditional songs can be heard on Pulaski of Texas Records. Played by the Steve Okonski Band, the songs are produced on records by Polish enthusiast J. L. Cicherski of San Antonio. Such music sets the tone of festivity for the Polish wedding celebration.

About ten the dancing begins, with the bride and groom leading the grand march. In the center of the hall, chairs are provided for the newlyweds, and the merriment increases. The groom is asked to choose between a jug of wine and his bride. In some areas, it is traditional for a cheap plate to be placed in the bride's lap covered with a napkin. Anyone who wishes to dance with the bride or her attendants must break the plate by throwing coins—usually silver dollars—at it. All coins thrown at the plate are gifts to the bride. In addition, guests usually give gifts of money to the bride and are rewarded for their gifts with wine and cookies. Laughter dominates the evening. Removal of the bride's veil ends the evening, for it is a symbolic moment when the young girl officially becomes a working woman. Years ago a meaning was attached to each pin that was removed from the veil. During the ceremony the older women and men sometimes sing songs. Some are comic in nature, as the following translation indicates:

> There's a valley, a valley,
> In the valley, green grass,

Tell me, my fair maiden,
Why you do not love me.

There's a valley, a valley,
In the valley, mushrooms.
And how am I to love you
When you're such an ugly fellow?

One informant remembers only part of one song that had motions as the singers sang: "The old woman was dancing, she didn't know how, / She just twisted herself to and fro." They sing sad songs, too, about how the young bride will have to work and feel pain:

A little cuckoo is cooing,
In the woods yonder.
A pretty bride is weeping.
Za stolem.

The bride places her veil on the head of the little flower girl, and the attendants usually provide more comedy by placing humorous hats on the bride and groom.

There are many superstitions associated with marriage. It is said that bad luck follows a girl who is present in church when the banns are read for her marriage. No jewels are to be worn by the bride on the wedding day; for each one worn, she must cry a cup of tears. The wedding bouquet is supposed to contain some hidden objects, including a bit of bread for luck and a lump of sugar to sweeten the marriage. Some say that whichever newlywed leaves the altar first will also be the first to die. Perhaps the large number of guests invited to a wedding celebration has something to do with the belief that if there is one vacant chair at the party, death will come.

The traditional superstitions, sayings, customs, recipes, songs, and tales of the Polish Texans are not to be regarded as merely curiosities or even vestiges of a different place and time. The traditions give insight into those aspects of life and character that are valued by this important and growing segment of Texas culture. For example, a recent author, speaking of thousands of Polish people who risked punishment from the Russians by visiting Our Lady of Czestochowa, described Polish character as persistent, peaceful, and religious: "The Poles have loved freedom, have fought to keep it and to help others win it. They have loved their Faith and held onto it against terrible odds."[10] No less can be said about the Polish Texans who braved the antagonism of man and nature to make a home in a new land, and no less can be seen in their traditional lore. In Polish sayings, for example, persistence is applauded. Idleness is disdained, as it is said of someone who is inactive, "It's a wonder he doesn't sprout mushrooms." The peacefulness of the Poles is indicated in the saying, "Don't stare into a well," suggesting one shouldn't look for trouble. Another traditional saying brings together Polish religious spirit and pride in country: "When the Czechs and Bohemians came to America, the first things they built were dance halls; when the Germans came, the first things they built were barns; when the Polish people came, the first things they built were churches."

If there is one story that typifies the Polish spirit, it is that of the trumpeter of the Church of Panna Maria, the church that inspired the name for the first Polish settlement in Texas. The young trumpeter was a watchman on duty in the tower of the church when Tartars besieged the city of Krakow in 1241. Because he had taken an oath to remain at his post until death, he did not leave when the city was taken and burned. His duty was to sound the Heynal—the hymn to Our Lady—every hour of day and night. He was shot with a Tartar arrow and died before he could finish the last notes of his song. The song is still sounded hourly from the church, and at the end the melody is broken off in memory of his devotion. That boy and his famous broken note typify Polish persistence, peacefulness, and religious devotion—the qualities that have aided the Polish Texans to survive, to grow, and to prosper in America. Such a spirit must be kindred with Father Leopold leading his flock through the wilderness, with Constantina Adamietz swimming a flooded river to deliver a baby, with Frances Moravietz digging the mill race out of nearly solid rock, as well as with the hundreds of men and women today who are joining forces to unify efforts for improving the position of Polish Texans and for educating their neighbors on Polish contributions to Texas and to America.

[1]This joke and other materials for the article were garnered from interviews with many Texans of Polish descent from all parts of the state. Of special help were Catherine Stearns, Alys Straach, Mrs. Neil Coulter, Helen Jureczki, Mrs. Coy Ross, Amelia Kalka, Christina Kalka, Benny Adamietz, Vince Anderwald,

Isabel Stokes, Mrs. H. V. Mazurek, Mrs. Eduard Englert, Pauline Gorski, and J. L. Cicherski.

[2]Kalikst Wolski, *American Impressions,* trans. Marion Coleman (Cheshire, Connecticut: Cherry Hill, 1968), pp. 3-18.

[3]Adolph Bakanowski, *Polish Circuit Rider,* trans. Marion Coleman (Cheshire, Connecticut: Cherry Hill, 1971), pp. 38-46.

[4]Marvin Hunter, *Pioneer History of Bandera County* (Bandera: Hunter's Printing House, 1922), p. 42.

[5]Unpublished journal of Mrs. Annie Christians. Quoted with permission of her granddaughter, Mrs. Catherine Stearns.

[6]Rev. Edward Dworaczyk, *The First Polish Colonies of America in Texas* (San Antonio: Naylor, 1936), p. 7.

[7]Hunter, p. 81.

[8]Dworaczyk, p. 124.

[9]Bernard Pajewski, "The Headless Ghost of Panna Maria," *Polish Folklore,* IV (March 1959), pp. 11-12. Also see Bakanowski, pp. 35-36.

[10]Caroline Peters, *The Black Madonna* (Paterson, N.J.: St. Anthony, 1962), p. 29.

Panna Maria and Płuznica: A Study in Comparative Folk Culture

By T. LINDSAY BAKER

IT IS NOT LIKE your village. . . . One cottage lies from the other 10 miles or even more. . . . It is difficult to go with bare feet because there are various thorns and reptiles. . . . There is no prepared land, but everybody must get it ready for himself, because the land is covered with trees and bushes and no one has ploughed it before. . . . Here there is no winter.[1]

In writing home to his family and friends in Europe, John Moczygemba, one of the original settlers at Panna Maria, Texas, used these words in 1855 to compare the new settlement in Texas with his home village of Płużnica in Poland. Panna Maria had been established by immigrants from the Polish region of Upper Silesia, in what was then the Kingdom of Prussia, only five months before John Moczygemba wrote the letter.

Both Panna Maria and Płużnica remain sleepy Polish villages today, although they are located on different continents and are separated by thousands of miles. Panna Maria is distinguished by being the oldest Polish colony in America[2] while Płużnica is distinguished by having supplied the founders for that colony.[3] Both communities have changed only gradually over the years, retaining their folk culture to a surprisingly high degree.

On first view, the most striking thing about Panna Maria and Płużnica is their similar outward appearance.[4] Both villages are small communities of farmers whose homes are built around small Catholic churches. Panna Maria was laid out on the American town plan with rectangular blocks[5] while Płużnica has the traditional Polish "main street" pattern with houses built on either side of a street the length of the village.[6] The agricultural fields in both communities are unusual by American standards. They are long narrow strips of land, sometimes only a few yards wide and up to a mile in length. Such design facilitated ploughing with draft animals and continues today as a legacy of the old agricultural techniques.[7]

The cottages built by farmers in Panna Maria and Płużnica are remarkably similar. In both communities the old style houses were built of wood or stone with steeply arched roofs designed for snow to slip off easily in the winter. Typical houses in both communities often have very low rear walls with roofs coming within five feet of the ground. Generally the upper rooms or lofts have access by way of outside ladders or inside staircases. The upper rooms are ventilated by pairs of square or rectangular windows at one or both ends. The major modification made by the Silesians in Texas to their traditional cottages was the addition of porches for protection from the summer sun. Such a classic Silesian house in Texas is the Gawlik house, north of the community hall in Panna Maria.

During the mid-nineteenth century, the most popular roofing materials for Silesian peasant cottages were wooden shingles and straw thatch. Both of these materials have been phased out of modern construction in Panna Maria and Płużnica, but they were commonly used in both places into the twentieth century. Some old wooden shingles continue to cover roofs in both villages at the present time. Although there are no longer any thatch roofs in Panna Maria, several people remember seeing them on different houses there as recently as the early years of the twentieth century. There are still several barns and one residence in Płużnica that have thatch roofing.[8]

The first shelter erected by the Silesians at Panna Maria was not so substantial as the stone cottages that remain today. The immigrants naturally used building techniques which had been passed down since the Middle Ages in the old country. Some of the colonists first built dugouts and covered them with thatch, or in the words of one of the original settlers, "We lived in burrows covered with brush and stalks."[9] Such shelters are still used by peasant farmers in Upper Silesia as cellars for the storage of potatoes and livestock feed. Although the instance was extremely rare, as recently as 1970 an old woman was known to be living in one of these "cellar houses" in Prudnik County, about thrity-five miles from Płużnica.[10]

At the beginning of their colonization in Texas, the dress of the Silesian Poles set them apart from the general American population. The best description of their dress at this early date comes from L. B. Russell, who moved to the Panna Maria area as a young boy in 1853.[11] Russell, later in life, recalled the Silesians as wearing:

. . . The costumes of the old country, many of the women having what at that time were regarded as very short skirts, showing their limbs two or three inches above the ankles. Some had on wooden shoes, and almost without exception they had broad-brimmed, low-crowned black felt hats. . . . They also wore blue jackets of heavy woolen cloth, falling just below the waist, and gathered into folds at the back with a band of the same material.[12]

The unusually short skirts of the women evidently caused some excitement among the Americans because only six months after Panna Maria was established, its founder, Rev. Leopold Moczygemba, wrote back to Płużnica advising: "Don't take any country dresses for Hanka, because she will not need them here. . . . Our dresses are the reason that the native people make fun of us and they cause sin."[13] Even as recently as the beginning of this century, people in Texas were surprised by the comparatively short skirts worn by women just immigrating from Silesia to Panna Maria.[14]

Though at first it seems outlandish to think of Polish peasants wearing carved wooden shoes, such footwear, known as *holzschoen,* were in everyday use by nineteenth century peasants in Silesia.[15] The old type *holzschoen* were carved from solid blocks of wood and looked very much like the wooden shoes still worn in Holland. A pair of these shoes is preserved at the Museum of the Opole Countryside near Opole in Upper Silesia.[16] Other wooden shoes worn in both Panna Maria and Płużnica were a modification of the solid wooden type. These' shoes had thick carved wooden soles to which leather tops were attached. Both types of wooden shoes were used at Panna Maria as recently as the early 1900's and at Płużnica until after the Second World War.[17]

The Polish language spoken at Panna Maria is the dialect that was used in the area around Płużnica over a century ago. The immigrants to Panna Maria came from a relatively small geographic area and once in America they were relatively isolated from contact with the larger Polish-American community. These two factors contributed greatly to the preservation of their original dialect. Because the dialect is no longer spoken in a pure form in Poland, linguists from Europe come specifically to Panna Maria to study and record the archaic Silesian Polish as it continues to be used in the American colony.[18] To the casual observer, however, the Silesian spoken at Panna Maria is still very similar to that used in Upper Silesia. After visiting Płużnica, a Silesian Pole from near Panna Maria remarked recently: "There was no doubt in our minds that our grandfathers came from there, because Polish is spoken in many dialects, but here it was spoken as we speak it."[19]

In both Panna Maria and Płużnica, large numbers of folk beliefs attend the birth and first weeks in the lives of infants. A great number of these customs are common between the two communities. A major base for the beliefs is the widely held view that a mother is so weak after the birth of a child that for six weeks she "has one leg in the grave."[20] Consequently, in both Silesian communities there are restrictions upon what a new mother can and cannot do.

In the old days in Panna Maria and at the present time in Płużnica, each mother is warned by older women that to ward off bad luck she must wear a scarf over her head if she goes out of the house within the first six weeks after her child's birth. This belief is so strong in Płużnica that despite the fact that the parish priest has preached against it as superstition, he readily admits that virtually all the young mothers in his parish observe it.[21] In both Panna Maria and Płużnica there are restrictions on the drying of diapers for babies during the first six weeks after birth. In Panna Maria the custom is not to allow the diapers to dry outside the house either at noon or after dark, but in Płużnica the practice is simply not to dry the diapers anywhere outside the house during the period.[22]

Several customs in both communities relate to the baptism of infants. In the past there was an extremely strong custom that a mother should not take an infant out of the house until it was taken to the church to be baptized. This baptismal ceremony generally took place one to three days after birth. At Panna Maria, in the early years of this century, it was customary for the father and the grandmother to take the infant to church for baptism. At the church they met the godparents who went with them to the priest who performed the ceremony. The procedures have now changed somewhat, so that at present it is normal for the father and godparents to take the baby to the church for baptism. In either case the mother remains at home in bed during all the proceedings at the church.[23]

People in Panna Maria and Płużnica interpret numerous occurrences as signs of bad luck. In both places howling dogs frequently portend or announce death. In Panna Maria in the summer of 1973, for example, neighbors reported that about midnight the dogs belonging to a certain man began howling so loudly that they were awakened by the noise. The next morning the same neighbors went to the man's house and found that he had died in his bed during the night. In Płużnica the beliefs about howling dogs are similar but more complex. There, when a dog howls with its head facing the ground, someone will die or has died; but when the dog howls with its head faced toward the sky, there will be a fire. In Panna Maria many people believe that when a hen crows like a rooster, bad luck will follow; the same sign in Płużnica portends death. In both communities there is a strong belief that if a holy picture falls from the wall and breaks, death or bad luck will surely follow. Such omens in both villages are so numerous that they can be listed almost without end.[24]

Stories of ghosts are known in both communities, although they are probably stronger in Płużnica. The great ghost story teller in Płużnica was the old man Franciszek Karkosz, who was a grandson of Johanna Moczygemba, sister of Rev. Leopold Moczygemba, the founder of Panna Maria in Texas. Karkosz related many stories to the children in Płużnica, but the best remembered of these was about "the Great Dog of Płużnica." According to the story, there was a huge dog that lived in the cellars of the manor at Płużnica, which came out at night and could attack children. This terrifying beast was described as being as large as a wolf, lion, or even a horse. According to one version of the story, the dog had shaggy hair around its head and fire coming from its mouth. Another version of the story described the dog as having legs and hoofs like a horse. Until very recently, all the children living in Płużnica learned a rhythmical verse about "the Great Dog" that they repeated whenever they walked alone at night as a charm for protection:

> In the evening at the manor Verona saw the big fiery wolf.
> Verona began to shout very much:
> "Go out, people, and ring the bell at the manor,
> "Take brooms, pitchforks, hoes, and spades,
> "Run the big wolf into the forest."[25]

In Panna Maria stories are told about a similar "great dog," but they are not so highly developed as in Płużnica. According to one version, there is a huge black dog occasionally seen along Cibolo Creek on the Piegza Ranch. According to another, a black dog as large as an automobile is to be seen racing at the sides of cars traveling on the road from Panna Maria to Falls City.[26] Yet another version of the story describes the dog as having "a tail as long as a broomstick with fire on the end."[27]

As a rule, most ghosts in the two Silesian communities are those of local people who have passed away. A typical encounter with a ghost in Płużnica took place early in the summer of 1972. The old man who related the story had lost his wife only a few weeks before the occurrence. As he drove his wagon into Płużnica late at night, the man saw the ghost of his recently departed wife approach him from the cemetery. He stopped his horse as the spirit got nearer and to his great surprise his deceased wife asked him why he was out so late at night. At this question the man's courage broke and he left the ghost as fast as his horse could pull the wagon.[28]

The most colorful ghost in Panna Maria is the so-called "headless ghost." Since the village cemetery was moved in 1867 for the construction of the school, the mysterious black-garbed headless being has been seen around the community. Most often people chance to see him somewhere about the church or school, traditionally on the veranda of the school. Since the mid-twentieth century remodeling of the school, however, people at Panna Maria have seen the headless ghost less and less.[29]

Separated by time and distance, the Silesian communities of Panna Maria and Płużnica obviously have had different histories, but at the same time they have retained surprisingly similar folk cultures. Both of them are located in areas dominated by large cities and will probably remain villages for at least the foreseeable future. The passage of time is taking its toll in folk life. As the older generations pass away in both places, they leave the younger people who are less in touch with their parents' and grandparents' life styles. Most of these young people go to the cities for education and employment, leaving only a remnant in the home communities to work the farms and to maintain the old family homes.[30]

[1]Johann Moczigemba *[sic]*, Panna Maria, Texas, to Relatives and Friends, Płużnica, Regency of Opole, May 13, 1855, in Regency of Opole Collection, Archives of the City of Wrocław, Poland. This letter has been recently reprinted in Andrzej Brożek and Henryk Borek, *Jescze jeden list z Teksasu do Płużnicy z 1855 roku* [One More Letter from Texas to Płużnica in the Year 1855] (Opole, Poland: Instytut Śląski w Opolu, 1972), pp. 14-19.

[2]Among the English-language sources for the history of Panna Maria are the following: Thomas Lindsay Baker, "The Early History of Panna Maria, Texas," unpublished M.A. thesis, Texas Tech University, 1972; Edward J. Dworaczyk, *The First Polish Colonies of America in Texas* (San Antonio: The Naylor Company, 1936); Jacek Przygoda, *Texas Pioneers from Poland* (Waco, Texas: Texian Press, 1971). The best single Polish-language source is Andrzej Brożek, *Ślązacy w Teksasie* [Silesians in Texas] (Warsaw, Poland: Państwowe Wydawnictwo Naukowe, 1972).

[3]The following Polish immigrants to Panna Maria are known definitely to have come from the Catholic parish at Płużnica: Albert and Mary (Friedrich) Dlugi; John and Johanna (Willczek) Dziuk; John and Marianna (Moczygemba) Felux; Rev. Leopold Moczygemba, the founder of Panna Maria, and his four brothers, Antoni, August, John, and Joseph; and John and Marianna (Felux) Moczygemba, a cousin of Rev. Leopold and the author of the letter cited in the beginning of this article. Baptismal Records (1812-1833), pp. 31-32, 69-70, 149-

150, 179-180, 237-238, 273-274; Baptismal Records (1833-1858), pp. 3-4, 55-56, 89-90, 105-106, 137-138, 173-174, 211-212; Death Records (1765-1847), p. 235; Death Records (1847-1890), p. 7; Marriage Records (1766-1886), pp. 96, 100, St. Stanisław Church, Płużnica, Opole Voivodeship, Poland.

[4]In the summer of 1972, the author and his wife, Krystyna Baker, visited the villages in Upper Silesia from which the immigrants of the 1850's came, taking numerous notes and photographs. Comparisons in this paper are based upon these observations.

[5]Dworaczyk, *The First Polish Colonies,* p. 11.

[6]For a study of the forms of villages in Upper Silesia see Halina Szulc, *Typy wsi Śląska Opolskiego na początku XIX wieku i ich geneza* [Types of Rural Settlements of Opole Silesia at the Beginning of the Nineteenth Century and Their Origin], Instytut Geografii Polskiej Akademii Nauk, Prace Geograficzne Nr. 66 (Warsaw, Poland: Państwowe Wydawnictwo Naukowe, 1968).

[7]Robert H. Thonhoff, "A History of Karnes County," unpublished M.A. thesis, Southwest Texas State College, San Marcos, Texas, 1963, p. 113.

[8]Mrs. Felix Mika, Panna Maria, Texas, to T. Lindsay Baker and Krystyna Baker, Interview, August 11, 1973; Elias J. Moczygemba, Panna Maria, Texas, to T. Lindsay Baker and Krystyna Baker, Interview, August 10, 1973.

[9]Unidentified Polish colonist to Rev. Adolf Bakanowski, c. 1870, cited in Adolf Bakanowski, *Moje Wspomnienia* [My Memoirs], ed. by Tadeusz Olejniczak (Lwów, Austrian Empire: Nakładem XX. Zmartwychwstańców, 1913), p. 29.

[10]Jacek Michałowski, Museum of the Opole Countryside, Bierkowice, Opole Voivodeship, Poland, to T. Lindsay Baker and Krystyna Baker, Interview, July 8, 1972.

[11]L.B. Russell, *Granddad's Autobiography* (Comanche, Texas: The Comanche Publishing Co., [1930]), p. 4.

[12]*Dallas Morning News,* January 24, 1932, Sec. IV, p. 1.

[13]Leop. BM. Moczygemba, Panna Maria, Texas, to Dear Fathers, Płużnica, Regency of Opole, June 18, 1855, in Andrzej Brożek and Henryk Borek, *Pierwsi Ślązacy w Ameryce: listy z Teksasu do Płużnicy z roku 1855* [The First Silesians in America: Letters from Texas to Płużnica from the Year 1855] (Opole, Poland: Instytut Śląski w Opolu, 1967), pp. 13-14.

[14]Mrs. Felix Mika, August 11, 1973.

[15]Alma Oakes and Margot Hamilton Hill, *Rural Clothing, Its Origins and Development in Western Europe and the British Isles* (New York: Van Nostrand Reinhold Company, 1970), p. 155.

[16]Jacek Michałowski, July 8, 1972.

[17]Franz and Maria Karkosz, Płużnica, Opole Voivodeship, Poland, to T. Lind-

say Baker and Krystyna Baker, Interview, June 23, 1972; Mrs. Felix Mika, August 11, 1973.

[18]Among the published linguistic studies that have considered the Silesian dialect at Panna Maria are the following: Franciszek Lyra, "Język polski w najstarszych osadach polskich w Stanach Zjednoczonych" [The Polish Language in the Oldest Polish Colony in the United States], *Zaranie Śląskie*, XXVIII, No. 2 (1965), pp. 562-566; Reinhold Olesch, "The West Slavic Languages in Texas with Special Regard to Sorbian in Serbin, Lee County," in Glenn G. Gilbert, ed., *Texas Studies in Bilingualism* (Berlin: Walter de Gruyter & Co., 1970), pp. 151-162.

[19]*The Karnes City Citation* (Karnes City, Texas), July 12, 1973, Sec. A, p. 4.

[20]The expression, in the original Polish as used in both Panna Maria and Płużnica, is "jedną nogą w grobie." Mrs. Felix Mika, August 11, 1973; Mrs. Krystyna Popanda-Jaksik, Płużnica, Opole Voivodeship, Poland, to T. Lindsay Baker and Krystyna Baker, Interview, June 25, 1972; Mrs. Ella Snoga, Panna Maria, Texas, to T. Lindsay Baker and Krystyna Baker, Interview, August 11, 1973.

[21]Rev. Rafał Kaczmarczyk, Płużnica, Opole Voivodeship, Poland, to T. Lindsay Baker and Krystyna Baker, Interview, June 23, 1972; Mrs. Krystyna Popanda-Jaksik, June 25, 1972; Mrs. Ella Snoga, August 11, 1973.

[22]Mrs. Krystyna Popanda-Jaksik, June 25, 1972; Mrs. Ella Snoga, August 11, 1973.

[23]*Ibid.*

[24]*Ibid.;* Mrs. Krystyna Popanda-Jaksik, Płużnica, Opole Voivodeship, Poland, to T. Lindsay Baker and Krystyna Baker, Interview, June 30, 1973.

[25]Franz and Maria Karkosz, June 23, 1972; Mrs. Krystyna Popanda-Jaksik, June 25, 1972, June 30, 1972.

[26]Bernard Pajewski, "The Headless Ghost of Panna Maria," *Polish Folklore*, IV (March, 1959), p. 11.

[27]Ben P. Urbanczyk, Panna Maria, Texas, to T. Lindsay Baker and Krystyna Baker, Interview, August 10, 1973.

[28]Conversation with unidentified villager at Płużnica, Opole Voivodeship, Poland, June, 1972, cited by Rev. Rafał Kaczmarczyk, June 23, 1972.

[29]Pajewski, pp. 11-12.

[30]Edward J. Dworaczyk, *The Millennium History of Panna Maria, Texas* (n.p.: privately printed, 1966), pp. 98-99; Maria Starczewska, "The Historical Geography of the Oldest Polish Settlement in the United States," *The Polish Review*, XII, No. 2 (Spring, 1967), pp. 30-32.

THE CZECHS

Mr. and Mrs. Joseph Peter.

St. Isadore Group, Czech Catholic Agricultural Society, Fayetteville, Texas. Courtesy Sister Maria Andrea Harrington.

Bordovitz School. Courtesy Sister Maria Andrea Harrington.

Baca Band member.

Wedding with Fayetteville City Band. Courtesy Sister Maria Andrea Harrington.

Texas Folklife Festival.

Czech Lore and Customs

By W. PHIL HEWITT

PRAHA, TEXAS, on August 15, bulges with Czech Texans and their friends celebrating the parish feast day. On this one day of the year the population of the sleepy village, located just off U.S. 90 between Schulenburg and Flatonia, grows from less than a hundred to about five thousand. The day begins with a mass in the morning. The local chapter of Catholic laymen with plumed hats blowing, ceremonial swords glittering, and already sweating a little in the Texas heat, lead the procession from around the side of the tan brick St. Mary's church and the festivities are under way. After mass the celebrants get down to some real eating, drinking, socializing, and dancing. The parish festival at Praha resembles a combination of family reunion, Fourth of July picnic, country western hoedown, carnival, and county fair, all rolled into one. Activities include reminiscing by the old folks, playing bingo, throwing balls at real or faked and weighted milk bottles, eating good rich Czech food, including the famous *kolache,* drinking beer, and dancing to music provided by one of the many polka bands that abound in the Czech-settled areas of Texas.

Czechs from as far away as Dallas and the Texas panhandle return each year to the Praha festival to maintain old friendships, visit relatives still living in the heart of Texas Czech country, and in general to reaffirm their Czech heritage. The visitor at Praha can hear the Czech language spoken by old and young alike, for Czech is far from dead or dying among Texas' second largest European immigrant group. If he could understand the language he could hear the wry humor and jokes with which the Czechs poke fun at themselves, their circumstances, and at life in general. The Praha festival also provides an opportunity for Czech women from cities and rural communities to swap recipes for various delicious and fattening pastries and other culinary delights like homemade chicken noodle soup with real egg noodles made while the pot is boiling.

The visitors come from all walks of life and from all parts of the state. But most have a common cultural heritage; they are descendants of Czechs who left ancestral villages and farms in Moravia and Bohemia for a chance at a better life in Texas.

Large numbers of Czechs began arriving in Texas shortly after the Civil War. They tended to settle in clumps of families, and most picked places near already established Czech and German settlements. The earliest settlements were concentrated in Fayette, Lavaca, and Austin counties. By 1900, though, Czechs could be found in virtually all parts of the state, but heaviest concentrations lay in an area bounded by Dallas, Austin, Corpus Christi, and Houston. Wherever they settled they took their language, their religious practices, their lore of superstitions and folktales, their proverbs and jokes, and a love of fine food, good drink, fellowship, and festivity.

The early settlers celebrated or commemorated important religious holidays in the traditional old-country ways. Those beliefs, customs, and superstitions which had little or no relevance to the settlers' new life were discarded almost immediately. Others survived in altered forms. The Czech ways of celebrating Easter, Christmas, and weddings lasted longest in the alien Texas environment. Czech proverbs, which seem to be an integral part of the language even today, are perhaps the best preserved bits of European folklore.

As late as the mid-1940's in some Czech communities, December 6, St. Nicholas Day, signaled the start of the Christmas season. On that day the children hung up their stockings to be filled by St. Nicholas. Some time during the day *Maticka* (Little Mother) and the Devil visited the children. *Maticka* went in first and asked if the children had been good during the past year. If they had, she left them fruit and candies as a reward. If not, she departed and the Devil came in, whipped the misbehaving youngster, and, adding insult to injury, even gave the unlucky child the switch.

Christmas was a time of prognostication for the coming year. At the Christmas Eve dinner a lighted candle was placed by each person's plate. It was believed that the person whose candle went out first would die first. Other customs supposedly foretold the marriage prospects of the maturing young people. For example, if a rooster answered a girl's knock on the chicken house at midnight Christmas Eve, she would marry within a year. If a hen answered a boy's knock, the same prediction held true.

On Christmas Day a girl of marriageable age stood with her back to the door and threw her shoes over her shoulder. If the shoes landed pointing away from the door, she could look forward to another year at home. If they pointed toward the door she would marry within the year.

The younger children often played a game which supposedly told their occupations, or in the case of girls, their future husbands' occupations. They would melt lead, then pour it into cold water. The fantastic shapes assumed by the lead were the subject of extensive speculation on the part of youngsters and oldsters alike.

During the Christmas season Czech children played a variation of the old pea-under-the-shell game with a rather morbid twist. They used three walnut shells. Under one a ring was placed; under another, some soil; and under a third, nothing. Then the usual razzmatazz and the child picked a shell. If he chose the one with the ring he would marry soon; if the soil, he would die within a year; if nothing, then he would remain single.

In the early days in Texas the Czech people began their celebration of Easter two weeks before the event. The children would carry a figure representing the goddess of death from house to house. Along the way they serenaded those they visited with songs heralding the coming of spring. At each stop they were rewarded with eggs, pastries, and little gifts. The ceremony ended with throwing the goddess into a river or stream representing the end of winter and the coming of spring.

Until the early 1940's, particularly in the more isolated areas, many Czech families observed the Easter custom of "washing faces." On Easter Sunday the boys would attempt to wash their sisters' faces, usually over the girls' protests. The girls returned the favor on Easter Monday. Supposedly this washing on Easter Sunday made the girls prettier.

Aside from this face washing, the Easter Monday celebration did not take root in Texas. This holiday in Europe was one of rejoicing, partying, dancing, and general merriment. It served as a release after the long lenten season, the solemnity of Good Friday, and the religious services on Easter Sunday. On Easter Monday the boys would cut switches and chase the girls. The girls could stop them by offering handpainted Easter eggs, called *kralice*. In Texas the *kralice* were given as part of the Easter Sunday observance. Some were merely boiled and painted with simple designs, like ordinary eggs. Others were hollow shells painted with elaborate designs and intricate detail. Today some Czech families still give *kralice* to their loved ones and to special friends.

In the old days, when most Czechs still lived on farms or in small rural communities, a wedding was a social occasion of some magnitude. It required much careful preparation to produce a satisfactory wedding and the sumptuous feast which followed. First, the young couple rented land on which to live. Then, still well ahead of the happy day, the groom selected two of his best friends to dress in Sunday clothes and ride to the neighboring farms and homes extending formal invitations. A few days before the wedding the female members of the family and close friends gathered at the home of the bride and began the task of cooking and baking the food for the wedding breakfast and for the reception-feast that was the heart of the occasion. Most of the rich, delicious pastries were baked as much as three days ahead. The meat dishes, Czech sausage, goose, and roast pig were prepared early on the wedding day. As always there were the numerous kegs of beer that would be consumed during the festivities.

On the morning of the wedding, breakfast was provided for the bride and groom, their immediate family, and members of the wedding party. In many weddings the groom was not permitted to see his bride in her wedding dress before they met in the church parlor shortly before the wedding. In others, the bride and groom met at the home of one of the families to receive the parents' blessing. The couple knelt before the parents and the fathers placed their hands on the heads of the couple and gave their blessing. Next the mothers of the couple performed the same act. In some weddings the couple met in the church parlor and were formally introduced by a mutual friend of both families. This man admonished the groom to be kind, gentle, and worthy, and the bride to be chaste, obedient, and submissive.

After the ceremony the wedding party and their friends returned to the bride's home or to a parish or fraternal hall for the feast. Sometimes the guests were stopped by friends who stretched a ribbon across the road and asked a donation. The money might be given to the newlyweds or perhaps to the musicians who played for the reception. At the reception the bridesmaids pinned sprigs of rosemary on each guest, symbolizing fidelity and constancy. In some weddings a person with a doll or shoe passed among the guests and collected money to buy the cradle for the first child.

Then the feasting and dancing began. Tables were loaded with pork, goose, chicken, and a variety of starchy and fattening foods that Czechs seem to favor. Pastries like the Czech *kolache,* with a variety of tasty fillings, and kegs and kegs of beer were all available to the guests. In fact some receptions used to be characterized by the number of kegs of beer consumed, as in, "I went to an eight-keg reception." And of course there was always the obligatory polka band. The whole atmosphere was sort of a relaxed free-for-all that lasted well into the night.

Nowadays the weddings of most Czech couples resemble those of most other young people. Occasionally a bride and groom will have their parents bless them in the traditional way, but that custom is slowly dying. One aspect of the celebration which is certainly alive and well in Texas is the magnificent feast put on by the family. If attending one, you will notice that some of the most traditional foods like goose and roast pork have been replaced with barbeque beef. But Czech sausage and potatoes are still served, and there is always plenty of beer, and the Czech pastries remain an integral part of the celebration.

Several times a year the Christian Sisters of the Taylor Brethren Church get together for a fund-raising effort that is both profitable, sociable, and a delight to the taste buds. Before the day is over these Czech ladies bake more than six-hundred-dozen *kolaches,* and sell them to eager buyers who stand in line for the yeast-dough rolls with poppy seed, fruit, and cottage cheese fillings.

The Taylor *kolache* bake begins the day before, when the women gather in the small church kitchen to fill earthenware crocks with pineapple, apricot, peach, prune, and cottage cheese fillings. Dozens of baking pans are greased and stacked for use the next day. The next morning some women report for the sunrise shift. They mix the first batch of doughs and set them on the back of the stove to rise. Then work begins on an assembly line basis that would put Henry Ford to shame. Eggs are beaten by hand, batches of dough are mixed with wooden spoons, and surprisingly, no one uses a recipe. At first glance, it appears that *kolaches* are made on the 'dash of this and pinch of that' principle. But really the women follow formulas handed down from generation to generation among Czech families.

The balls of dough are placed on baking sheets, patted into round shapes, and filling is ladled into the centers. After another rising, the pans of *kolaches* are baked in the huge commercial baking oven the Sisters purchased expressly for the project. The oven holds fourteen pans of *kolaches,* each pan containing fifteen *kolaches.* After baking, the *kolaches* are brushed with a generous coating of butter. Recently the women have taken to using paint brushes, but it's only because they can no longer find goose feathers with which to do the job.

According to tradition the first batch is the crew's breakfast. But after that the *kolaches* come out of the oven at a steady pace. By mid-morning other women in the next room are busy taking phone orders and waiting on the people lined up to buy boxes, cartons, and bags of the delicious goodies.

The conversation in the kitchen and in the adjoining rooms is bilingual, jokes, witticisms, and gossip being exchanged in both English and Czech, sometimes drifting back and forth from one language to the other all in the same sentence. The lunch break is taken in shifts. Czech bread is often served, and the standard meal is homemade chicken noodle soup. In fact, you can stand in the kitchen and watch one of the women slowly pour the mixture into the boiling soup pot. The aromas coming from the kitchen of the Brethren Church on *kolache* day would tantalize and delight the most hardened steak and potatoes man.

In the days of the early Czech settlers and before the coming of radio and television, Czech parents, like those everywhere, often told fairy tales to impress virtues of thrift, honesty, and obedience upon their children. Other tales were told simply for their entertainment value. Today virtually all of these heroes, heroines, villains and assorted evil-doers have been superceded by the American success story, the proverbs of Benjamin Franklin, and Texas tall tales.

At one time the central figures in Czech fairy tales included these: the *vodnik* or water sprite; *rusalka,* a nymph; *bludnicka,* a will-o-the-wisp; *mura,* a vampire-like spirit that rose from the grave to suck people's blood; *rarasek,* the devil; *sotek,* a mischievous imp; *trpaslier,* dwarfs of both good and evil; *carodejnice,* witches; *obniny mus,* a man who became lightning; and *jitrenda,* a good fairy who brought good luck to those who were working while she, the last star of the morning, was still in the sky. The *vodnik* seems to have been a popular figure in stories detailing the value of honesty and hard work. Other figures such as the vampire-like *mura* probably sent shivers of delicious terror down the spines of countless Czech children.

Most of those who have studied Czech Texan folklore agree that the Czech proverb remains probably the most well preserved of the lore brought by the early Czech settlers to Texas. Those learning the language quickly learn to incorporate the proverb into the speech pattern. Like proverbs everywhere they run the gamut of human experience and like most proverbs from other languages, they lose some of their original sharpness and linguistic individuality when translated into English. Some of the more interesting ones are as follows:

Some people have more luck than brains, but you must have brains before you have any luck.

Treat the devil well and he gives you hell.

Without money, do not go to the music.

What is on the heart is on the tongue.

If you get a big dower, you'll feel your wife's power.

Foolish is he who gives; more foolish is he who does not take.

The hour of death is the hour of truth.

As the loan, so the payment.

When you're behind the wagon, you walk.

Every fox praises his own tail.

Where there is nothing but feasting, hunger is not far away.

Who wants too much usually has nothing.

Who chooses too long, in the end chooses wrong.

Who chases two rabbits will catch neither one.

If there were no plowman, there would be no rich man.

He who is ashamed of his native tongue deserves the scorn of all.

There are as many opinions as heads.

When the game is most enjoyable, stop.

Better one's own piece of bread than another's roast.

A lie has short legs.

Silence is often a good teacher.

At a feast everything smells good.

Look back at the rear wheels.

I like to listen to him when he is silent.

When promises are promised, fools rejoice.

At the farmer's are black hands, but white bread.

Little thieves they hang, big ones they let go.

Everything has an end, but a sausage has two.

The Czech musical tradition is almost as viable as Czech Texan proverbs and certainly more readily apparent to the interested observer. Although opinion varies as to the exact year, the first all-Czech band in Texas was organized sometime around 1880. By 1900 virtually every settlement boasted at least one such group. Few of these men were professional musicians, but almost all had received some musical training in Europe. At picnics, weddings, and festivals they played their polkas, marches, and waltzes for enthusiastic and appreciative audiences.

Over the decades Czech music has grown and changed along with the Czechs themselves. The first bands featuring brass instruments gave way in the early 1920's to bands composed primarily of reed instruments. Lately Czech musicians have adopted electrically amplified instruments, but traditional instruments such as tubas, drums, and assorted horns remain popular.

Wherever Czechs gather, a polka band is sure to be. These bands, composed of men and women who usually have other jobs during the week, still play the traditional songs. But now in response to changing tastes they spice-up the polka music with an occasional country-and-western tune. This blend of old and new reverberates in a hundred lodge halls across the state. From the country club to the country picnic and the parish festival, fourth and fifth generation Czech musicians do their best to play the old favorites and improvise the new requests. The climactic event for polka aficionados is the National Polka Festival held at Ennis in May of each year. For an entire weekend Czech polka bands from across Texas and the United States compete for one of the national championships in polka music. But in most areas of the state one does not have to wait until May or even until Saturday night to hear polka music. Many radio stations in heavily populated Czech areas feature hours and hours of traditional Czech music every day. Some stations even feature Czech-speaking disc jockeys who broadcast to large and receptive audiences.

Between 1850 and 1920 several thousand Czechs left Europe and came to Texas. And any but the most diehard Czechophile must admit that in many ways Czech Texans resemble Texans whose ancestors came from Norway, Lebanon, or Tennessee. Their dress is similar; most speak with the familiar Texas twang, and they pursue life with the usual Texan and American vigor. The Czechs' impact on Texas culture and traditions was never earthshattering; they were simply too few and the land too large for that. But their coming has enriched life in Texas in a number of ways. You can buy *kolaches* from the

Christian Sisters in Taylor; visit a town like Fayetteville where many of the last names read like the bottom line on an eye chart; and eat, drink, dance, and joke with Czech Texans at Praha, Ennis, or Sefick Hall near Temple and a hundred places in between.

The Czechs who came to Texas brought along their cultural baggage, including their religion and their language. Packed in someplace was a wry, droll humor that they used to poke fun at themselves, their situations, and at life in general. They also brought along their folk and fairy tales, their superstitions and proverbs, and their religious and festive customs. Many of their customs and much of their folklore has been muted or transformed by time. But much thrives today in the rural communities, small towns, and large cities where Czech Texans live.

Much of the material in the sections on fairy tales, Christmas customs, and proverbs is from Olga J. Pazdral's "Czech Folklore in Texas," M.A. thesis, The University of Texas at Austin.

THE NORSE

Mrs. Sadie J. Hoel, age 5. Courtesy Mrs. Sadie Hoel.

Karl Questad and family. Courtesy Mrs. Sadie Hoel.

Norse band. Courtesy Mrs. Sadie Hoel.

Charlie Swenson's new thresher in the 1890s or 1900s. Courtesy Mrs. Sadie Hoel.

Old Swenson Cotton Gin in 1890s. Courtesy Mrs. Sadie Hoel.

Four Mile Church. Courtesy Judge Derwood Johnson.

The Norse of Bosque County

By SADIE J. HOEL

THE HISTORY of the Norwegian emigration to America is a fascinating one. Courage and love of adventure proved to be among the many strong Norse characteristics which sent them in search of land in Texas.

When God made Cleng Peerson, he must have thrown the pattern away, as there isn't and never has been another man like him. He was born on the western coast of Norway, near Stavanger, May 17, 1782. We have little knowledge of his early life. However, we assume that he became a sailor. We do know that he traveled extensively in Denmark, France, Germany, and England, and learned to speak English.

When he returned to Norway in 1821, he became a Quaker. Because of his religious belief, he turned his attention to the opportunities in America. Accompanied by a friend, he sailed for that country and landed in New York in 1821. For two and a half years he studied the opportunities and possibilities for a more abundant life, and then he returned to Norway where he began recruiting colonists, urging his friends to emigrate to America. He returned to New York in 1825 to personally greet the "sloopers" (ships) as they arrived that same year. Of all his travels, it is evident that he preferred Texas, since he eventually came to Bosque County and settled at Norse. In exchange for a section of land, he made his home with one of the pioneer Norse families.

Cleng Peerson was tall and lanky and walked with a long stride. He possessed a horse and saddle, but he relied on his legs to get him where he wanted to go. He was an extrovert and was more interested in others than in himself. He often went to Austin to transact land business for the new arrivals from Norway.

His dress was not conventional. Tradition tells us that the members of the Texas Legislature gave him a frock coat and a top hat out of appreciation for his efforts and his kindness to others. When he returned home, his new appearance frightened the neighbor children when he called at their house for buttermilk.

He boasted that he was never broke, for he always had a quarter in his pocket. He was a great storyteller. In his travels, he would spend the night wherever he could. In the morning, he would offer to pay for his night's lodging, but fortunately he never had to. He was so entertaining and his hosts were so enthralled with his stories that they would never accept any kind of remuneration, not knowing, of course, that he had only twenty-five cents in his pocket.

The settlement called Four Mile Prairie in Kaufman County acquired its name from its location. It was located at the east edge of a prairie that was four miles long and four miles wide, and it became the first Norwegian settlement in Texas. Some of those who came with Johan Reierson in 1847 or shortly thereafter, included Bervend Swenson, Karl Questad, Ole Nystel, Wilhelm Warenskjold, and Elise Tvede. Reierson also started the nearby town of Prairieville, which is older than Dallas. Many other Norwegians came directly from Norway to the Four Mile settlement and later moved on to Bosque County. In 1854 a large group left the Kaufman County area and moved to the newly created Bosque County. They called their first settlement Norse.

The church has been the heart of the Norwegian community since its inception. Our Savior's Lutheran Church at Norse was established in 1869. Previous to that date, services were held in the settlers' homes. At one of these services at the Karl Questad home, Gustave Belfrage, the famous entomologist, was in the loft, guzzling whiskey, while preaching and praying were going on in the *stuen* (living room) below. Madame Questad wept with humiliation.

The business of the church was entirely in the hands of the men. The offering was given once a month when the members marched around the altar, laying their money on the altar. It was the custom for the women and children to sit on one side of the aisle, and the men on the other, during services.

After Sunday services, there was much visiting in the homes. Hospitality was extended to all, especially to those from a distance. Many invitations were given and accepted for dinner or for coffee and cake before they made the long ride home. It is said that women living near the church (within five miles) would often invite as many as thirty persons for dinner, preparations having been made on the previous day. Socializing after worship services is still a happy custom in Our Savior's Lutheran Church.

Confirmation was, and still is, a very impressive and important rite of the church. Martin Jenson, a Lutheran minister, gives a good description of the event of the day. The rite consisted of the instruction, public confession, and affirmation of faith, but many a youngster was more concerned about the externals, for on this day, the girl could wear a long dress and the boy could wear long pants. Proudly they sat at the first table for confirmation dinner. It was perhaps the first time that many of them discovered that a chicken had breasts and drumsticks.

The boys usually had horses of their own before confirmation age. Later they acquired a cart or buggy, according to how prosperous their fathers were. Parents were understanding. They figured a vehicle of some kind was essential to having dates in order that the young people fall in love and get married.

Weddings have always held priority in social events, perhaps because they were events in which the entire community participated in the early days. Days, even weeks before the appointed day, riders on horseback went from place to place spreading the news of the approaching wedding and extending a most cordial invitation to everyone in the community.

When Mr. and Mrs. B.P. Hoff celebrated their Golden Anniversary, the following account of their wedding day was read. The account of the event had appeared in *The Clifton Record*, Clifton, Texas, on February 25, 1892.

"Bernt P. Hoff was united in marriage with Miss Carolina Swenson, daughter of Otto and Elena Swenson; the Rev. J. K. Rystad officiating." There were four couples of waiters (attendants), as they were then called. They were as follows: Helge P. Hoff and Miss Annie Bronstad; Thomas Jenson and Miss Matilda Hanson; O. E. Schow and Miss Belinda Swenson; and John Arneson and Miss Augusta Strand.

Since the church was only approximately one-half mile from the bride's home, the entire wedding party and all the guests set out on foot across the pasture to the St. Olaf's Rock Church. It was customary that the Norse Band always furnish the marching music whenever one of its members was to be married. Since the groom was the trumpeter, he had to march with the band, leaving his bride to walk alone. While the group was proceeding across the pasture, the music was heard by cows and horses, which hurried to the scene out of curiosity. Ofttimes the horses would lay back their ears and take flight to the other side of the enclosure, but frequently the cattle accompanied the band with mooing.

The ceremony was performed at twelve o'clock noon; and immediately after it was concluded, the friends and kinsmen joined the wedding party in marching back to the home of the bride, where the reception was held. And truly, it was an old-time reception, many days having been used to prepare four kinds of cake, several kinds of cookies, and a large wedding cake which had been decorated with large and small candy hearts. This was in addition to one hog and one calf which had been made up into different kinds of meats.

The splendid and delicious dinner was served from a large table, housed in a huge tent that had been made from all the borrowed wagon sheets in the neighborhood. The table accommodated seventy-two people, and it had to be filled three times before all the guests had been served. The good neighbors were free with their help before the wedding day and during the serving of this fine meal to so large a gathering.

Since there were no flowers at this time of the year, and as greenhouses were almost unknown at that time, the table had been decorated with garlands of green cedar and with paper flowers, another tribute to the ingenuity and versatility of the pioneers.

By the time the supper had been served and the dishes had been cleaned, nightfall had come. It was the tradition that the feast was followed with dancing to the accompaniment of stringed instruments. If no instruments were available, a caller would still call the dancers to swing or square dance or do Norwegian folk dances. When musicians were available the waltz, the polka, and the schottish were favorite dances. By sunup the next morning, the entertainment was over. The remainder of the day was spent in returning all the things which had been borrowed for the reception.

Another form of entertainment (or punishment) was serenading a recently married couple with a charivari, or shivaree. After the newlyweds had been in their new home for only a very few days, these friends would stealthily gather near the entrance to their house after dark, and when the lights were out, with one accord, all instruments and noise makers would be struck. The noise was deafening! After the serenading, the group would storm in expecting refreshments. Then they would depart as hastily as they had come, making the house a disaster and leaving the couple to clean it up then or face it the next morning. This was considered an experience to be remembered.

Dancing became an art with the pioneers. Shoes were hard to get; consequently, if the distance wasn't too great, the dancers would carry their shoes as they walked to the party, putting them on just before reaching the home of the hosts.

Funerals were, in a way, like social gatherings, with the exception that the wedding was a joyous beginning, whereas the funeral was a sorrowful ending. As many persons came a long distance, they needed to be refreshed with food soon after arrival.

Services were held either in the home, or at the church. The tolling of the church bell accompanied the body to the grave side and was the last rite of the sorrowful occasion.

One of the superstitions handed down was that when a person died in his home, all the mirrors in the house should be draped or covered immediately. This was often practiced even though the reason for this tradition had already become unknown.

Those first Norwegian settlers of Bosque County lived through experiences that have now become legendary.

During the Civil War, a Mrs. Linberg lived in a log cabin with her two small children while her husband was away at war. She was not a brave woman according to the standards of that time. She asked her neighbor, Karl Questad, who lived across the valley, if his daughter Martha, aged twelve, could spend the nights with her. Permission was gladly given.

One night they heard someone trying to open the door. As there were still glowing coals on the hearth, they took some slats from the bed to use as fuel in order to heat dish water boiling hot. Then they stood with vessels in their hands, ready to scald the intruder whoever he might be. During this time Martha wanted to put the gun through a crack in the log cabin wall and fire, but the older woman would not let her. But near daybreak, Martha did it on her own. The shot was heard across the valley and the men came quickly. However, by the time they arrived the intruder had fled.

Life during the pioneer days was never lacking for excitement, especially for Martha. One day the teen-age girl was out looking for some of their cows when a wild stallion took after her. Knowing that he would overtake her, she fell down in the tall grass and crawled. Then she would jump up and run a distance before again crawling on hands and knees. She repeated this procedure several times until the stallion finally lost sight of her.

Another time she was looking for horses and was riding her favorite horse, Selem. She was quite a distance from home when she caught sight of an Indian who was also looking for something. As soon as she saw him, she wheeled her horse around and raced for home. In the chase that followed, she forced Selem to jump across a gulch so wide that the Indian did not dare make the attempt. She arrived home safely, but her horse dropped dead under her.

Then there is the unforgettable Indian episode so well known in Bosque County. This incident took place in the late 'sixties. It was in March, 1867, that Ole Nystel, age fourteen, went with his neighbor Karl Questad to the mountain in an ox-drawn wagon to cut cedar posts. Karl left Ole to unhitch the oxen and had gone only a short distance when he heard an Indian war-whoop. He turned just in time to see the Indian shoot Ole through the knee with an arrow. When he realized that he could not rescue the boy, Karl ran, and to escape the Comanches he jumped off a thirty-foot bluff onto a pile of cedar cuttings. Carrying his gun and his ax, he ran four miles, largely through brush. He reached home in tatters, telling his frightening story. Martha jumped on her horse and alarmed the neighbors, and because of her action a posse was quickly formed and was soon in hot pursuit. They were never able to overtake the Indians, although at one time they found a campfire of smoldering coals.

Three months later, Ole was exchanged at a trading post in Nebraska for staples such as flour, sugar, and coffee. These kindly merchants grew fond of Ole and wished to keep him as their own, but eventually he was delivered to his own home, wiser for the experience.

Another Ole, Ole Hoel, had a mother who was quite a remarkable woman, and was the epitome of self reliance. If she couldn't accomplish a task one way, she would do it another; consider the making of her son's suit, for instance. One of her neighbors had bought a ready-made suit for one of the boys. Mrs. Hoel also had a boy who needed a suit. But instead of buying one, she borrowed her neighbor's "store-bought" suit, ripped it apart, cut a pattern by it, sewed it together again, pressed it, and returned it to her neighbor the following day, thereby saving the price of a suit. That was like putting silver in the cottonseed bin.

In pioneer days when silver was the currency, and before there were local banks in the rural areas, it was a real problem to find a safe place to hide a quantity of silver.

Ole Hoel, who was in his early teens, was sent to town to bring home the money that had been paid for the wheat—some over $300. The money was placed in a large wheat sack, equally divided so it would balance, tied securely, and then thrown over the pommel of the saddle. He rode twelve miles with the jingling money, arrived home safely, and deposited the silver in the home "bank"—deep in the cottonseed bin! At one time the family had several thousand dollars hidden in that bin.

Although the Norse settlements in Kaufman County have been absorbed by the surrounding farming communities, the Bosque County settlements still retain the strong Norwegian flavor and celebrate their traditions and ancestry. An annual Smorgasbord is held at Norse in Our Savior's Lutheran Church. Visitors are served a large variety of Norwegian foods by the ladies of the community dressed in traditional costumes. This fellowship of the Norwegian community in Bosque County is strong and has been, since, of necessity, they banded together as pioneers over a century ago.

Frank Bean

By PALMER H. OLSEN

FRANK and Patsy Bean had been slaves, but somehow, unknown to descendants and younger friends, had become free and lived and worked during the Civil War and for some years afterwards on the farm of Grandma Swenson about nine miles southwest of Clifton in the Norse community. When Grandma Swenson moved to Clifton about 1890, Frank and Patsy moved to Clifton's "old-town," but continued to work for Grandma and her married children. Both Frank and Patsy learned to speak Norwegian and Frank, especially, was fluent in simple, conversational language.

Norwegians came in an almost steady stream in the '90's and Frank became a regular greeter of the Santa Fe trains. Readily recognizing the newly-arrived and puzzled Norwegians, Frank greeted them with smiles and in perfect Norwegian asked solicitous questions as to their welfare and wishes. Having hardly even seen a Negro before, they were naturally thunderstruck. Their expressions and actions indicated strongly that they were not only highly puzzled, but also not a little concerned. Frank's ebony color startled them. And they were hardly comforted in the scorching Texas sun when Frank deadpanned, "I wouldn't worry; things will be all right. When you have been here in this hot sun as long as I, you may be black, too."

FRENZENY & TAVERNIER

THE GREEKS

The Rev. Archimandrite Theoclitos Triantafilides.

Greeks aboard immigrant ship, ca. 1911.

Capt. George Economon with mother and brother Stavros.

Greeks in Houston dancing the *kalamantianos* wearing the *Euzon* man's costume and the *Queen Amalia* women's costume. Courtesy Kit Van Cleave.

The Mike Galanos family. Courtesy Mr. and Mrs. Mike Galanos.

Texas Folklife Festival.

Greek-American Life Styles

By KIT VAN CLEAVE

GREECE has an old and rich heritage of traditions, shaped through centuries of unbroken national life. Contemporary Greek music, dances, folklore festivals, and religious feasts all have their roots in the ancient civilization. Their forms and names may have changed, but they always remain the same in essence. Today, the holy ground of the Greeks is not Delfi but Tinos; Goddess Athena is no longer the vanguard of Athine, for it is the Holy Virgin who now watches over all Greeks. At Eleusis, the descent of Demeter into Hades is no more a cause of mystic celebrations; now, in every part of the country, Good Friday symbolizes the entombment of Jesus, and is celebrated with great religious solemnity. The tantalizing aroma of roasted meats no longer reaches the heights of Olympus from the sacred slaughter grounds; on Easter Day, however, a pre-eminently Greek religious feast, the family's roasting lamb, sends its spicy aroma from garden barbecues, inviting all to feast and drink.

For those whose parents and grandparents immigrated to Texas from Greece, the hardship of being different in an America of the 1930's and 1940's was offset by zealous devotion to Greek Orthodox church ritual, family traditions, and community intimacy. Today, in most Houston Greek-American homes, Orthodox religious holidays and celebrations are the core around which family members gather for the warmth of closeness, familiarity, and continuing tradition.

While Easter is the biggest holiday with Greeks everywhere, Holy Week and Christmas are also important in both religious and family contexts. In addition, Greek-Americans in Houston have created for themselves another religious-family-community event which helps keep traditions alive: an annual Greek Festival, held in October on the grounds of Annunciation Greek Orthodox Cathedral, 3511 Yoakum Street. Greek foods and wines of all kinds, beer, paintings, sculpture, weavings, artifacts, and other gifts are offered for sale; and the dancing goes on for all three days. It's a phantasmagorical block party given by the Greek-American community for the people of Houston.

During the Festival, more than 45,000 pieces of pastry and other rolled foods are consumed. These are created solely by the women of the church, who begin preparations in July. Dancers in the children's, teenage, and adult groups start rehearsing at about the same time. This year, some 14,000 people crowded into the churchyard to participate in the three-day Festival.

The annual celebration is but one reflection of the concept held by Greek-Americans in Houston that, as Mary Bellos puts it, "Orthodoxy is a way of life," which weaves church, family, and life continuum together. Greek-American women in Houston, for example, firmly support the patriarchal tradition which is held by the church and is orally transmitted from parents to children.

"My husband is the head of the house," Elizabeth Lewis, a Greek-American woman, states. "When he comes in, I do for him. This is a traditional, not a theological, matter, but it's our way."

While this patriarchal lifestyle is changing slightly for younger Greek women in Houston, Mary Bellos says, "Our mothers came from Greece, and they asked no questions of their husbands, but simply obeyed their wishes."

The emphasis on the male's importance starts early in life; a boy is devoutly hoped for. The first boy is named after his paternal grandfather. According to the ancestral region of origin, the family's first girl is usually named after her maternal grandmother. Celebrations of one's Christian name-day, more important to Greeks than birthdays, are big bashes if the honoree is a boy; girls are wished well and occasionally honored by other women with a kitchen coffee.

Part of the reason for the closely-knit relationship between church and family is historical with Greeks, and stems from the oppression by the Turks during some four hundred years of their occupation of Greece. Prejudice and hostility which Greeks hoped to escape in America were often equally severe in the New World, and sometimes worse early in the twentieth century. As "foreigners," these new Americans had to struggle to survive, to learn the English language, and to work in new trades. The pressure to assimilate grew greater as they stayed longer. Curiously, Greeks in Houston say today that there was much less discrimination in the South than in the North, although many Southern Greek-Americans still associated mostly with other Greeks during the 1930's and 1940's.

Life during the early years in America was church, choir, going to school with other Greeks,* and making family-unit visits to such events as name-day parties. As a result, the sense of community became quite strong, and oral traditions spread easily from generation to generation.

Any joining of the family and the church in a social context is usually eagerly anticipated, and turns into a terrific party. Greek weddings, for example, are virtually unchanged from immigration days. Depending on area of family origin, the groom today still buys the bride's gown, and *koufeta* (candy-covered Jordan almonds) is distributed to the guests in lieu of rice. *Koufeta* is wrapped in a square of tulle and tied with a ribbon, five or seven almonds in a bag, and set out on a table or distributed to the guests by young girls.

The bride and groom are crowned with *stefana*, two wreaths of orange blossoms tied with a single ribbon, and placed on their heads by the best man. The crowns are interchanged three times during the ceremony and represent both eventual attainment of the kingdom of heaven and the couple's reign as king and queen of the family during married life. Wine is shared by drinking from a common cup; this ritual anticipates sharing the bitter and sweet of life.

Family traditions are multiplied during christenings, when the child's parents select and welcome the godparents. In Greek Orthodox circles, godparents are extremely important, for they have a real obligation to aid in the child's moral development, and, in the case of the deaths of the parents, to rear the child. The godparents provide new white clothes for the christenee. After the service, when the child has been properly chrismated, these clothes must be washed carefully, and the water poured onto clean ground. Because it contains holy oil, it must be returned to the earth. Even today, participants in the service are given *marteriko*, a pin emblem designating witnesses who have observed the child's initiation into Christianity.

Seven sacraments tie the Greek-American family to the Orthodox Church: baptism-confirmation-unction (all occur at the same service), marriage, communion, confession, and ordination. Within the framework of these rituals, and with reinforcement from family and community, Greek-Americans find that their children rarely become delinquent or criminal.

"Because the family unit is close, the family name is important, and even in Houston the community is like a small town," says Elizabeth Lewis. "So everybody knows what the children are doing." In addition, Greeks have a tradition of taking care of their own, and they pride themselves on seeing that no Greek, even a stranger, takes welfare. Such services are provided by the whole community through the auspices of the Philoptochos Society ("friend to the poor"), the ladies' auxiliary of Annunciation Cathedral.

Particularly during Holy Week and New Year's do the social and religious lives of Houston Greek-Americans intertwine.

The stage is set for Holy Week by serving fish on Palm Sunday, followed by a complete renunciation of meat, fish, and dairy products during Lent. The family exists on olives, bread, lentils, and such contemporary additions as peanut butter. The regimen, however, is not so hard as it sounds; the artful Greek way with food combines Holy Week specialties such as *faki* (lentil soup with vegetables) and *fasoulatha* (bean soup) with fresh breads, wine, coffee, and tea.

Holy Week services are held every night; Saturday night, at midnight, the Resurrection service is held. Usually after the regular weekday and Sunday liturgy, bread pieces called *antitheron* ("instead of the gift") are distributed. After this Resurrection service, congregation members file out of the church and are given eggs instead of *antitheron*. These hardboiled eggs are dyed red, a symbol of everlasting life. Pairs of service participants crack the eggs against each other; one person says, *"Christos anesti* (Christ has risen)," to which his partner responds, *"Alethos anesti* (Truly, he has risen)." This statement and response has always been the proper greeting for forty days after Easter as well; but this tradition is slowly being assimilated out of existence, for it is hard, Greeks in Houston say, to continue this in an English-speaking and not particularly religious American society.

The traditions surrounding the red eggs and Easter follow an old legend about Mary Magdelene and the Holy Land. Reportedly, she came to the palace of Emperor Tiberius, where she had been rich, after she was older and had voluntarily given up her wealth. To celebrate the Resurrection, she brought a gift to the emperor, but it was the smallest gift, the kind the poor gave, to show that she had given up everything for Christ, and had become poor for his sake. Rich in faith only, she offered the emperor faith in Christ, holding out a white egg, and saying, "Christ is risen."

"I can no more believe that than I can believe the white egg in your hand is red," Tiberius replied. But as Mary Magdelene spoke about Christ, the egg in her hand turned pink, then red.

After the late Saturday night Easter service, all families retire to their homes, bearing lighted candles which signify the New Light, the promise of eternal life. This practice, which also probably once helped Greeks find their way home, causes a sensation among other auto drivers, says Mrs. Bellos. An early Sunday breakfast is served consisting of *magerista* or tripe soup, with dill and green onions, egg and lemon sauce, and *tsourekia,* a sweet, braided Easter bread with a red egg baked into the center.

On Easter Sunday afternoon, the *agape* service, or "lovefeast," is held. From the Bible, *John 20,* heralding the Resurrection, is read in Greek, Latin, French, German, Italian, Spanish, and English, so the whole world can understand the good news. Afterwards, several families go home together for a real feast, with a roasted spring lamb, and *baklava* dessert and *koulourakia,* their twisted cookies. Where legal, fireworks are set off, and everyone dances late into Sunday night.

"Holy Week is mournful, meditative, and quiet," says Catherine Dameris, "and Holy Thursday evening is more sorrowful. There's no social life during this week; the church is draped in black, and no entertainment is allowed." Early on Good Friday, the community women decorate the *epitafion,* a symbolic tomb of Christ, with fresh flowers. The *epitafion* is then carried around the exterior of Annunciation Cathedral by selected male church members.

At New Year's, the emphasis is again on mixing of religious and family traditions and food. *Vasilopeta* (bread or cake of St. Basil) is baked in preparation of the celebration, with a gold coin inside. At the family meal, immediately after New Year's, the head of the family cuts the *peta* in a traditional way, three times in the shape of the cross. Slices are cut first for St. Basil (the *Agios Vasilios),* for *Christos,* for the house, for each member of the house, and finally for attendant relatives. He who receives the slice with the coin has good luck for the coming year. In some homes, gold jewelry, fresh fruit, and a cross are draped over the *vasilopeta* prior to its cutting.

The emphasis on bread in Greek-American family life comes from the concept that bread is the staff of life. "During World War II," says Mary Bellos, "Greeks often lived on nothing but bread and olive oil."

Quite alive in Houston is the custom of passing the Greek traditional dances from one generation to another. These folk dances express a wealth of sentiments through movements and the rhythm.

While women are not allowed to dance all the folk dances, there is an increasing interest by family members in knowing and frequently dancing the native steps. Most popular is the *kalamantiano,* a national dance. Regional dances frequently seen in Houston are the *pentozale,* a fast Cretan dance, the *tsamiko,* a warrior's dance performed in ancient times by men going into battle to demonstrate masculinity, and the *hasapiko* (Zorba's dance), performed by two men who grasp with straight arms one shoulder of the opposite partner.

Macedonian and island dances, particularly the *kerkyrakieko,* are also often seen in Houston, as is the *zembekiko,* wherein one man dances solo, and executes his most difficult steps, and is followed by a competitor who tries to outdo him. In the *andekristo,* two men dance across from each other.

"We used to learn the dances by hooking on the end of our parents' dance lines," says Catherine Dameris, "or we learned alone. Since babysitters were not part of our family lifestyle as Greeks, we went everywhere with our parents and danced with them at parties. Now we have instituted dance classes at the church for others interested in the native dances." Dancing is essential on Greek national days, she says, and once were presented as end-of-the-year exercises in gymnastics classes.

Wherever he may live or wherever his origins may lie, whether he lives on airy, almost inaccessible heights or on a sunny plain in Greece and dresses in an ancient *chlamys,* or is a businessman or housewife in Houston, the Greek remains ever-faithful to his traditions, and builds on them daily, for they remain the essence of his Greekness.

*While Greek schools were not available in the days when these Greek-Americans grew up in Houston, Annunciation Cathedral has established a parochial school. In addition to regular curriculum, children also receive one hour of Greek a week. Open to anyone, classes now only cover the first and second grades, but expansion is planned next year.

THE ITALIANS

Wedding picture of Mr. and Mrs. A. J. Falsone, 1924. Courtesy Frank E. Tritico.

Italians who worked on the N.Y., Texas & Mexican Railroad. Courtesy Mr. and Mrs. Charles Innocenti.

Italian Club Picnic, Thurber.

Josephine Lucchese. Courtesy Mr.
Florentine Donato.

Shrimp boats.

Texas Folklife Festival.

Magic and Ritual
Among Italian Fishermen
on the Gulf Coast

By PATRICK B. MULLEN

FOLK BELIEFS play an important part in the cultures of various ethnic groups of the Texas coast. I collected the following beliefs and customs from Italian fishermen on the Texas Gulf Coast in the summer of 1967.[1] These Italian fishermen have retained many of their old country traditions, but they have also become a part of the mainstream American culture in a number of ways.

The Italian community of fishermen is located in Galveston where they form a sizable minority of the overall population. The older Italians were born in a small fishing village near Catania, Sicily. My informants were all fishermen in Sicily before coming to the United States, and they have continued this occupation here. Their migration from Sicily follows a set pattern: most of them came to Florida to fish and stayed there until a big general migration of fishermen to Texas in the 1930's and early 1940's. One man was a leader in the move to Galveston. He came to Galveston in about 1920 in advance of the heavy wave of migration. He shrimped and established his own fish house which became very successful. He then began to bring friends and relatives from Florida and Italy into Texas which explains the fact that so many Italians in Galveston are from the same village in Sicily. His son now runs the fish house and shrimp packing business his father founded, which is presently one of the largest on the Gulf Coast.

The eleven informants of Italian background ranged in age from eighteen to ninety. Eight of them were born in Sicily, and the youngest three were born in the United States. Most of the older men had a limited education, less than high school, but two of the young men were enrolled in college. All of the informants were Catholic, as the entire Italian community seems to be. Seven of the informants were married and had children. Several were members of the same family; one man and his two sons and two other men with one son each were all informants. Seven families were represented by the eleven men, and three of these families were related to each other. The men were ages eighteen, nineteen, thirty-six, fifty-seven, fifty-eight, seventy-five, and ninety. The other four did not give their exact ages, but all seemed to be in their fifties except for one man in his seventies.

The older men had been fishing all their lives, and only the ninety-year-old man was completely retired, and his retirement came at age eighty-eight. The younger men have worked on their father's boat, and the thirty-six-year-old runs his own boat. The five active fishermen owned at least one boat each and had prospered in the fishing business. One man was wealthy from his huge fish and shrimp packing business. The rest did not approach his wealth, but they all had comfortable homes in middle-class neighborhoods. Their friends seemed to be mainly people with the same ethnic background, but there was no complete separation geographically or socially from the rest of the community. Four of the men owned and ran their own medium-sized shrimp boats. They mainly took one-day trips into the Gulf, although at times they stayed out for as long as a week or two. One old man worked at a shrimp house; another worked on his son's boat; two worked part-time for their father; one ran a grocery store; one was retired; and, as mentioned, one owned a shrimp house and a fleet of boats.

A few of the Italian fishermen expressed attitudes about ethnic group identity. There was a definite difference in attitude between the Italian-born first generation and the United States-born second generation. The older people still talked about their home and relations in Sicily. They were familiar with traditions of the old world, but the younger generation has severed its cultural ties with Europe. One day I observed a graphic instance of the difference between the generations. I was in the home of one Italian family when one of the boys asked what they were having for dinner. His mother said they were having an Italian dish, and the boy made a face. I asked him about his preference in foods, and he said he did not like Italian foods. Both of his parents eat them regularly. This is just one way in which the second generation has rejected the customs of the first. The same boy was engaged to a non-Italian girl, and his mother remarked that this was the first time this situation had existed in their family. The younger men seem to be rejecting their father's traditional occupation, fishing, since they are studying unrelated fields in college. The older people speak Italian part of the time, but the younger ones do not seem to have a knowledge of it. Thus, the customs and traditions brought from Sicily to the United States by one generation are being discarded by the next, which is becoming more assimilated into the dominant culture.

This social background is helpful in analyzing the occupational folk beliefs of the fishermen. Most of the beliefs of the fishermen with an Italian heritage are parallel to those of the rest of the fishing community of the Gulf coast. For instance, seven of the Italians mentioned a taboo against turning the hatch cover upside down, a taboo that is widely practiced among all fishermen. The Italians believed that the hatch cover taboo was not found exclusively in the United States; two men said they had heard the taboo in Italy, and another said that it was "universal." They reported other widespread beliefs. Five of them knew of a custom of putting money under a mast for good luck. Three said that horseshoes were good luck on a boat. Three said they launched new boats with a champagne bottle. They also reported many popular weather signs. Four of the fishermen mentioned a ring around the moon as a bad weather sign. A red sunrise as a sign of wind and a rainbow at night as a sign of good weather were common beliefs of Italian fishermen. In their folk beliefs, Italian-American fishermen are part of the overall occupational tradition of sea-faring men.

They do have a few magic beliefs and one weather sign which seem to be exclusively their own since they did not appear outside the circle of Italians in Galveston. The sign was that when the shrimp turn red a storm is coming, and it was reported four times by Italian fishermen and only once by a person outside this group. None of them said it was originally from Italy so that it may have been a common observation since they have been fishing in the Gulf of Mexico. This was the only sign that belonged to the group alone, but they had several magic beliefs.

One of these magic beliefs was linked to their religion. Two of the men said that they carried blessed palms on their boats once a year on Palm Sunday for good luck. This is a belief which is supported by their Catholicism so that they do not think of it as a superstition, and they can believe it with little or no conflict forming in their minds.

The belief is enhanced by the social support which the entire ethnic group provides through their common religion. This would also hold true for the blessing of the fleet among Italian fishermen.

Another magic belief which was widely held by Italians concerned evil spirits. Four of the fishermen offered various magical means of ridding a boat of evil spirits, but the most popular way was a red cloth. "A red cloth is waved to scare evil spirits away by old Italians. Some still do it." The thirty-six-year-old man reported this and then laughed. He did not believe in the practice and attributed it to "old" Italians. Older native-born Italians presented a different attitude toward the belief: "Some of them believed that the red flag was like voodoo. Even young people still do it." The fifty-six-year-old man who said this did not want to admit that only the old-timers practiced the belief. He may also be telling a fact; some young men may practice the belief without openly avowing it. Here in the beliefs is cultural evidence for the generation gap among the ethnic group which is aggravated by the rejection of ethnic traditions by young people striving to fit in with the rest of society. The concept of evil spirits sounds too "superstitious" to a generation educated in modern American public schools. Thus, they would have no need for a red cloth or any of the other remedies for evil spirits, such as sprinkling salt or putting garlic on board the boat. The younger fishermen trust technology and rationality under hazardous situations on a boat because they have grown up in a society which teaches dependence on these values. The older men cling to their traditional beliefs for psychological support because they have not been influenced as much by modern non-fishing non-Italian society.

The Italians had one magic control device which was more popular than any of their other beliefs. Seven Italians had this belief and only one non-Italian reported it, and he was a man who had also fished in the Mediterranean before immigrating to the United States. The belief was that making the sign of the cross in some way would break up a water spout. I collected this basic belief with a varied amount of details in each case. The first time I heard it was from the two boys, eighteen and nineteen, who were working on their father's boat: "If you see a water spout and you make the sign of the cross with your hand, it will go away. I heard this from my mother who got it from her father in Italy." Their testimony was void of any of the details which I later collected, but it was obviously an old magical practice which had been brought from Europe. I talked to their mother about the belief, and she said that most old Italians are "superstitious," and she admitted a belief in some of the practices herself. An older man who was in his fifties added some details to the belief: "They used silver knives to get rid of, to cut the water spout. They make the sign of the cross with silver knives. Some kind of words were said with it." The next man, who was fifty-seven, remembered one more detail. "The oldest boy in the family, they hand him a knife and say a prayer." As the informants increased in age, they knew the belief in more detail and had more faith in its efficacy. The young boys simply dismissed it as an old "superstition."

I was still to receive more information about the ritual. Finally I talked to a seventy-five-year-old fisherman who spoke only Italian; his son-in-law had to act as translator for us. The old man remembered practicing the belief in their old fishing village in Sicily:

Old-timers used to do the thing with knives and water spout. There was a special day when they had to learn the words, some feast day. They had to use special knives. Christmas Eve was when you had to learn the words. Had to use a white-handled knife. It was supposed to cut the water spout. Use scripture and holy attitude and make the sign of the cross. They said "tail of the rat" so that you might not harm any human beings. It was a secret thing for sea-faring men. It was an elderly lady who said she had cut the spout.

His version details a complete magic ritual which was an important part of the fishermen's life in their Sicilian village. There are all sorts of stipulations controlling the belief: special knives have to be used, and there is only one day a year when the ritual can be learned. The belief is related to their Catholic religion by its use of the cross symbol and the "scripture and holy attitude" used with it. This would have much more strength in Sicily since virtually all of the community had the same religion. The "tail of the rat" statement was used to offset the dangerous consequences of dealing in magic. Despite the religious overtones, the belief was basically magical, but by saying "tail of the rat," human beings were protected from the magical effect. The ritual established fishermen as an esoteric group since only sea-faring men were supposed to learn the belief.

From this strong, complicated ritual, the belief has degenerated in its migration to the United States and through three generations into an interesting but not vital "superstition." It serves no function for the teenage boys because they have no faith in it. It serves only a limited function for the men of their father's generation because they have forgotten many of the details. The old man, who is representative of men their grandfather's age, is the only one who still remembers the belief in detail and who would still practice it if the occasion arose. The belief illustrates the generation gap in its widest spectrum, and it shows how ethnic traditions are dying out in a new context.

Internal conflicts arise in the minds of old and young Italian fishermen because of their disagreement over magic beliefs. The conflict is probably greater for the older men since their beliefs are being ridiculed by sons and nephews who represent the values of the surrounding non-fishing society. The young men also feel some inner conflict since they are denying the traditions of their fathers which go back for many years. The second generation who continue in fishing have an easier time accepting old beliefs because their conflicts are lessened by their psychological need and their involvement in a small group which gives social support to the beliefs.[2]

The second generation is usually more actively involved on the social level of the community. By this I mean that they are interacting with other members of society more fully than their fathers or grandfathers. This has come about because of their education in public schools where they have freely mixed socially with non-Italian people to the point where they are now marrying outside their ethnic group. This is not to say that the Italian parents are not also socially interactive with the rest of the community, but they are not so to the same degree because of their strong ties to the ethnic group.

In order to understand the complicated process of acculturation better, the terms society and culture will have to be clearly defined. In doing this I am following Clifford Geertz's distinction between the two. Culture is an "ordered system of meanings and of symbols, in terms of which social interaction takes place"; it is "the framework of beliefs, expressive symbols, and values in terms of which individuals define their world, express their feelings, and make their judgments." Folk beliefs would be a part of this framework, since they are symbolic expressions which often reflect values. Society can be defined as the "pattern of social interaction itself, . . . the ongoing process of interactive behavior"; the social system is the form which culturally directed action takes.[3] Folk beliefs would also be a part of the social system when they are actually practiced or manifested as a ritual. Culture is what man passes on from generation to generation; society is the putting into action at any particular time of what has been passed on. These two levels are not always well integrated; at times societal pressures come into conflict with cultural beliefs. It is this area of conflict which brings about some of the changes in folk belief. This is a two-way process; society changes culture and culture changes society.

The folk beliefs of the Italian fishermen can be considered a part of their cultural framework according to Geertz's definition. These same beliefs are a part of the first generation's social structure since they do not practice them. A discontinuity exists between the cultural framework of values of older Italians, a framework which was established in Italy, and the new social structure of their children in the United States. Geertz says that this discontinuity is to be expected in societies where change is a normal occurrence.[4] Change is certainly taking place in the Italian ethnic group as they have migrated to a new country and come into contact with a new social structure which is in conflict with their old cultural beliefs. A conflict also exists between the cultural values of the two communities. The surrounding society has the values of rationality and dependence on science which are in conflict with the ethnic group's magic folk beliefs and some of their Catholic beliefs. Thus, discontinuity can exist on the cultural level alone, on the social level alone, or between the cultural and social levels. But since the social structure tends to change at a faster rate than the cultural framework, the discontinuity will most often exist between these two.

[1] For further information on the folklore of Texas fishermen see my previous articles on this subject: "The Function of Magic Folk Belief among Texas Coastal Fishermen," *Journal of American Folklore*, 82 (1969), 214-225; "The Relationship of Legend and Folk Belief," *Journal of American Folklore*, 84 (1971), 406-413; and "The Function of Folk Belief among Negro Fishermen of the Texas Coast," *Southern Folklore Quarterly*, 33 (1969), 80-91.

[2] The theories on which this analysis is based are from Leon Festinger, *A Theory of Cognitive Dissonance* (Stanford, California, 1957).

[3] Clifford Geertz, "Ritual and Social Change: A Javanese Example," in *Reader in Comparative Religion: An Anthropological Approach*, eds. William A. Lessa and Evon Z. Vogt (Evanston, Illinois, 1948), 501.

[4] *Ibid.*

THE SLAVS

Courtesy Allison Wittliff.

The Slavonian Stave Makers of the Big Thicket

By A. R. (DOLPH) FILLINGIM

JUST A FEW YEARS BEFORE the Kaiser sent the German army to invade France, a bunch of about forty Slavonians came into the Big Thicket of southeast Texas to make white oak barrel staves. The wine makers of France, Italy, and Germany knew that the war was coming, and that while it lasted, it would be hard to get staves for their wine barrels and vats for fermenting alcoholic beverages. No other kind of wood would do except white oak. The best place to get white oak was in the United States, and one of the best places in the United States was in the Big Thicket.

There were about forty Slavonians in the crew. They came by train to Kountze and then went on into the Thicket in wagons. They went down on Black Creek about one-half mile from the Highway 326 crossing. All they had brought was their bedding, pots to cook in, groceries, their stave-making tools and nails, and plenty of whiskey.

They unloaded their supplies in a forest that had never had a saw or axe put to it. They went in the woods and began to cut trees and saw blocks about three feet long. Then they took their big hammers that weighed about ten pounds, their iron wedges that weighed about four pounds, and their axes, and they split the blocks in billets about six inches through. Then they took their froes and split the billets into boards about one-half inch thick and four to six inches wide.

The staves were to be shipped to the wine makers in Europe, and all of the white outside, or sap of the tree, and all of the knots and other defects were removed by hand with a drawing knife. The stave makers made a rack for holding the stave while they sat and finished it with the drawing knife. The choice billets of wood from each tree were ready to be finished with the drawing knife.

White oak wood was the only wood that I ever heard of that was good to make vats and barrels for fermenting and aging alcoholic beverages, wine and whiskey. It seems that the Creator made white oak wood for that purpose. In the white oak tree there is a hard flinty grain that runs from the outer edge to the center, or pith, of the tree. These streaks of hard flinty wood not much thicker than a sheet of writing paper are about one-sixteenth or one-eighth of an inch apart. Alcohol will not penetrate or go through this hard streak in the white oak wood and evaporate out of the barrel that it is put in.

The tannin or tannic acid that is in the wood turns the wine or whiskey red and gives it a sparkle. If the oak wood didn't have this tannin in it, two or three years later the juice would still look like the grape juice that was put in the vat or barrel. I don't mean that it would look like the grape juice you buy at stores with artificial coloring in it, but that it would still look clear, and the whiskey would be as clear as water without the tannic acid in the oak wood to turn it red. (When my friends and neighbors were making whiskey during the Volstead Drouth in the 1920's, they put in the whiskey color.)

The Slavonians worked in pairs, but just one man stayed at the tree while his partner went to another tree to work. They would sit on a seat that they moved from tree to tree and draw the staves for several hours. I heard that while a stave maker was sitting quiet, drawing staves, a panther slipped up to him and jumped on him. He called to his partner for help, and his partner ran to him and ran the panther off and saved his life, but he was badly bitten in the neck and shoulder.

They set posts about three feet apart in the ground where they wanted a camp house and nailed boards to the posts to form the wall. They put a roof of boards over it, leaving an opening two or three feet big in the center of the roof for the smoke to go through when they built their campfires in the center of the camp house, which was about fifteen feet square with a dirt floor. They made bunks around the wall and had the fire for cooking in the center of the camp house. They were the hardest working men that we ever saw. When it was light enough for them to see how to make their way through the forest, they would cut the tree that they wanted to work on that day before the wind started to blow. We could hear the trees fall before sunup.

A few days after a big storm hit the Thicket I walked about a mile east from my father's house to the five hundred acres that Enoch Grigsby traded the French family of Beaumont. The storm had blown down hundreds of hardwood trees. The pine had already been cut and hauled off to the saw mill at old Nona about three miles south of Kountze. On the French five hundred acres were hundreds of white oak trees that were big enough to make barrel staves.

After the storm that came I set out to find some of the heirs to the land and tell them what had happened to the trees on their five hundred acres. I located one of them who was living in Dallas, Texas.

I wrote to him and told him about his fallen timber and asked him if he would sell it. He wrote back that he would. I knew two Slavonian stave makers who were camped in the woods a few miles away. I went to them and asked them if they wanted to buy the trees that the storm had blown down on Mr. French's land; they said yes. I wrote Mr. French and told him that I had found somebody that would buy the white oak logs.

I helped the two Slavonian stave makers buy the trees and they immediately went to work on it and hired two men with a cross-cut saw to saw blocks forty-two inches long while they split the blocks and finished the staves with long drawing knives about two feet long.

It took them about five months to work up the fallen white oak on the five hundred acres.

The Slavonians had left their families, the ones that had families, in central Europe and many of them wanted to make all the money they could and go back to their families, or have their families come to them. Many of them never returned to Europe.

They didn't bother the wild animals, and they never went hunting. Deer would come up and lie down two or three hundred yards from where the stave makers were working. We soon learned that when we went hunting with our deer dogs the dogs would start trailing a deer where it had passed through the woods, while feeding the night before, and trail it up near the stave makers and jump it up. I don't know if the deer were just daring, or if they thought they would be safer there.

After the stave makers had worked the timber up around the camp on that tract of land, they moved out, perhaps some of them to another job and some of them back home.

That was the beginning of white oak stave making in the Thicket, and it lasted until all of the best white oak timber was cut out.

Besides the Slavonians, Austro-Hungarians and others, I don't know how many nationalities were represented among the forty men that were there. When they moved out they left camp houses standing.

The houses were soon occupied by hogs, woods rats, and chicken snakes, and fleas. I can't forget the fleas that the hogs raised.

From then on there were Slavonian stave makers' shacks all through the Thicket. In about 1920 Big Fox and his father Old Fox had their whiskey stills in an abandoned stave makers' camp when it was discovered by hog hunters and reported to the law. They moved out that night, and set up in a new location. The law came the next day and traced them to the new place and arrested them.

THE LEBANESE

M. K. Hage, Sr. Courtesy M. K. Hage, Jr.

Albert Jabour, peddler by wagon, Austin, 1908. Courtesy Mrs. Mary Jabour.

Assad Khoury and son Abe.

Albert Jabour, in front of his grocery store. Courtesy Mrs. Mary Jabour.

Anthony Ferris on the *oud* (lute), M. K. Hage, Sr., on the tambourine, and William Shea on the drum-baki.

Texas Folklife Festival.

Ya America!
Ya Beledee!

By JAMES P. MCGUIRE

WHEN Austin's Lebanese community gathers for its Labor Day celebration (a social event called a *sahria* which has been held now for forty-four years) or in the local Lebanese parties, it is not unusual to hear "The Eyes of Texas" or "The Star Spangled Banner" sung in Arabic. But, when an oldtimer calls for the singing of "Ya America! Ya Beledee!" (pronounced "Be-lady") he is hitting on something which has special meaning for the Austin group. For it is perhaps the only Arabic song composed and recorded in Texas by a Lebanese immigrant as a tribute to his new homeland. Its patriotic words expressed the collective sentiments of the entire Arabic-speaking community in Austin and in Texas at the outbreak of World War II. "Ya America!" was dedicated to President Franklin D. Roosevelt, and the copy sent to him was acknowledged by the White House.

A few years ago while researching the history of the Lebanese minority in Texas (about ten thousand, according to best guesses), I came across a stack of recordings of Arabic songs in an old Victrola case in Margaret Joseph's living room in Austin. Her father, Isaac Joseph, an immigrant merchant, bought most of them from a dealer in New York for entertaining his many guests. What attracted me initially was the mention of Roosevelt, the only word in the songs which I could understand. For the first time that hot afternoon I really listened during what was my initiation to the unfamiliar yet appealing melodies of Arabic music. When Margaret said that she had helped record "Ya America!" I really listened. In fact, she said that three of the four singers were still living in Austin. The composer, Anthony Rizcallah Ferris, died there in 1962. How he came to write and record this tribute certainly deserves to be part of Texas' folklore—even in Arabic.

Anthony Ferris, a young Lebanese intellectual, came to Austin during the early 1930's, first to visit an uncle who immigrated earlier, and then as a permanent resident on the Lebanese quota. Ferris attended and later taught at the University of Texas at Austin and became a consultant on foreign languages at the Texas Education Agency. His translations of Kahlil Gibran's Arabic works can still be bought in Texas' bookstores. At the outbreak of World War II, Ferris entered the Army as an instructor at Randolph AFB in San Antonio. At about the same time, he composed and recorded "Ya America! Ya Beledee!"

During the late 1930's in Austin a small group of Lebanese immigrants gathered around Ferris to form an amateur band. Ferris and Father James Rottle of St. Elias Syrian Orthodox Church played the *oud,* a lute popular in the Middle East; M. K. Hage, Sr., played the tambourine; and William Shea kept the beat on a small clay Arabic drum. Their little group provided flavor and fun for family parties, club meetings, and especially for Austin's large Labor Day Lebanese gathering. Ferris himself composed much of the music for the dances. He recruited Margaret Joseph and Tameena Dawood to help with the singing. In traditional Arabic songs the women sang answers to questions posed during the verses and on all choruses.

"Ya America!" featured Ferris and Father Rottle who accompanied and sang with Margaret and Tameena. After many well remembered rehearsals during the summer of 1941, their recording was made, and one thousand copies were produced in New York. The records were sold from the Ferris Drug Store on East 6th Street where Anthony worked with his brother, Elias. The latter recalled that they sold copies by mail as well and that many more were just given away to friends. The record lost money. Since few have survived, the little melody may soon be lost. The other day I dusted off my tape recording at the Institute of Texan Cultures and asked Elias and Margaret to make a translation.

An understanding of the deep love for America which grew in the hearts of the Lebanese immigrants would help to appreciate Ferris' tribute:

OH AMERICA! MY COUNTRY!

Chorus:

Oh America! My Country!
You are my beloved and affection,
For you we live, for you we die,
In you are liberty and equality,
Oh America! My Country!

Ya America, Ya Be-lay-dee. Inthe
   Roo-he wah-wah da-dee;
Fee-kill Ha-yath; Fee-kill Ma-maythe;
Fee-kill Huh-rhee-ya; Wol Moo-sa-
   waithe,
Ya America, Ya-Be-lay-dee.

Verses:

Oh, Uncle Sammy!
We are your children,
Forever we protect you,
and forever we defend you.
Patriotism is faith and love
and duty we owe to the end of time.
God bless you, Uncle Sammy!

Ya Om-mi, Sammy,
Nah-noo Ow Wa-lay-dak
Abba-dan Nah-me-ka; Wah Nah-mee
   Be-lay-dak
Hub-bil Ow-than; Min-al E-man;
Fahr-dan Mah-thoom, moon Ma-dal
   Iz-main,
Rob-bee U-bayrek-cock, Ya Ommi,
   Sammy.

Let us all march on
in Unity and peace.
Protect our America
Against enemies forever and ever.
The love of a country is faith
and sacrifice.
Oh America! My Country!

Doo-mee America,
Ma-dal Az-may-nee;
Oom-mil Op-thal-lee
Wash-shoe-zhanee
Al-lom Ahl Kha-thoob
Dow-min Ya Doom.

With our blood, we defend you,
Oh America, our hope.
The dawn of progress has appeared
By the leadership of Roosevelt,
the messenger of peace.
Oh America! My Country!

Fowk Al-ak-lamee
Dow-min Ya Doom
Rob-bee U-bayrek-cock
Ya Ommi, Sammy.

Oh, people of Lebanese extraction,
Live in peace in the land of freedom;
The land of knowledge and prosperity.
Oh, America! Live in glory forever and
   ever.
Oh America! My Country!

See-ro Zha-mee-aan; Lil a-may-mee
Bith thee Hay-din, Wah Sa-laamee
Wah-moo Al Ow-than; Min Al Id-wane
Fee-kul Heen-nin; Ma dahl Ill-yame
Ya America, Ya Be-lay-dee.

A-yoo-ha Soo-ree-yo Nad-dee
Bine-na Ab-nekh Ill Be-lay-dee

The Lebanese   **287**

Hub Al Ow-Thon
Min Al E-man; Far-done Mah-thoom-
min
Al-lahl In-sane
Ya America, Ya Be-lay-dee.

Nah-noo Naf-deek-kee
Fe De-man-na
Ya America, Ya Rz-zhon-na
Fazh-roo Nazh-zha
Fee-kee Cod-lah
Fee Fod-lee Roosevelt, Mal-lik ill Is-lah
Ya America, Ya Be-lay-dee.

Sha-ib Lub-nay-nee; Issh Bil Sa-laam-mi
Fee De-yohr Ill Om, Sammy; Ahrd el
Oor-fane
Ahr el Oom-ron, Bil Iz ill Doom-mi
Ma-dahl Iz-main, Ya America, Ya
Be-lay-dee.*

This emotional acknowledgment was often heard in Austin during the war on Margaret Joseph's half-hour radio program of Arabic music on Sunday afternoons. Things have changed a lot since those days. Austin has changed. The chances of hearing another Arabic radio program in the heart of Texas are remote. But Father Rottle, Margaret Joseph, Tameena Dawood, Elias Ferris and many others remember "Ya America!" and are proud. Anthony Ferris helped them express their love for America. Perhaps no other song will be composed in Arabic in this state. Too many of the second and third generation Lebanese Texans cannot speak or understand the ancestral tongue. And most all of the oldtimers are now gone.

*Elias Ferris of Austin and Margaret Joseph said that a verse for verse translation was impossible, and that the original six Arabic verses translated down to four in English.

(Guitar accompaniment in strict eighth-notes)

(F)   (C)

Chorus: Ya- a A- mer- i- ca,   Ya- a Be- lay - dee'

(C)   (F)

In-   the Roo - he - wah - wah - da- dee;   Fee-kill Ha-

(C)   (F)   (C)

yath;   Fee-kill Ma- maythe;   Fee- kill Huh-   rhee - ya;   Wol Moo- sa-

(F)   (C)   (F)   (C)   (F)

waithe,   Ya - A- mer-   i- ca,   Ya- Be-lay- dee.

* The music of the verses and chorus is identical, but each verse repeats from here.

Lebanese Song Style

By DAN BEATY

"YA, AMERICA" is sung in a moderate tempo by a small chorus of male and female voices with guitar accompaniment. Although the voices sing mostly in unison, there is some alternation between the men's and women's sections in the verses. The relative range of the melody is narrow—a perfect fifth—incorporating the first five tones of a diatonic major scale. The cadential raised-seventh scale step (E) lends further "key" feeling. Melodic ornamentation (indicated by small sixteenth-notes) is typical of this style of song. The shifting rhythms of the melody are also typical of Lebanese folksong and, in this instance, are the most uniquely identifiable elements of Arabic style. Harmonically, the tune employs alternating tonic and dominant triads (F major, C major) found in the music of the western continents but not so typical of Arabic folksong.

THE WENDS

A Wendish bride and groom.

Interior of St. Paul's Lutheran Church, Serbin.

Loeban Hunting Party.

Rev. Johan Kilian and daughter.
Courtesy Anne Blasig's Collection,
Wends of Texas.

Texas Folklife Festival.

Folklore of the Wends

By GEORGE R. NIELSON

ON THE MORNING of December 16, 1854, the immigration authorities at Galveston went out to meet the *Ben Nevis*, an English sailship, which had arrived in the harbor. On board they examined the papers and the physical condition of the five hundred Wends who had come to settle in Texas. Seventy-three had died since the band had left their homes in Germany; but since none on board were ill, the authorities permitted the settlers to land.

Although these Wends came from Prussia and Saxony, they were not Germans, but descendants of the Veneti of ancient times and the Polab Slavs of the Middle Ages. They called themselves Serbes or Serben, but to avoid confusion with the Serbs of the Balkan region, anthropologists named them Serbo-Lusatians or Wends.

These once numerous people had become more restricted in area until they were surrounded by Germanic tribes, and as far back as 1346 the Germanization of the Wends had begun. The Wendish culture was not related to that of the Germans. Their language resembled that of the Czechs, Poles, and Russians, and their dress, folklore, and literature were more Slavic than German. In 1815, however, the Congress of Vienna divided Lusatia, giving Upper Lusatia to Saxony and Lower Lusatia to Prussia. That was the beginning date of an organized and ruthless program launched by the Prussian government to make the Wends Germans.

In 1840 the 140,000 people speaking Wendish were dissatisfied and unhappy; and when the king, the "Pope in Berlin," forced the union of the Lutheran and Reformed churches, emigration increased and approximately 580 Wends under the leadership of Pastor John Kilian left their homes for Texas.

After landing in Galveston, they quickly took a boat to Houston, thus avoiding contact with the yellow fever epidemic in the Island City. From Houston they crossed the fertile prairie until they came to the Post Oaks near Rabb's Creek in what was then Bastrop County. For fifty cents an acre they got some of the worst land in Texas, whereas for fifty cents more they could have had the fertile prairie or bottom lands. They realized as much, but nearly all were completely without money. They had had little in Germany and after the trip they had even less. If they settled on the prairie, in addition to paying the higher price for land, they would have to buy wood for their houses, fences, and furnishings, whereas in the Post Oaks they could cut their own timber.

Under these conditions it is not difficult to see why the Wends kept little European folklore. Much of their folklore had been associated with trees, animals, and land; so when they saw mesquite, scrub oak, and oleanders instead of birches, chestnuts, and alders; and coyotes, skunks, possums, armadillos, scorpions, and tarantulas instead of the few wolves, rodents, and deer of Europe, the stories must have lost their meaning. And how could one possibly imagine that spirits and fairies would exist in the same woods with the wild Indians? Any costumes that were brought over were soon ruined by living under primitive conditions, and if there was money, it would be spent for land and not on new clothes.

As a result, the folklore which developed in Europe was almost completely lost in this new environment, with the exception of those customs which were practical and necessary, such as cures, planting and harvesting ways, and those practices associated with the church. This loss can probably be illustrated by an incident related by my grandmother. Once when her father was telling the children some stories, the mother interrupted the story-telling because she wanted the children to amount to something. By that she meant that she wanted them to work or learn something that would yield financial returns.

Ironically, the Wends did not escape from German influence. There were Germans in Texas when the Wends landed in Galveston, and in 1860 a large migration of Germans brought many to the vicinity of Bastrop County. In this instance the church was the unifying factor for the two groups and fraternization and intermarrying resulted. The question of language was the only real problem, but the pastor and the people were bilingual, knowing both Wendish and German. Services were conducted in both German and Wendish until the 1920's, when German became the only language used in public worship. Folklore, as a result, is also a combination of the two cultures, and it is impossible to separate the German from the Wendish folklore.

The most common and rich category of German Wendish folklore is that of the folk cures. My first memories of these cures go back to my childhood when I stepped on a nail. In the hot summers of central Texas, going barefooted was taken for granted, and along with the pleasure went the occasional injuries from grass burrs, mesquite thorns, and goatheads. A wound from a rusty nail, however, was a different matter, and in modern times the injured person would be punished further with tetanus shots. In the days when doctors were far away and the transportation was slow, the remedies had to be applied at home. In this case the treatment was painless and effective. A piece of bacon rind was placed on the wound, and then the foot was set in a shallow pan containing turpentine. The combination of the two caused a drawing effect on the wound, and the strong odor of the turpentine had the desired psychological effect. This remedy was said to be good not only for wounds, but also for curing boils and chest colds. For curing the chest colds, strips of fatty bacon were sewn on a woolen cloth, saturated with turpentine, and then applied to the chest of the patient. The uncomfortable person had to sleep all night with the sticky, gooey, and evil-smelling poultice, but in the morning the cold was broken.

Our skins suffered not only from the sharp spines of the thorns, but also from the sharp stingers of the yellow jackets and bees, and the painful bites of the big red ants. These were unavoidable. Sometimes we asked for it by standing on the anthill while holding our breath, or by knocking down the yellow jackets' nest from underneath the eaves with fishing poles, but at other times we were innocently playing or picking cotton. If we were near my uncle, we would go to him for aid, and he would remove part of his chewing tobacco cud and place it on the bite. If we were closer to the house, we would run in to Mother who would then place a teaspoon of baking soda on the wound and pour on a little vinegar. It fizzed, and the cooling relief was felt immediately.

Not all the remedies were from materials in the home; occasionally the adults ordered some from Germany or bought them in town. One such medicine, called *Blitz Öl* (Lightning Oil), was, in my grandfather's opinion, the final word in pharmaceutics. If any of the children hurt themselves, he would administer the medicine, even though it was hated and feared because its burn was worse than the pain of the original wound. One day, however, as Grandfather was splitting wood, the ax slipped and grazed his knee. Quickly he went onto the back porch, for this was his first opportunity to apply the medicine on himself. When he did so, the burning was as fierce as lightning and he gave the bottle a good heave into the pasture. Needless to say, the children were not sorry to see it go.

If this medicine was not effective, there were others that were. The efficacy of one of them was proved by an injury suffered by my Great-grandfather Schneider. He was binding oats, and it took a great deal of skill to drive the four horses as well as operate the machine. In an attempt to obtain additional leverage, he wrapped the lines controlling the horses around his thumb; but on this occasion the trailing lines got caught in the big bull-wheel, and the thumb was wrenched off. All that held it was a bit of skin on one side. He went home, doused the thumb in *Heil Öl* (Heal Oil), and wrapped it snugly with cloth. The thumb healed, and he regained its complete use.

A very popular cure was the *Lebenswecker* (Life Awakener), which was used to cure sore muscles, stiff joints, strokes, mastoids, and nearly everything else. It was a contraption the main part of which was a handle with a head the size of a fifty-cent piece made up of hundreds of little needles. The instrument was placed against the ailing part and the handle was drawn back and then released, causing the many small needles to prick the outer layer of the skin. No blood was drawn, but tha areas would be red from irritation. Then a little *Lebenswecker Öl* was applied with a feather. The patient was forbidden to get his hands wet for the next three days.

The *Lebenswecker Öl* was also used internally, but with great care. A girl, by the name of Alma Leitco, was taken to the Hamilton hospital with a severe case of locked bowels. Drs. Beecher, Chandler, and Cleveland tried everything but finally had to give the case up as hopeless. When Oswald Melde heard of it, he got some of the oil from Great-grandmother, went to Hamilton, and asked for permission to use the oil. The doctors said that since they had given up twelve hours earlier, they would consent. The father hesitated, but then gave his permission. Several years before, he had had a constipated mule and had tried the *Lebenswecker Öl*. A few minutes after the application, the mule had gotten up, jumped, and run, but then dropped dead. The only reason Mr. Leitco now gave permission was that he had prayed for help only fifteen minutes before, and he believed that Oswald Melde was the answer to the prayer. Nevertheless, Mr. Leitco went home. Three drops of the oil were mixed with the yolk of an egg and administered orally. Several hours later the girl passed a tapeworm thirty feet long, and when the father returned she was on her way to recovery.

Some of the cures that interested me, but were not used by my immediate family, were the numerous teas. The older women in the community placed great faith in them. For general health, tea made from linden, rose, or camellia leaves was good. As a specific remedy *Shreck Tee* (Fright Tea) was among the most popular. Anyone who was startled or shocked could get sure relief from a drink of this tea. About three heads of dried *Shreck Kräuter* (Fright Herb) were boiled for about thirty minutes in two cups of water. The patient drank the brew and went to bed, enjoying complete relaxation. The part of the plant that was boiled resembled the blooms of a thistle. It was not purchased, but usually grown in the corner of the garden, and after it was dried, stored in a fruit jar. Some people say that for added effect, the patient should take part of the object that startled him and boil it along with the tea. If it was a dog, he should take one of the hairs, place it in a tablespoon, roast it, and add it to the tea.

Few of the cures are as unpleasant as the cure for bedwetting. The ingredients are several newly-born mice without hair. These are chopped up (without being cleaned), fried, and fed to the child. To keep the child ignorant of what he was eating, the cook would chop up steak in a similar way and give it to the others.

Unpleasant in odor was the preventive measure used especially during epidemics. Asafetida was carried either in a bag around the neck or in the pocket. It was used to ward off the germs. Because it was an evil-smelling resin, the nickname for it was *Teufel's Dreck.*

Present in several of the cures is the element of mysticism. It is most difficult to find a complete recitation of one of the curing verses. Most seem to mention the name of Jesus and the number three. Here is one used to cure bleeding:

In meines Jesu Garten	In my Jesus' garden
Steben drei bäumelein	There are three trees
Eins heist . . .	One is called . . .
Das zweite heist . . .	The second is called . . .
Das dritte heist . . .	The third is called . . .
Blut halt stille.	Blood stop.[1]

The bleeding would stop almost immediately, but this help should only be used in extreme cases, because while this verse would stop the bleeding, the healing of the wound would be slow.

Since there was also a verse to promote healing of the wound, possibly these two should have been used together. The only line known is: *"Est stehn drei blumen auf Christi grab. . . ."* ("There are three flowers on Christ's grave. . . .") Many of the mystical cures of the Wends centered around Mutter Spielert, who lived in Giddings. Great powers were attributed to her, including the ability to cure erysipelas, a common Wendish disease.

The cure for warts requires a person to hold a silk thread over the wart and tie a knot in it. The thread is then buried next to the house where there is moisture. When the thread rots, the wart will be gone.

The remedy for side-ache caused by walking is even simpler. To cure the side-ache, the person should stop, pick up a rock, spit on it, and replace it.

When you ask the *Grossmutter* (Grandmother) if the cures are any good, she will smile and say, *"Sie leben noch"* ("They are still living").[2]

[1] The informant, Mr. Melde, did not know the names of the trees, but believed that no other names could be substituted.

[2] "Folklore of the German-Wends in Texas" is taken from *Singers and Storytellers* (PTFS XXX, 1961), Mody C. Boatright, Wilson M. Hudson, and Allen Maxwell, eds.

THE JEWS

Rabbi Henry Cohen. Courtesy Harris Kempner.

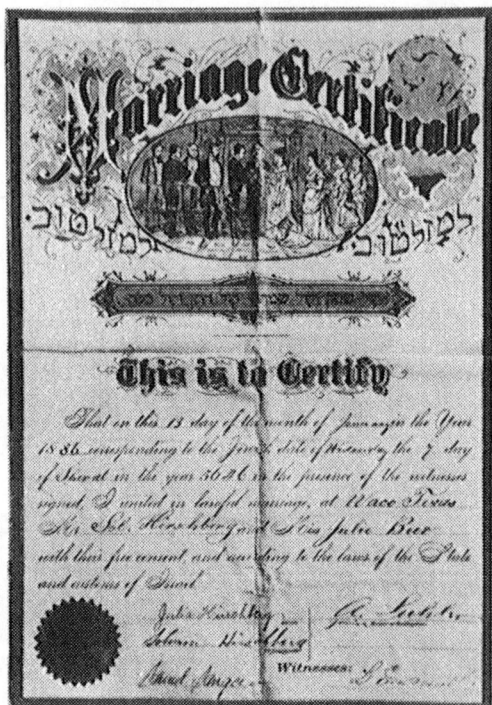

Certificates courtesy Texas Collection, Baylor University.

Adolphus Sterne of Nacogdoches.
Courtesy Archie McDonald.

The ladies of the Isaac Loewenstein family, Waco. Courtesy Texas Collection, Baylor University.

The Julian Schwartz family, ca. 1913. Courtesy Hirsch Nathan Schwartz.

Jewish Folkways

By LARRY LAUFMAN

THERE IS a Jewish saying: "Before I begin my speech, I'd like to say a few words." Before we start to follow the Jew through life, it should be noted that in ethnic studies there is a problem trying to deal simultaneously with the particular and the universal. What often happens is that we concentrate on one extreme or the other. Here we shall attempt to depict the customs of Jewish life in their uniqueness as well as in the psychology and mythology which they share with other ethnic groups. Before examining these customs, it should be remembered that there are eight synagogues in Houston: three Reform, four Conservative, and one Orthodox. Each group interprets the laws and customs to varying degrees, sometimes interpreting them out of existence altogether. One may therefore meet Jews who have never heard of some of these rituals and Jews who practice much more than is described here. However, for several years now in Houston, on the second day of Passover, children and youths have hiked to the Jewish Community Center from their respective synagogues. At some point, they jump across Braes Bayou, symbolically "crossing the Red Sea." The Exodus March is on its way to becoming a local Jewish tradition—but the question is, "What life style produces a group which commemorates the three thousandth anniversary of leaving one country for another?" What really sets these children apart from their neighbors in the community at large?

The new-born Jewish child almost immediately sets out on one of two ritual paths determined by his or her respective sex. At the age of eight days, a boy is circumcised. The ceremony is called *Brit Milah* ("Covenant of Circumcision") or *Bris,* to use the common Yiddish term. The rite goes back to the Biblical story (Genesis 17) where God commands Abraham to circumcise himself and his family as a sign of the agreement between them that God would stay with the Jews if they would stay with Him. This is the traditional Jewish explanation of the ceremony, at which the baby boy is named and thus acquires his identity, both personally and culturally. The particularly Jewish attitude is that the infant boy is not only being admitted into a social group but is having physically impressed upon himself a symbol of commitment to the Jewish faith and fate.[1] January 1 is eight days after December 25 and is the church holiday known as the Feast of the Circumcision.

The procedure involves a *minyan,* or quorum of at least ten men required for all public religious assemblies. The infant is held on the lap of the *sandek* ("godfather"). The chair beside that of the *sandek* is empty and is called the chair of Elijah, the prophet who traditionally will announce the coming of the Messiah. This is interpreted in terms of the potential of every child to become the Messiah who may save the world.[2] The operation is performed by the *mohel* ("circumciser"), who is specially trained and nowadays may himself be a physician. As with all Jewish rituals, the ceremony may be postponed if the child's health is endangered. Just before the operation, the *mohel* recites the benediction, "Blessed are You, Lord our God . . . who has commanded us concerning circumcision." Afterwards, both the *mohel* and the father recite several more blessings, culminating with the *mohel's* saying the blessing over the wine, announcing the child's name, drinking some of the wine and putting a few drops on the child's lips.

Traditionally, girls are named much less elaborately. On the Sabbath after birth, or as soon as the mother is well enough to visit the synagogue, the father is called up to the *Torah,* the scroll of the Pentateuch which is read liturgically at Sabbath services. He recites the appropriate blessings over the *Torah;* a blessing is said by the rabbi for the child and the mother's health, and the name of the girl is announced. Congregation Beth Yeshurun has just initiated a new ceremony in addition to that just described. Both the parents will bring the baby up to the pulpit. The grandparents will open the ark in which the *Torah* scrolls are kept, and the parents will recite the traditional blessing of joy and thanksgiving. It should be noted, however, that this is only a new custom at Beth Yeshurun. It remains to be seen whether the custom will really become a congregational tradition or be copied at other synagogues.

The ceremony of *Pidyon Ha-ben* ("Redemption of the Son") takes place on the thirty-first day after birth of a (mother's) first-born son. The ceremony is based on the Biblical verses (Exodus 13:13 and Numbers 18:16) in which the first-born of all animals and the first fruits of all produce are dedicated to God. In ancient times, this meant that the first-born animals from each year's new flocks and herds, as well as the first crops to be harvested, were reserved for God as sacrifices and offerings in the Temple before they could be used by the populace. Obviously, first-born children could not be so dealt with, even though surrounding cultures in the Biblical period evidently did sacrifice their first-born sons. The famous story of Abraham nearly sacrificing his son Isaac (Genesis 22) clearly and poignantly interdicts such action. In the Biblical passages cited above, human first-born are exempted, i.e., redeemed, by the father's paying the sum of five shekels to a priest, who represented God by virtue of officiating in the Temple.

While the roles of the Temple functionaries obviously ceased with the destruction of the Temple in the year 70, Jews still maintain from father to child the respective lineages of *Kohen* ("priest"), *Levi* ("levite," the assistant to the priests), and *Yisrael* ("Israelite," the general population). At the ceremony, the father hands five half-dollars to the *Kohen* and they both recite blessings and passages from the Bible, including the appropriate verses referring to the ceremony. If either parent is a descendant of a *Kohen* or *Levi*, the family is exempted from the ritual since the priests and levites were already consecrated to God because of their roles in the Temple cult.

Childhood is spent in school. The Bible itself commands the Jew to educate his children: "And these words which I command you this day shall be upon your heart; and you shall teach them diligently to your children. . . ." (Deuteronomy 6:6-7). By the time of Jesus, rabbinic law required every father to teach his son to read and to swim. The importance of learning in Judaism, plus the centrality of religious texts like the Bible, the Mishnah, and the Talmud, among others, have combined to make the Jewish school a universal element found in practically every congregation, even when there may not be a sanctuary for worship.

There are three main types of Jewish school, and examples of each are to be found among the eight synagogues in Houston. Most religiously traditional is the day school, or parochial school, combining religious and secular classes, and providing the deepest exposure to Jewish studies. There are two day schools in Houston. One is the South Texas Hebrew Academy, which meets in, but is not affiliated with, the United Orthodox Synagogues. Another is the day school of

Congregation Beth Yeshurun. At the opposite extreme is the Sunday School, providing the most limited contact with students. The majority of Jewish children today go to afternoon religious or Hebrew schools for four to six hours a week in addition to public school. Most congregations maintain either a Sunday School or an afternoon Hebrew school, and sometimes both. In addition, most of the synagogues send students to participate in the National Bible Contest. A local Bible quiz is held and the winner goes to the national contest. In the past, two Houston Jewish students have won the national quiz and gone on to the international contest, which is held in Jerusalem, Israel.

However, even more widespread than childhood education is the rite of *bar mitzvah* ("son of the commandment") at the age of thirteen for boys. A girl is a *bat mitzvah* ("daughter of the commandment") at the age of twelve. The term refers to the fact that the child is now to be considered religiously an adult, i.e., responsible for his or her own actions and able to be counted as a member of the adult congregation. Before this, the father is considered responsible for the child with regard to religious law. There is even a blessing which the traditional Jew may say on the occasion: "Blessed are You, Lord . . . who has released me from responsibility for this child." Certainly, familial responsibility does not end at this young age. However, the ceremony, which goes back to the Middle Ages, originated in a time when the child at puberty actually became eligible for marriage and assumed adult status in the community. The *bat mitzvah* is a liberal attempt, since the nineteenth century, to equalize the status of women.

It is often mistakenly stated that a child has a *bar mitzvah.* In reality, the child is a *bar mitzvah,* i.e., he has come to religious majority and may thus celebrate his becoming a *bar mitzvah.* The ceremony is thus analogous to voting for the first time after coming of age. The boy is called up to the *Torah* scroll in the synagogue and says the blessings traditionally reserved for adult males. After this day, the boy may begin to put on *tefillin,* leather amulets containing small parchment scrolls on which are written passages from the Bible and which are worn by adult men at daily morning services. The boy is now counted as part of the *minyan,* the quorum of ten men required for public worship services. Traditional Jews do not count women in the *minyan,* while liberal Jews do.

Traditionally, in addition to reciting the blessings over the *Torah*, the *bar mitzvah* would give a *derashah*, a presentation or speech on some legal problem from the Talmud or on some aspect of the *bar mitzvah* ceremony, to show how much he had learned. In addition to reading from the *Torah* itself, the boy would read the *haftarah*, a selection from the prophets which corresponds to the respective weekly portion of the *Torah*. The ceremony thus took on the aspect of a graduation from elementary to secondary religious study. At the same time, the boy showed that he had mastered what it takes to be Jewish, i.e., knowledge and understanding, in accordance with the rabbinic dictum that "an ignorant person cannot be pious." Nowadays a child often just reads the *haftarah* portion and possibly leads part of the services. Usually he also gives a talk thanking his parents for their love and devotion and expressing his commitment to Judaism.

Starting with the Reform movement and spreading to the others in varying degrees, a new ceremony of "confirmation" has been added to Jewish observance in many congregations. Usually this service is performed at the festival of *Shavuot*, or Pentecost, which comes at the end of the spring. According to tradition, God gave the Torah to Israel at Mount Sinai on *Shavuot*, seven weeks after the exodus from Egypt on *Pesach*, or Passover. The festival thus commemorates both education and covenant. The confirands are two years older than at *bar mitzvah* and the declaration of their commitment to Judaism is therefore felt to be perhaps more meaningful than at age thirteen. The Reform synagogues (Temple Emanu El, Congregation Beth Israel, and the Houston Congregation for Reform Judaism) all have their confirmation ceremonies on the first night of *Shavuot*. The Conservative and Orthodox congregations celebrate the holiday for two days, and usually have their ceremonies on the second night of the festival. Besides denoting one of the differences between the liberal and the more traditional congregations, this also facilitates many of the confirmands' going to their friends' confirmation services, which might otherwise be impossible if all the congregations had the ceremony on the same evening.

Whether or not the Jewish child continues his or her religious studies, the day eventually comes when most men and women get married, and the Jewish wedding ceremony has a long development from ancient times till now. The Biblical commandment to be fruitful and multiply was taken very seriously by the early rabbis. "To neglect that duty," writes Gaster, was considered just "as serious a crime as to commit murder," because "the law prohibiting homicide is in fact followed by that enjoining the propagation of the species!" (Genesis 9:6-7).[3]

In ancient times marriage originally involved a business arrangement between two families, with little or no concern for our modern notions of romantic love. Certainly such love was not to be ignored, as in the Biblical story of Jacob and Leah. Even today, however, a *ketubah,* or marriage contract, is signed before the wedding and then read at the ceremony. The document follows specific legal forms identifying the names of the couple and the locality. Usually the name of Buffalo or Braes Bayou is mentioned as a landmark, following the ancient custom of citing local bodies of water to indicate the geographic area. The contract then lists contingencies regarding inheritance, divorce, financial settlements, etc. In modern wedding ceremonies, these latter formalities are not read out to the congregation. By the end of the Middle Ages the business-like aspect had practically disappeared, although it may be added that the contract was actually a safeguard for the woman, should the husband die or simply decide to stop supporting her. As a modern, non-Jewish development, we note that some participants in the women's liberation movement have re-instituted the marriage contract for just this purpose, to insure equality in the relationship.[4]

The groom is called *hatan,* which originally meant "one who is circumcised" and which reminds us of the pre-Israelite and primitive custom of circumcising at puberty, i.e., prior and prerequisite to becoming a marriageable adult. The groom traditionally wears a *kittel,* a white linen coat which the observant Jew wears at the High Holiday services and at the *seder,* the paschal meal at Passover, and in which he is buried. In Houston I have seen a groom wear a *kittel* only at the United Orthodox Synagogues, as the custom is seldom followed in Conservative and Reform congregations. The bride is called *kallah,* which originally meant one who is shut in or secluded. She also is adorned in white, and wears a veil, following the almost universal custom. All these aspects of the ritual originally stem from the ancient belief that any major change of status was fraught with danger from demons and dark forces. Through the rituals, the participants were protected against these dangers: the bride and groom fast on the day of the wedding; they do not see one another prior to the ceremony; their clothes are the white of purity, which drives away demons; candles are lit against the powers of darkness. While most of these original meanings have been lost in modern society, the customs are nevertheless shared by many cultures.

The wedding ceremony itself is preceded by the signing of the marriage contract. The bride and groom stand under the *huppah,* or canopy, harking back to the outdoor bowers under which marriages took place in former times. Under the *huppah,* the *ketubah* is read, followed by a blessing over the wine. The groom places the ring on the bride's right index finger and says, "Behold you are consecrated to me by this ring, according to the religion of Moses and Israel." The service proceeds with seven blessings over the marriage cup. The blessings praise God for creating the fruit of the vine, the world, man, man in God's image; for the rebuilding of Zion; for causing the joy of marriage; and for the combination of marriage with the anticipated joy at the rebuilding of Jerusalem and the return of the Jews from exile. The bride and groom then drink from the same cup of wine, the important thing not being the wine but the sharing of food or drink as a symbolic means of making and demonstrating an alliance. The word "companion" and the custom to drink a toast after an agreement are based on similar notions.

The ceremony is then ended by the groom's stepping on and smashing a glass. This custom is again a conventional ancient and medieval means of frightening away evil spirits. The Jewish interpretation has "historicized" it into the Jewish tradition by saying that breaking the glass is in remembrance of the destruction of the ancient Temple in Jerusalem. The congregation in attendance belies this interpretation, however, by immediately shouting *"mazal tov"* ("Good Luck"). The rest is joy and festivity.

The final *rite de passage* is at death. Jewish law requires that the dying should be made as comfortable as possible and ought not to be left alone. The dying Jew tries to have on his lips the words "Hear oh Israel, the Lord is our God; the Lord is One." (Deuteronomy 6:4). This verse is the closest thing to a credo in Judaism. Mirrors, which are signs of human vanity and which reflect life, are covered in the house of the deceased. The body is not supposed to be left alone, and traditional Jews may recite psalms continually until the funeral. To prepare the body of the deceased and to participate in his funeral is considered one of the greatest good deeds in Judaism. This may seem strange; however, the reasoning is that this is the only time when one can be said to be doing a favor truly with no hope of reward! While most Jews use a Jewish mortuary, there is in Houston a *Hevra Kadisha* ("Holy Fellowship," or burial society), made up of volunteers who will prepare the body in the traditional way, if the family requests their services.

The dead man is buried wearing his *kittel* and wrapped in his *tallit*, or prayer shawl, with one of the corner fringes removed. Traditionally, the dead are to be buried on the day of death, if possible, unless the death occurs on the Sabbath. In that case, the funeral is put off till the next day. Cremation is not allowed by Jewish law because of man's being created in God's image, which would thus be destroyed. The ceremony and preparation of the body are, by rabbinical law, to be kept as simple as possible, both out of humility and out of concern for the poor, who should not be made to feel embarrassed if they cannot afford luxurious burial accoutrements. The coffin is to be of simple wood, often with holes drilled in the bottom so as not to impede the return of the body to the earth. This follows the Biblical phrase regarding man's creation from and ultimate return to the dust of the earth. (Genesis 4:19). Orthodox Jews sometimes place in the coffin a sack of earth from the land of Israel so that the dead might lie in holy earth and also to ease the return to the Holy Land when the Messiah will come and resurrect the dead.

Traditional signs of mourning are to let the hair and beard grow without shaving, to sit on the floor or low benches, not to wear ornaments, to read from the Biblical book of Lamentations, and to tear the outer garment of clothing. There are two theories as to the origin of this last custom. One is that it is simply an understandable form of expressing anguish. A second possibility is that it is a sublimated form of actually mutilating the body. This was a common mourning practice in the ancient Near East, but was expressly forbidden in the Bible.

Mourning for the dead falls into four main time periods.[5] First, the period between death and burial. Second, *Shivah* ("seven"), referring to the seven days after burial, during which the immediate family stays at home, does not go out to work, and receives visits of condolence. Third is *Shloshim* ("thirty"), the month following burial, during which the family may begin to resume normal activities. Finally, there is the first year after death (actually, only eleven months). During this period members of the immediate family say the *kaddish* prayer at daily services. This prayer is a doxology, praising God's greatness, but significantly not mentioning a word about death or dying, and so "the mourner acknowledges submission to God's judgment and the acceptance of His justice."[6] The mourners do not go to joyous celebrations or entertainment during this year. At the end of the year, the tradition is to unveil the tombstone at the grave.

Every year after that, on the anniversary of the Jewish date of death, the immediate family commemorates the *Yahrzeit.* On this day the family recites the mourners' *kaddish* at the three daily services. In addition, at the three yearly festivals and on the Day of Atonement, a special memorial service is held. It is called *Yizkor* ("He will remember") and at this service everyone who has lost anyone of his immediate family recites special prayers of remembrance in addition to the mourners' *kaddish.* These customs parallel beliefs common in antiquity that the living must propitiate deceased spirits, lest they become angry with the living and cause mischief. However, as Gaster suggests, the Jewish interpretation has turned these prayers of remembrance into a renewal of bonds with the past as well as a commitment to the future. It is the same commitment which was sanctified on the eighth day after birth and which cuts across the lines of life and death.

Thus a Jew in Houston may watch the Foley's Department Store parade on Thanksgiving Day and also walk in the Exodus March at Passover. He may celebrate San Jacinto Day and also light candles at the Hannukah festival, which commemorates the first rebellion for religious freedom in world history. Of course, I have not discussed the yearly, weekly, and daily cycle of holidays and liturgy or the dietary laws. Nevertheless, the feeling which I have endeavored to share is that of a particularistic yet universal art which, when applied to life, produces meaning and commitment. We may look at these customs and see truth or fairytales or a host of other positively and negatively valenced terms. Looking at the protean changes which these rituals have undergone and which many cultures share, I am tempted to side with William Blake, who tells us of a conversation with two Biblical prophets.[7] They declare, "We of Israel taught that the Poetic Genius (as you now call it) was the first principle and all the others merely derivative. . . ."

[1]Theodore H. Gaster, *Customs and Folkways of Jewish Life* (New York: William Sloane Associates, 1955), p. 53.

[2]C. G. Montefiore and H. Lowe, *A Rabbinic Anthology* (Philadelphia: Jewish Publication Society, 1963), p. 257.

[3]Gaster, *Customs and Folkways of Jewish Life*, p. 94.

[4]Harriet Mary Cody and Harvey Joseph Sadis, "To Love, Honor, and . . . Share: A Marriage Contract for the Seventies," *Ms. Magazine*, June 1973, p. 62ff.

[5]*Encyclopedia Judaica*, s.v. "Mourning."

[6]Abraham Isaac Sperling, *Reasons for Jewish Customs and Traditions*, tr. Abraham Matts (New York: Bloch Publishing Co., 1968), p. 298.

[7]*The Complete Writings of William Blake*, ed. Geoffrey Keynes (London: Oxford University Press, 1966), p. 153.

THE CHINESE

Harry Gee and family.

Dr. Joyce Fan and family.

Chinese students in El Paso.

Chinese working party, 1917.

中国红十字會 在棉加 旅館 我號 柒月拾 日

THE CHINESE ORIENTAL N⁰
for the Red Cross at the Menger Ho
JULY 12-1917

Chinese refugees in San Antonio, 1917.

Meeting of Kou Min Tang.

Texas Folklife Festival.

Un-Organizations:
The Family Associations of the Chinese

By THOMAS M. WOODELL

EVEN AMONG Houston's many organizations, the Family Associations of the Chinese community are unusual. To begin with, they are really un-organizations; that is, they lack the typical manifestations of formal structures: charters, permanent offices or staff, specifically defined objectives, and the like. Further, the Family Associations are largely an American development of Chinese immigration, although they maintain certain of the traditional ways. What, then, are the characteristics by which the Family Associations in Houston can be described?

Although not all Chinese living in Houston are members, there are at present, eight Family Associations, all of which have come into being in the last thirty to thirty-five years. This in itself reflects the fact that the Chinese community in Houston is a recent development, since, in the older centers of Chinese population on the West Coast, Family Associations date back to the mid-nineteenth century. Of the eight Houston associations, four represent single families and reflect the family name: the Gee Family Association, the Gor Association, Lee's Family Association, and the Lim Family Association. Two associations—Gee Tuck and Oak Tin—are composed of smaller families banded together by ancient and, sometimes, putative family ties. Gee Tuck includes the Choi, Wu, Chow or Joe, Young, and Tow families; Oak Tin, the Chin, Woo, and Yuen families. The Wong Family Association extends membership to the Wangs and Engs, if, as in Houston, there is not an association of each of the latter two families. Lung Kong takes its name from a small village in south China. Its members trace their relationship and family names back thousands of years to a local king and three of his generals: Low (the king), Quan, Chang, and Jew.

The basis for membership in any of the associations is the concept of the extended family, including sons-in-law. Because of the practice of including sons-in-law, it is not unusual to find that an association counts among its members persons bearing the name of some other family. Sons-in-law are not required by custom to give primary allegiance to one or the other of the two associations to which they may belong. In practice the wishes of the wife frequently determine the family association in which the son-in-law is most active. In addition to the uncertainties of membership involving sons-in-law, an accurate count of the membership of a given association is complicated by the practice of including in the tabulation only those male members over eighteen years old. Membership of the various associations, then, is an estimate, though there is some agreement that each numbers between fifty and two hundred members who are active to varying degrees.

As has been mentioned, there is little in the way of formal organization among the Family Associations in Houston. The annual head of each association is informally agreed upon by the most active members; sometimes the agreement assumes the form of a good-natured, "You have volunteered." There are no mandatory dues as such, although family members may be asked for small donations at the annual banquet so that the association can support its few activities. Among such activities is support of the Grand Lodge, which, like its member lodges, is an un-organization, defined now in an informal fashion and dependent on largely voluntary support. The Grand Lodge of most associations is located in San Francisco. Only the Gor Association is headquartered in Houston.

The Family Associations in Houston exhibit the lack of clearly identified activities and goals that is typical of informal organizations. By and large, the only activities common to all the Houston associations are support of the Grand Lodge and sponsorship of an annual banquet. Several associations make a practice of monetary awards for academic achievement, the worth of an "A" depending on the student's year in school. Unique among activities of the Houston associations (and among Houston's financial institutions) is the Lee Credit Union. As one might gather, eligibility for the services of this particular credit union is restricted to Lee's Family Association; in fact, unless a person is eligible, he is unlikely to suspect the existence of the institution.

Despite the lack of regular activities and specific goals, the Family Associations stand ready to provide for their members in much the same way as does any family. For example, an association may be called upon to settle a family dispute, although such a function is now rare and the sanctions which can be imposed are only social. Such a case occurred locally when the elders of a Family Association judged that the monetary estate of a dead member should be sent to his closer kin in Macao rather than be divided among his more distant relatives in Houston. Another potential function of the associations is to provide welfare services for members. Instances of such a function are difficult to document, however, for two reasons: the financial success of the Chinese in Houston and the loss of face in acknowledging that a family member is a failure. There is, nonetheless, one case of an association's fulfilling a welfare function that is without embarrassment. A few years ago an elderly Chinese was struck and killed while crossing an expressway on foot. Because he carried little identification, his body was taken to a municipal facility from which an anonymous disposition seemed inevitable. City authorities, however, contacted representatives of the Chinese community who were able to identify the Family Association of which the man was a member. The association claimed the body, provided a proper burial, and saw to it that affairs of the estate were lawfully handled.

In one instance the Family Associations acted concertedly to right a wrong done to a member. Some ten years ago a college-educated young woman was denied a job by a locally-headquartered, international oil company because she was Chinese. Members of the associations returned their credit cards *en masse,* accompanied by a letter of protest. A Family Association member who knew the company's board chairman through a professional organization repeated the community's protest. As a result, the company apologized, offered the young woman a position, and made broad changes in its hiring practices among minorities.

Activities such as the last three examples are not the usual ones for the Family Associations in Houston; the most often stated purpose of the associations is a social one. "Social," however, does not convey the underlying, serious accomplishments of the Family Associations in maintaining some traditional aspects of Chinese culture. The generally tacit, perhaps unrecognized, purpose of the associations is to perpetuate family identity, the implications of being a family member, and those modes of behavior which bring honor to the family. In so doing, the Family Associations are important means by which

Chinese ethnicity is maintained. Seen in such light, perhaps it is fitting that the guardians of such a hard-to-grasp notion as "culture" are themselves un-organizations.

I am indebted to Mr. Wallace C. D. Gee and Mr. Bill Woo whose generous gifts of time and information have made this description possible.

THE JAPANESE

Fuji Kishi.

Kichimatsu Kishi.

Japanese field workers transplanting rice, Deepwater, Texas.

Taro Kishi.

442nd Regiment, U. S. Army.

S. A. Kondo.

Texas Folklife Festival.

The Kishi Colony

By GWENDOLYN WINGATE

RICE LAND, rich loamy Gulf Coast rice land, was the lodestone that drew Kichimatsu Kishi and a colony of Japanese farmers to Orange County, Texas, one of at least three such groups that settled in the coastal Texas bayou country just after the turn of the century. The others were the Saibara colony at Webster and the Mayumi group near Fannett.

What were the reasons that led these settlers with a culture foreign to their adopted home to pull up their roots and transplant them to the sparsely-settled Gulf Coast of the early 1900's?

"I believe my father had a natural urge to own land," said Kishi's son, Taro, whose Japanese name translates "First-Born." "My great-grandfather was a big landowner in the northern coast of Japan—that was still in the medieval system—and I think Father inherited the desire to own land."

Taro Kishi remembered stories of the predictions of a Japanese soothsayer who, when his father was very young, foretold that Japan would not hold him, that he would seek his destiny elsewhere.

Kishi had thought of buying land in Manchuria, where in 1904-05 he had fought in the Russo-Japanese War and had been decorated with the Kite medal, but he discovered that land there was as high as thickly-populated land in Japan. The demand for land, the natives told him, was because of bandits who could take away a man's riches; but if he invested in land, they could not carry that away.

Whatever motives drove him, in 1906 Kichimatsu Kishi, father of two small children, Taro and a baby daughter Toki, left his home in the town of Nagaoko in the Prefecture of Niigata on the Sea of Japan and came to America to search for farming land. He had been widowed and had remarried, but he left behind his children and his young wife Fuji, or in English, "Wisteria."

After a search that took him through California, the Carolinas, Mississippi, and Texas, he settled on a site at Terry in Orange County. A graduate of six years' study at the University of Tokyo, Kishi believed he had found the land for which he had been looking. It was flat and fertile with some timber. A study of records showed adequate rainfall, and he could irrigate from Cow Bayou.

On September 20, 1907, Kishi signed a lease and purchase contract with Theodore M. Walker to buy 3,500 acres of land in the James and William Dyson Survey. But it was not until October 10, 1908, that Kishi and Walker signed the final agreement by which Kishi agreed to pay $72,000 for the land, part of that in cash and the rest in notes. Taro Kishi said the cash was provided in part by Japanese investors from whom his father had secured the money.

By that fall in 1908, Kishi and his farmers were harvesting their first rice crop from the land. He had brought back with him from Japan about fifteen Japanese tenant farmers as well as his wife Fuji and his six-year-old son Taro. Two-year-old Toki remained in Japan with her banker grandfather for two years because they feared he would be lonely.

S. A. Kondo of Fannett, whose father Sataro was among those farmers who came with Kishi, recalled stories his father told of those first crops.

"They plowed all winter long," said Kondo. "They used a single-blade sulky plow pulled by three mules or a two-blade gang plow with four mules."

"The drill and binder too were pulled by mules," said Kondo. At first Kishi and his farmers built levees in a checkerboard pattern, as they had in Japan, to hold water on the rice. But Kishi soon employed C. B. Daniell of the county surveyor's office to lay out levees that followed land contours, and he contracted for the building of a gravity flow canal.

Sataro Kondo came from the Prefecture of Niigata too. It was 1911 before he could send for his wife, Fumi, and his three children. Eventually the Kondos would have seven children.

"My father came for the opportunity," said S. A. Kondo. "My mother used to tell me how they farmed along the foothills in Japan. The work was all done by hand. They worked the ground with something like a hoe, but with sharp fingers to dig the soil. Most families had just a few acres. They put water on it, muddied it up and transplanted the rice from another little patch by hand. Nothing was wasted—along the levees of each little plot they planted soybeans— they called them levee beans."

"They harvested by hand too—tied the rice in bundles and hung them on racks to dry and then threshed it off the straw by hand."

Most of the fifteen or sixteen men who came to the Kishi colony were bachelors.

"They were striking out for adventure," said Taro Kishi. "But I recall a newspaper man once telling Father that if a colony didn't have as many as thirty families, they scatter. They get lonesome and have no opportunity to intermarry." The words were prophetic.

The men who were married, as was Kondo and a few others, sent for their wives and families. But at least five arranged marriages with brides from Japan after their arrival in the United States.

"When I was about five years old," remembered Mrs. Toki Hirasaki, daughter of Kichimatsu Kishi, "I was pleased to find that I had acquired five new aunts at one time. Tora Kishi married in Japan and brought his new wife with him and wives for Junzo Nagai, H. Kishi, and men named Moriyama and Hasagawa—I don't remember their first names."

It was not an unusual custom, said her husband Tokuzo Hirasaki, for the families of a young man and woman to arrange a marriage deemed mutually suitable, with the consent of both parties, of course.

Orange County marriage records show two of the marriages. On February 2, 1912, H. Kishi, younger brother of Kichimatsu, married Moto Sokai, and Junzo Nagai married Hisa Kitabara.

The men built homes or repaired and lived in homes left by earlier Terry residents. Some of the men who made up the colony besides the Kishis, Kondo, and Nagai were Yagama, Onozaki, Soji, Kato, Moriyama, Okuma, Tanamachi, Otsuki, Toba, Nomura, Okabayashi, and Kasuagi.

The colony was almost self-sufficient. The men came as tenant farmers, not as laborers. Most of them were well educated—one was a Cornell graduate, and several had finished college in Tokyo or in California—and each had some special ability to contribute.

However, most could speak little English, although Kishi himself had had an English tutor in Tokyo, and Junzo Nagai also spoke the language. Kishi was concerned that his children speak flawless English.

" 'You speak Japanese to me in our home and English outside. That way the accent will remain pure,' " Taro Kishi said his father told him.

Whether through necessity or by deliberate design, the Japanese

Japanese adopted the customs of their new home. Their children attended the Terry school along with other community youngsters, except for the Kondos, who attended the Granger school nearer their home. However, in accordance with Japanese custom, Kishi's son, Taro, was sent away to school after finishing fourth grade, living with friends in Houston while he went to school there.

"There is a saying in Japan," Taro Kishi remarked, " 'If you have a son you love, make him travel.' He will appreciate his home."

A few of the older colonists clung to the old ways. In Japan they had followed Buddhist teachings, and in their new home they continued to follow the Eightfold Path of Love and Renunciation taught by the Enlightened One.

In Japan all Buddhists had a family altar. On one of his trips back there, at the insistence of family members, Kichimatsu Kishi brought back a small shrine which is still treasured by his descendants—not for its religious significance, for they are Christian, but for its beauty and the memories that surround it.

In the shrine that Kishi brought from Japan is the delicate porcelain figurine of Kwannon, goddess of compassion, as well as scrolls with prayers and names of the family's dead inscribed in carefully brushed Japanese characters, and pictures and relics of the dead. A beautifully fashioned brass incense burner, candle holder, and vase where fresh flowers were traditionally kept complete the altar.

"At certain times deceased family members were remembered in special ways," said Mrs. Tokuzo Hirasaki. "I remember my mother used to bake a cake and leave it before the altar for a while before we ate it."

Kishi's wife, the diminutive Fuji, did not expect to enjoy the luxuries she had known in Japan.

"We are here as pioneers," she told her daughter, Toki, now Mrs. Hirasaki.

She learned to sew Western clothes on a Singer sewing machine, and she abandoned the intricate coiffures that in Japan were polished to a silken gloss with a camellia nut, in favor of more practical hair styles. Left behind was the *kato*, a large, stationary stringed instrument she had once played, as was the *samisen*, played by the farm superintendent's wife.

"I did see a couple of woodwinds, though," recalled Taro Kishi, "a bamboo flute and a kind of saxophone, also made of bamboo."

One of the few things the gentle Fuji did bring with her to Terry were her fragile blue and white dishes in which to serve in gracious style the traditional Japanese meal. She cooked for ten or twelve men and her family with little help. At first they ate the familiar Japanese foods, bean paste soup, vegetables pickled in brine, eggs—and the rice without which no meal could be complete. In Japan the very word for "meal" is *"gohan,"* rice.

Sashimi, raw fish dipped in soy sauce or pungent horse radish, which they had once enjoyed in Japan, was sometimes available, as was occasionally chicken or pork. Soybeans, the only rival of rice, were used in a variety of ways: *miso*, a fermented soybean paste used along with other dishes; *tofu*, a soybean cake of whitish custardlike consistency; and *shoga*, soy sauce used to flavor Japanese cooking.

There was *aemono*, mixed things, tossed with a thick sauce, the main ingredient of which was *miso* or *tofu* or ground sesame seeds; and *sunomono*, vinegared things, which consisted of raw, crisp vegetables, cold cooked fish or shellfish and a thin dressing of rice vinegar with a dash of sugar and soy sauce. Red pickled ginger was used when available for color and seasoning, as was *nori*, or seaweed.

Dessert was usually fresh fruit, when it was available, peeled and presented by the hostess herself. The meal was accompanied by rice wine, or *sake*, and hot green tea.

Japanese food is served in small, carefully prepared, esthetically beautiful portions with the emphasis on subtlety of taste and appearance. Arrangement and presentation of the food is disciplined artistry, and each small dish has its assigned place on the table.

Somehow, between her chores, Fuji Kishi found time to teach the children, Taro and Toki, a little of Japanese letters and the lore of that ancient land. The stories she told them resembled *Aesop's Fables*, said Taro Kishi, often pointing up a moral lesson.

One of the stories she told was about an honest man who had a dog of which he was very fond. One day the dog barked excitedly at a spot in the back garden, and when his master dug there, he found a rich treasure of golden coins.

When his neighbor, a wicked man, saw the treasure he borrowed the dog. The dog barked as he had expected, but when he dug at that spot, he turned up only roof tile and bits of porcelain. At that, the cruel man killed his neighbor's dog.

In sorrow, the honest man buried his dog, and a fine tree grew there, whereupon the jealous, wicked neighbor chopped it down and burned the wood. The honest man asked to collect the ashes, and they turned out to have miraculous powers. As the lord of the territory was passing through, the honest man scattered the ashes to the wind, and the ashes caused dormant trees to bloom out of season.

The lord of the territory, seeing this, rewarded the honest man. But when the wicked man, hoping for a reward also, scattered ashes from the tree to the wind, they only got in the lord's eyes, and he punished the miscreant severely.

Another tale of which the children were fond was the story of Urashima Taro, a young fisherman who one day at the seashore came upon some children who had captured a sea turtle and were tormenting it. When the children refused to stop the torture, saying the creature belonged to them, he pulled out some money and bought it. Releasing the turtle, he admonished it to stay in the ocean and away from the shore.

But one day when he was again at the seashore, there was the turtle in the guise of a beautiful maiden. She asked Urashima Taro to go with her to her ocean realm. He rode on the back of the turtle to a lovely underwater kingdom where he was feasted and entertained.

But soon he realized he must return to his own land, and he prevailed upon the maiden to take him back. As she bade him farewell on the shore, she gave him a mysterious box wrapped in a silk scarf. She told him, however, never to open the strange gift.

When Urashima Taro returned to his home village, everything had changed, and nobody remembered the young fisherman who had lived there such a short time ago. Only the very old ones said yes, long ago there was such a young fisherman who lived there.

In perplexity, Urashima Taro sought the answer to the puzzle, and finally he opened the mysterious box. Instantly he became an infirm old man with snowy hair. In little more than a breath his life passed by.

Sometimes the children themselves told stories in song. A few phonograph records of Japanese folk songs had been brought to the colony, and a few of the colonists knew the proper dance movements to go with them.

There were harvest dances for the time on the moon calendar known as O-Bon, a three-day period beginning August 13 when the spirits of the dead were said to come back to earth. Then the cemeteries were cleaned, candles and incense burned, and flowers and food placed by the graves.

While Fuji Kishi took care of her children and her house, the men planted and harvested their crops, or sometimes on the long evenings when the work was done, they talked, perhaps remembering friends or family in faraway Japan, or played Sho-gi, Japanese chess. The flat, ivory pieces with different inscriptions, represent the *Sho* or King-General; the *Kin* and *Ghin*, Gold and Silver Generals; *Ka-Ma,* Horse or Knight; *Yari,* Spearmen; *Hisha,* or Flying Chariot, the Rook; *Kaku,* the Bishop; and *Hio* or *Fu,* Soldiers or Pawns. The game, however, is much more complicated than European chess, said Taro Kishi, since the value of the pieces is increased after entering the opponent's territory.

The first few years of farming were successful ones for the Kishi colony. There were disturbing rumblings of new land laws in California that might force out the Japanese landowners there, but it seemed distant thunder.

What was more immediate was the death of Kichimatsu Kishi's father in 1912, and the incursion of salt water into Cow Bayou, Kishi's source of irrigation water for his rice. With the deepening of the ship channel through Sabine Lake and the Sabine River and the straightening of the bayou, he picked up salt water each time he pumped on the rice, and the crops were lost.

One disaster followed another. Kishi bought more land in 1919, but in 1920 the rice market hit rock bottom, and in 1921 the California land laws were passed in that state forbidding Japanese to own, lease, or control land there. Many of the California Japanese migrated to the Rio Grande Valley and began to raise vegetables. H. Kishi, Kichimatsu's younger brother, led a colony to Harlingen.

"The Californians must have gotten excited," said Taro Kishi. "They even sent word that the Japanese would take over the Rio Grande Valley. That's when my father told them to come right on over to his settlement. And that's when vegetable farming intensified in Orange County."

By this time the Kishi colonists had bought tractors, and with the California group and recruits of Louisiana French and Mexicans, they farmed several hundred acres in cotton, corn, sweet potatoes, cauliflower, lettuce and cabbage, as well as forty-five acres of fig trees. They sent the figs to a canning plant in Orange, and the vegetables to local markets and by the boxcar-load to markets in the North.

Kichimatsu Kishi felt an obligation to provide schools and religious instruction for the increased number of workers required to harvest the vegetables, and he approached the Rev. W. W. Watts, a Methodist minister in Orange, about establishing a church at Terry. Enthusiastically, the Rev. Watts went to the bishop in Houston, and mission workers were sent to establish the Terry Methodist Chapel. Kishi deeded three acres of land for the church, naming as trustees R. E. Markle, Taro Kishi, and H. F. Banker.

"The quality of the people who came was very high," said Taro Kishi. "Miss Cleta Kennedy, a deaconess and church organizer, requested that she live in our house. Mother was getting aged and tired, but she finally consented. Mattie Eva Lane, a professor at Canyon College, took a cut in pay to come to Terry to teach and play the piano for church services."

Other teachers boarded in the Kishi home too, and they may have had a further influence on that family's adapting to Western ways.

Land for the Orangefield school came from Kishi too. On July 31, 1928, he deeded 7.71 acres of land in the James Dyson Survey to trustees of the Orangefield Independent School District.

With laborers of several nationalities working on the Highland Kishi Farm, there were often fifty or sixty in the Terry Methodist Chapel on Sunday. For the older Japanese colonists who spoke little English, Kishi himself taught a Sunday School class, translating the Bible into Japanese for his charges.

Although they had been Buddhists, that religion is not antagonistic to any other, and many of them became Christians. But some, like Sataro Kondo, could follow none but the way of his youth.

"For you," his son, S. A. Kondo, remembers his saying, "for you who are young, maybe it is good to change. But for me, there is only the old way. I cannot change."

The small white frame Terry Chapel with its stubby steeple was the scene of the wedding of Kishi's daughter, Toki. The bridegroom, Tokuzo Hirasaki, had come from Japan to join his father in California when he was sixteen. After graduating from college there, he came to the Kishi farm, where he became the manager. On December 21, 1935, after several years' betrothal, the couple was married in the small church.

The building stood until the mid-1940's, when it was torn down and the lumber used in the building of the old St. Paul's Methodist Church in Bridge City.

Along with his vegetable crops, Kishi acquired about three hundred head of mixed cattle and a few head of Brahmas, which were looked after by Peter McDonald. He organized an oil company and got production on a small portion of his land near Orangefield. He later sold his oil interests to the Kawasaki Shipping Company of Japan. With the money from that sale, said Kishi's son, Taro, he repaid threefold the investors who had put money into the venture when he first came to Orange County.

But hard times came upon Kishi's vegetable farm too. Cabbage seeds contained cabbage yellow disease, and severe winters froze their crops. Then the depression of the '30's heralded the end of the little colony. As the journalist had foretold years before, the colonists began to scatter. Some like Kondo and Okuma moved to Maricopa County, Arizona, where they farmed lettuce and cantaloupes. The Tanamachi and Otsuki families went to the Rio Grande Valley, where some of their descendants remain today. The younger people moved into other fields, and the colony dwindled away.

Kishi's courageous struggle to make the land pay off was over in 1931. In September of that year mortgagees, whose notes on the land he had been unable to pay, foreclosed, and the land, the rich, promising land in which he had invested so much of himself and his treasure, every acre of it, passed from Kishi's hands.

In that same year the Kondos returned to Orangefield, where they farmed until 1936. That year they moved to Fannett, where members of the family and their descendants live today, some of them farming rice and soybeans. Japanese-American descendants of those early colonists remain too in Arizona and in the Rio Grande Valley farming vegetable and fruit crops. Tokuzo and Toki Hirasaki reared their six children and farmed rice on leased land on the old Kishi farm until his retirement a few years ago, and they now live near the old Kishi homeplace. Their son, Henry Hirasaki, in the family tradition, plants three hundred acres of rice and fifteen hundred acres of soybeans. Kahnji Nagai, a descendant of the colonists Junzo Nagai, remains in Orange County, and A. Kasuagi lives in Beaumont.

The Kishis and the Hirasakis weathered the storm of World War II. They had long since become loyal Americans. Taro Kishi graduated from Texas A&M, playing on the college football team. But because of Kichimatsu Kishi's ties with the Kawasaki Shipping Company in the sale of his oil interests, he was required to appear before a board of inquiry made up of F.B.I. and Army and Navy intelligence officers presided over by the Hon. Steve King. After questioning, Kishi was released without restrictions.

"They told me he answered their questions magnificently," Taro Kishi said of his father. "I know he was very patriotic."

Kichimatsu Kishi died in 1956, following his wife Fuji by five years. They are buried along with Sataro and Fumi Kondo and others of the colony in the Kishi family cemetery at Terry.

Few remnants of Japanese culture remain in Terry today, perhaps because of the determined effort the colonists made to adapt to the ways of their new homeland. Of that gallant venture at Terry there is left an abandoned, faintly foreign-looking farmhouse shaded by a gnarled giant camphor laurel tree, whose seeds were transported from its native Japan by the Kishis; a Buddhist shrine treasured by Christian descendants of the colonists; a yellowed ivory game of Sho-gi; and fragile blue and white dishes once used by the dainty Fuji and now enjoyed by her grandson's wife.

But in many places and many occupations the progeny of those colonists have become a part of American life. They are artists, engineers, oil company employees, farmers, housewives, accountants—and sometimes soldiers. At least one, Saburo Tanamachi, who was killed in World War II, lies buried in Arlington National Cemetery.

Perhaps common to all of them and a part of their ancient heritage is their appreciation of simple beauty. Taro Kishi explained it in a story about his Japanese grandfather:

"My father recalled once how my grandfather said to a man newly rich, 'Take this incense burner and train your eye to something truly beautiful.' Grandfather was disgusted with the man buying cheap, gaudy things without being able to appreciate the beauty of a small incense burner."

Later as he stood beside the living green of plants he tends as head gardener at Schlesinger's Geriatric Center in Beaumont, he added, "All my life I worked to make money. Now I think I will raise something beautiful."

*I am indebted to the following people for information about the Kishi Colony: Taro Kishi of Orange County (interviews July and October, 1973), S. A.

Kondo of Fannett (interview July, 1973), Mr. and Mrs. Tokuzo Hirasaki of Orange County (interview August, 1973), Mrs. Henry Hirasaki of Jap Lane, Orange County (interview September, 1973).

THE FILIPINOS

Dancers at the Philippine Fiesta, San Antonio.

Typical Philippine dress at the Philippine Fiesta, San Antonio.

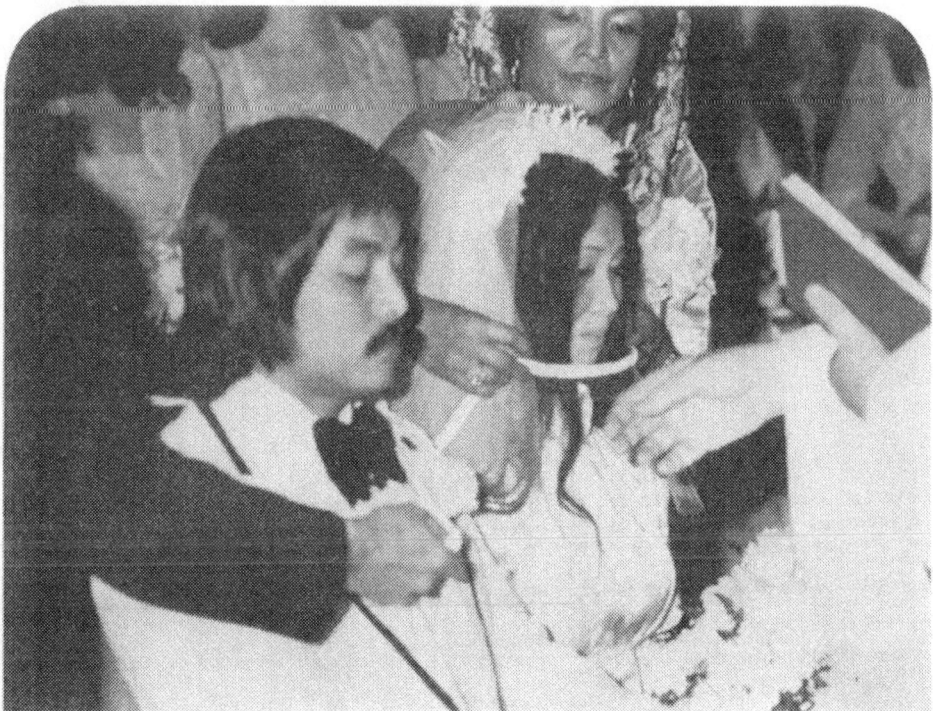

A Philippine wedding, San Antonio.

Traditional food at the Philippine Fiesta, San Antonio.

Traditional-style house built at the Philippine Fiesta, San Antonio.

Filipino Beliefs and Customs

By JIM HARRIS

ACCORDING TO the 1970 census, a total of 4,999 individuals from the Philippine Islands now live in Texas. Many of the Islanders came to the United States following World War II, most settling in San Francisco, Chicago, and New York. In Texas they have continued to come since the war, and they have migrated to the Dallas and Houston areas, although some are scattered about rural Texas. Ties with other Filipinos are maintained with organizations like the Filipino American Association. Many in the organization came as brides of servicemen, but professional and business leaders comprise a significant percentage of the Filipinos in Texas.

Although Filipinos have not received the extensive publicity other ethnic groups have in Texas, Filipinos do influence Texan culture in a variety of ways. For instance, one Filipino in the Dallas area works at a day school and teaches the Anglo children Filipino games and tells them Filipino stories. Mrs. Charles Hurt, born in the Philippine Islands, is of Spanish parents and married an American soldier before moving to the United States after World War II. Mrs. Hurt, who just returned from a visit with her relatives in Manila, supplied me with some of the following superstitions and customs that her friends and relatives have brought to Texas.

Many different actions bring good luck, according to Filipinos. If one wears polka-dot clothing at the beginning of the year he will be prosperous for the rest of that year. As in many cultures, certain types of coins bring good luck. At a christening, if one catches any of the blessed coins thrown on that occasion, he will have good luck. In addition, the giving of a birthstone brings good luck to the giver and the receiver of the gift. Finally, good luck may be associated with the New Year. On New Year's Eve the Filipino believes he should open all the windows in his house and let the smoke from firecrackers enter. If he does this, he will have plenty of money in the future.

Just as prominent as good luck actions are those that bring bad luck. While eating, the Filipino never puts his arms or hands behind his head. He never borrows salt from a neighbor. He never pays bills on a Monday or he will always be spending. And he never gives shoes as a gift to anyone he likes, because from that time on he will quarrel with that person.

Filipinos maintain close family ties and many typical attitudes come through in their customs concerning the family and the home. When a Filipino moves into a new home, if he stores rice, salt or sugar first, he will never run out of food. Sweeping or dusting the home at night will cause him to spend too much money in the future. Even worse, placing a bed facing a doorway will cause a death in the family. Unwelcome visitors can be removed by placing a broom beside the door. Family members are always welcome in the Filipino home. Old relatives remain in the home of, and are cared for by, the children. When a child starts to work, he gives half of his income to his parents.

Parents are involved in the courtship and marriages of the young. Rather than the young man asking the girl for her hand in marriage, the whole family goes to the bride's house to get permission for the marriage. In another variation of roles, the groom pays for the wedding expense. Before the marriage, if the girlfriend writes the name of her boyfriend on a paper, burns it, wraps up the ashes, and places them under her pillow, the boyfriend will think of her forever. During the wedding ceremony, if the bride steps on the groom's feet, he will become henpecked. If the first-born are twins, the couple will be lucky for life.

A final group of customs centers around church and religion. The Filipino should not have an accident during Holy Week—he may never recover. A short person can become taller by jumping on Easter morning. Young Filipino lovers should never exchange religious articles or share religious responsibilities; to do so will prevent them from ever marrying. If a couple is married and a child is born, the tossing of blessed coins at the christening will bring happiness and prosperity to the child.

These are only a few of the Filipino superstitions and customs that have found their way to Texas. The degree to which they are maintained and remembered depends, in part, upon the closeness of ties the Filipino maintains with others from the Philippine Islands. Many have remained close to other Filipinos in Texas by forming groups and organizations that bring together doctors, teachers, and housewives to talk about the Islands and the transplanted Filipino experience in Texas. That experience has added to the already healthy stock of Texas superstitions and folk practices. If Mrs. Hurt has her way, more and more Texas children will be playing Filipino games and learning of the contributions of Filipinos to Texas folklife.

THE GYPSIES

Drawing by Harry D. Brunner.

Le Rom And'o Teksas

By IAN F. HANCOCK,
General Secretary, Komitia Lumiaki Romani

THERE ARE more Gypsies in the USA than in any other country, perhaps as many as a quarter of the total world Gypsy population, which is conservatively estimated to be about six million. In Texas alone there are probably between two and three thousand.

A great deal of fiction has attached itself to Gypsies and their way of life, admittedly sometimes originating from Gypsies themselves to satisfy inquisitive outsiders, but more usually as a result of romantically inclined *Gazhé*[1] (non-Gypsies) supplying data of their own in lieu of firsthand knowledge. It is not easy for a Gazhó to gain the confidence of a Gypsy, making fieldwork sometimes difficult. For this reason, most people are unclear as to what a Gypsy really is.

To start with, the name "Gypsy," although used here, is not the usual term among Gypsies themselves, who prefer *Romani* or *Rom*. "Gypsy," a form of "Egyptian," is technically a misnomer, and has in any case pejorative overtones for many people.

The ancestors of the modern Rom originated in northwestern India, leaving there perhaps a thousand years ago and migrating through the Middle East into Europe and central Asia.[2] Because of lack of political and military unity, and because of Gazhó opposition to much of the Romani way of life, Gypsies came to be an oppressed group. The enslavement of many thousands of Gypsies in central Europe lasted for several hundred years, and Gypsies were well represented among the earliest unwilling immigrants brought to the Americas under the auspices of the Spanish and Portuguese. It is the centuries of European slavery and resulting misuse of Romani women by Gazhé slave-owners which makes the majority of Gypsies now largely European in ancestry.[3]

Although Gypsy slavery was repealed in 1856, persecution has continued until the present day,[4] with many countries still not allowing their entry. During the Second World War, an estimated half million

Gypsies were mutilated and gassed in Hitler's ovens as part of the Nazi final solution, which was to exterminate the entire Gypsy race. It is practically impossible for Gypsies to enter the USA or Canada legally *as Gypsies,* but since nearly all of those attempting to do so have passports listing them as nationals of this or that other country, a Gypsy from Hungary will enter as a Hungarian, a Gypsy from France as a Frenchman, and so on. For this reason, there is no official government census of Gypsies in America, although as a race, Gypsies in this country are classified as "other non white" regardless of actual complexion, which may range from dark to blond. Numbers given here are personal estimates.

Gypsies are then, broadly speaking, an Indo-Caucasian people, retaining a greater or lesser proportion of Indian characteristics and racial heredity. Time and geographical diversity have resulted in linguistic heterogeneity, different degrees of interbreeding with Gazhé, and loss of indigenous customs and folklore. There are instances of Gazhé being adopted by Gypsies or marrying into the race, and becoming *culturally* Gypsy themselves, but it is not possible for a Gazhó to *become* a Gypsy except metaphorically any more than he could become an Apache Indian. Blood connection with the race is one of the main criteria for acceptance, another being a knowledge of the Gypsy language; and a *stréno Rom* or new Gypsy in a community is closely questioned as to his family affiliations before being made fully welcome, or in some cases, rejected.

Although migrations have fragmented the Gypsy population, giving rise to many sub-groups different in dialect, appearance and custom, representatives of all Romani groups may be found in the USA. In addition, there are other non-Romanies such as the Irish Horse Traders in the southern states, whose life style bears some resemblance to that of some Gypsies, and who are sometimes classified with them.[5] Romani groups include, among others, the Vlakh-speaking Kalderásha, Machwáya and Lováría, the Anglo-Romani-speaking Romnichals or Ghipsuria from Britain, Sinti-speaking Gypsies from Italy, France, and Germany, and Caló-speaking Kalé or Gitanos from Spain and Latin America. (Vlakh, Anglo-Romani, Sinti and Caló are all dialects of the common language, Romanés.)[6] There is not a great deal of intercommunication among these, and the fierce group loyalties, scorn for other Gypsy groups, and for racially mixed communities such as the Romnichals is less in evidence here than in countries such as Britain where the so-called "pure" Gypsy way of life is in danger of extinction.[7] In one North American city, the locally estimated Romnichal population of ca. 2,000 people inhabits a fairly large district, and dominates two beer parlors in particular where it socializes, but the much smaller Machwáya population in the same city is largely unaware of them. They do know of the local Lovaro population, however, whom they avoid. Reasons may be at least partly due to their respective occupations, which tend not to overlap: the Romnichals engage in used car dealing, carnival operations and sometimes house painting, the Machwáya in fortune telling and stove repair, and the Lovária in taxi driving and entertaining as musicians.

In Texas, the largest groups are Machwáya and Kalderásha. They are for the most part all settled, and own considerable amounts of property in the form of cars, houses and land. They arrived from Serbia and Rumania by way of Russia and other countries during the second half of the 19th century, and speak Vlakh, i.e. Wallachian dialects of Romanés which are almost identical with each other. Both *nátsiyi*, i.e. "nations," make a distinction between those of them who are settled *(andé le kherá)* and those who remain nomadic *(trawlín)*, such as the Meskáya or Mexican Kalderásha who travel throughout Mexico with movie shows, and who still live in elaborate tents, occasionally visiting Texas and other southwestern states.[8]

Each *nátsia* consists of a number of clans or *vitsúri*, which are further grouped into family units *(famíliyi)*. Each clan or *vítsa* is named after a group characteristic or shared prominent ancestor; thus, members of the Lovaro *Imréshti tserá* (vítsa) share the ancestor *Imré*, while the Kalderash *Sapuréshti* are "snake people" *(sap,* "snake"), *Kashtaré* are "wood-working people" *(kash,* "wood"), &c. While each Gypsy may have any number of non-Romani names *(nava gazhikané)*, he or she has but one Romani name *(nav romanó)* which is patronymic; thus o *Wórka le Tanasésko* would be "(The) Worka, son of Tanas." This Gypsy name is never used in non-Gypsy situations. Besides this, a nickname is commonly used within the family; a rather squat and plain-looking individual in this community is known as *Zhámba* which means "Toad," but such an epithet is not used unkindly.

To give an idea of daily life, I describe here some aspects of the affairs of a family of six living in a small northeastern Texas town, the total sedentary Gypsy population of which is around thirty individuals, most of whom are related to each other by marriage. Represented are Kalderásha and Machwáya; Romnichals and Lovária sometimes pass through and are occasionally entertained when they do, but none is a permanent resident.

In this family, as in most, the principal breadwinner is the wife, who operates an *ófisa* or fortune telling parlor (known in police jargon as a "mitt joint") in her home. Advertizing is done by means of handbills distributed by younger members of the family outside theatres, in supermarkets, etc., and since fortune telling, usually called "advising," is technically illegal, consultations are given by donation. This means of livelihood is tenuous in this particular community where there are four other such establishments,[9] and income from it fluctuates considerably. The two daughters, who are both less than ten years old, do not attend school but remain at home to learn the technique of fortune telling *(drabarimós)* from their mother. The husband and two teenage sons supplement the income by soliciting such work as the repairing of steam radiators, vats, stoves, boilers, ovens, etc., in hotels, factories and restaurants, using a combination of traditional and modern methods with results usually superior to those of more formally engaged workmen.[10] Plumbing jobs, however, are avoided, this being considered a *marimé* (unclean or taboo) profession. Other occupations involve car dealing and repairing, the buying and selling of gold and sometimes jewelry, clothing and small arms, etc., usually obtained illegally from a Gazhó connection who receives some share of the profits. The quality of the first job of the year is an indication of the kind of luck a man will have during the next twelve months, so dirty or strenuous work is avoided to begin with, in case this is the only kind of work which will come his way.

The concept of certain activities being taboo pervades all aspects of daily life. Gazhé are treated with great circumspection, and socializing with them is minimal. Because of this there is a very high incidence of in-group contact, and gatherings *(kidinimáta)* are frequent— sometimes for a social evening for no special reason (a *shásto)*, sometimes to entertain a particular individual or his family (a *paikív)*, or else to commemorate a saint's day or other holy festival (a *sláva)*. Other occasions for gatherings are baptisms *(bolimáta)*, birthdays *(biandimáske djes)*, wedding feasts *(abiáva)* and feasts in memory of the dead *(pománi)*. For some of these, time is important. Birthdays for example are not celebrated on Saturdays, nor are memorial feasts held after sunset. At a festive gathering, a pig *(baló)* or sometimes a goat *(buzhnó)* is traditionally spit-roasted in the back yard, and served with *sármi,* which are cabbage rolls stuffed with rice and highly-spiced meat. Some other dishes are *yanía* or *djinéchi,* a compote of vegetables, meat and tomatoes; plain white bread in great quantities *(manró parnó);* rice boiled with chicken and peppers *(herézo kainiáko le piperiása); pirógo,* which is made from layers of flat noodles, cream cheese and raisins, baked in the oven; and *ritéshka,* a hot currant cake served with boiled fruit. Water *(pai)* is drunk with meals, and beer *(bíria),* coffee *(káfo),* spirits *(rakyá)* or tea *(cháyo)* otherwise—the last not with milk as the Gazhé drink it but in a glass with sugar and sometimes mashed strawberries or peaches. Thus the social activities revolve almost exclusively within the vitsúri, and from household to household.

For Gypsies in Texas, fishing and hunting are popular outdoor sports, although few will go near a river or lake after dark, believing the waters to be inhabited by the spirits of those drowned there. Such beliefs are deeply ingrained in the Romani mind. A gun will not be purchased if its previous owner is unknown, in case it was ever used in unfortunate circumstances and carries bad luck as a result. A house will not be inhabited by a Gypsy family if a death has ever occurred there, and elaborate steps of questioning the agent or previous tenants are taken to ascertain this. Even so, a newly occupied house is scrubbed and redecorated throughout, brightly and expensively. Couches and long, low coffee tables have replaced the cushions and brass trays on the floor of earlier years in most homes, but heavily draped windows and carpeted walls are everywhere still to be found. Religious icons, candles and crucifixes are prominently displayed in the room used for fortune telling, in most cases more for the benefit of the clients than as an indication of religious fervor on the part of the occupants. Much of the indigenous religion has given way to Christianity (especially Eastern Orthodox) or Islam. In some areas of Asia, the older animistic, ditheistic faith is more in evidence among Romani groups there.

Customs related to eating and hygiene are upheld with some tenacity. Each member of the family ideally has his own cutlery and crockery, which are supposed to be washed in bowls of their own. Most families no longer do this, but wash all together, keeping special utensils only for offering food or drink to Gazhé. More strictly observed is the use of separate basins for the washing of eating utensils, dish-cloths, men's clothing and women's clothing. For some time after childbirth, and during menstruation, a woman is considered unclean and must arrange for another woman to take over her duties. A man will not walk under women's clothing left to dry, nor live in a house with an upstairs, lest a woman walk above his head and defile him. At such times a woman should not cross water or it too becomes *pokelimé* or defiled. One may see women sidling around the walls of a room to reach the door rather than walk across the floor and risk crossing a water pipe. Some conservative families will go so far as to obtain architect's blueprints of the house to find out where the water pipes are located.

Dogs in particular are considered to be unclean animals, and any plate, knife, etc. which a dog has touched is immediately destroyed. Traditionally, the same end meets any eating utensil which may acci-dentally fall onto the ground.

In matters of dress, Gypsy women above the age of puberty are expected to keep their legs covered, and ankle-length dresses are still commonly worn. Married women wear a kerchief on the head. The stereotypical Gypsy male with embroidered vest, bandanna and ear-rings is a very rare figure, although other forms of personal jewelry are in abundance both for their cosmetic effect and as a means of storing wealth.

At a typical kidinimós, entertainment may take the form of indi-vidual exhibitions of step-dancing, or sometimes the more energetic *kelimós basó,* a dance known by various names to most Romani groups and of great antiquity, to recorded Gypsy music obtained from larger centers such as Los Angeles or New York. Drinking, discussion, card playing (one of the favorite card games is *prásta)* and story telling are also forms of relaxation and amusement, although the last is an art which is fast disappearing, few Rom now being skilled in relating the old tales *(paramícha).* Some of those which are remembered tell of a folk hero called *Frakpétre,* a giant who could grind rocks to pow-der in his fists. At such *kidinimáta,* the women usually disappear to another part of the house after the meal.

To a Gazhó, the furtiveness connected with the process of relieving one's bladder might seem odd. While Gypsy houses are equipped with bathrooms, for a man to be noticed going into one is for him a source of embarrassment. Instead, he will call to another, ostensibly for a private conversation outside in the yard, and perform the necessary function there. This, like so many surviving customs, originates from the days of life on the Road, where conventions of modesty were very strict. Also at variance with Gazhé ideas of etiquette is the lack of parallel word taboos. Outsiders have been shocked to hear Gypsy mothers and children using what to them would be considered very foul language. What seems equally rude to Gypsy observers on the other hand is the disrespectful way in which some Gazhé children are allowed to address their parents.

Even for settled Rom, life on the Road has not ceased entirely. Families may still travel for several hundred miles, usually for a pomána or a wedding, or else in search of work, but occasionally merely to break the monotony of living in one town too long.

Sometimes a wedding can be an expensive affair. At one such, held in December, 1973, at which several Gypsies from this community were present, the bride cost $7,000 and the trappings for the ceremony and feast, another $3,000. The bride price *(daró)* is not really a fee for the bride, but a gift to the father-in-law in compensation for the potential earning capacity of his daughter who is now leaving to earn for another family. Some girls may be married at as young as fourteen years of age, though rarely these days. In the case of an unsuccessful marriage, some, but seldom all, of the daró is returned to the groom's family, and the bride goes back to her father. In cases of mistreatment of one partner by the other not resulting in permanent separation, a fine *(glába)* may be paid to the family of the aggrieved in compensation. One man in this community recently knocked his wife to the floor in an argument, and had to pay a glába of $500 to her father as a result. Such decisions and arguments concerning work territory, abuse, etc., are discussed at another kind of gathering called a *Kris.* The Kris is often a heated affair lasting several days, during which time no drinking is permitted, and where impartial outsiders, even Gazhé, might be allowed to attend to give non-biased points of view. At a recent Kris held in a southern Texas town, several thousand dollars changed hands. This sum was for the settlement of hospital bills resulting from a vendetta over adultery charges, as well as appeasement money for the offended party and travel expenses.

While some of the customs and much of the folklore are submitting to pressures from the Gazhó way of life, the language—Romanés— is transmitted intact from one generation to the next. But while

Romanés may be the mother tongue, it is a distinctive variety of English that is most frequently spoken. Its speakers are aware of this kind of English, and maintain that it is especially characteristic of American Rom; nevertheless, it gives way to a much more typically Texan-American variety in conversations with Gazhé clients. An outstanding feature of this dialect is the high frequency of malapropisms (noted in the speech of Gypsies in other countries too), for example, "sonority house" for "sorority house." Widespread and recurrent mispronunciations such as "stiffick" ("certificate"), "bapatism," "cockaroach," "mens and womens," etc. may also be listed. Redundant endings are also heard, as in "loveded" for "loved," "bootses" for "boots," and so on.

Romanés itself is a fairly highly inflected language sharing much of its structure and vocabulary with modern Indian languages such as Punjabi or Hindi, but in the course of the migration from India through other lands, the vocabulary has become overlaid with words picked up from many other languages encountered along the way. Not unnaturally, this is happening here too, with English words being adopted into the vocabulary sometimes replacing earlier words, and sometimes existing alongside them. In all cases, however, the English words are modified to conform with the phonology of Romanés, e.g. *tóila*, "toilet"; *aiskrímo*, "ice cream"; *bára*, "butter"; *bádla*, "bottle"; *tenksgíwin*, "Thanksgiving"; and so on. These usually also take Romanés grammatical endings, thus *fréno*, "male friend"; *frenáki*, "female friend"; *frenúri*, "friends," etc. Very few Gypsies in Texas can read or write English proficiently, and Romanés is never written at all except by Gypsy scholars, who are very few in America. In some European countries on the other hand, there are Romanés-language newspapers and books published, a fact regarded with some skepticism and disbelief by Rom in the United States.

Certainly the Gypsies in Texas deserve recognition as one of the many ethnic communities making up this cosmopolitan state, even if they are out of the mainstream of Gazhó society. Centuries of persecution have resulted in an abiding mistrust of the Gazhé, and the reason that the two or three thousand Rom in Texas are so little in evidence is that they prefer it to be so. Dressing much like Gazhé, looking like Anglos or southern Europeans, Gypsies here take Gazhé surnames and, if especially dark-complexioned, may claim to be Greek or Italian.

ANTHEM OF THE ROMANI NATION

Opré, Romá   *Rise Up, Gypsies*

Gyelem, gyelem, lungoné droménsa,   I travelled, travelled long roads,
Malaidílem baxtalé Roménsa.   Everywhere meeting happy Gypsies.
A, Romále, katar túmen áven,   Oh Gypsies, where do you come from?
E tsarensa, baxtalé droménsa.   With tents on this happy road?
A, Romále, A Chavále.   Oh Gypsies, Oh my Gypsy boys.
A Romále, A Chavále.   Oh Gypsies, Oh my Gypsy boys.
Vi man sas-u bari familíya,   Once I had a great family,
Mudadárla e Kalí Legíya;   But they were killed by the Black
Aven mánsa sar e lumnyátse Roma,   Legion;
Kai phutáile e Románe droma.   Come with me, all Gypsies of the
Ake vriáma, wushti Rom akána,   world,
Amen xudása mishto kai kerása.   Help swell the Gypsy roads.
A, Romále, A Chavále.   Now is the time, rise up Gypsies,
A, Romále, A Chavále.   We will rise high through action.
                                       Oh Gypsies, Oh my Gypsy boys.
                                       Oh Gypsies, Oh my Gypsy boys.

MUTRÁS-AMEN ANDÉ TUMÁRI PIRÍ-LE-BILARÉNGI.

[1]*Gazhé* is masculine plural; the singular is *Gazhó.* Feminine singular is *Gazhí;* plural, *Gazhiá.* In this spelling, *zh* is similar to the "s" in "leisure," and *kh* like "ch" in Scottish "loch" Not distinguished here (although significant in the language) are retroflexed and non-retroflexed varieties of *sh* and *zh,* the dental and uvular *r,* and aspirated and non-aspirated *p, t, k,* and *ch.* The stressed syllables are indicated by an accent.

[2]This journey has been pictorially documented in Bart McDowell's *Gypsies: Wanderers of the World,* National Geographic Publications, 1970.

[3]Werner Cohn, in his *The Gypsies* (Reading, Mass: Addison-Wesley, 1973), estimates that forced interbreeding has resulted in a sixty percent admixture of European blood.

[4]For a full factual account of this, see Donald Kenrick and Gratton Puxon, *The Destiny of Europe's Gypsies* (Sussex, England: Sussex University Press, 1972).

[5]See J. Harper and C. Hudson, "Irish Traveler Cant in Its Social Setting," *Southern Folklore Quarterly,* XXXVII, no. 2 (June, 1973), 101-104; J. Harper, " 'Gypsy' Research in the South," in J. K. Morland, ed., *The Not So Solid South,* Southern Anthropological Society Proceedings, No. 4 (1971), pp. 16-24; and Ian F. Hancock, "Shelta: A Problem of Classification," in D. DeCamp and Ian F. Hancock, *Pidgin-Creole Studies: Current Trends and Prospects,* Washington, 1974, pp. 130-137.

[6]These are not mutually intelligible in ordinary conversation, although it is possible for one group to make itself understood to the other by speaking slowly and employing only those words common to both vocabularies. The common ancestor is not spoken now.

[7]For recent descriptions of the British situation see Jeremy Sandford, *Gypsies* (London: Secker and Warburg, 1973), and Manfri Frederick Wood, *In the Life of a Romany Gypsy* (London and Boston: Routledge and Kegan Paul, 1973). The latter writer is himself Gypsy.

[8]In October, 1973, about 50 Meskáya were in San Antonio, Texas, attending a wedding.

[9]Compared with the situation in a small town 150 miles from here where her sister-in-law operates the only ófisa, and consequently has no competition. On the other hand, the latter family must frequently travel considerable distances for their social activities, being the only Gypsy family in the area.

[10]A graphic and accurate account of some of these techniques and of North American Gypsy life generally is found in the autobiographical novel *Goddam Gypsy* (Montreal: Tundra Books, 1971) by the Romano author Ronald Lee.

Contributors

FRANCIS EDWARD ABERNETHY is a professor of English at Stephen F. Austin State University, Nacogdoches, Texas, and the Secretary-Editor of the Texas Folklore Society.

H. C. ARBUCKLE, III, of Kleberg Station, Corpus Christi, teaches mathematics in the Tuloso-Midway Independent School District.

T. LINDSAY BAKER is a Research Associate in history at Texas Tech University, Lubbock. He has studied the history and folklore of the Silesian Poles in both the United States and Poland.

GORDON BAXTER is an author, columnist, and Beaumont radio announcer who lives on Village Creek in the Big Thicket.

DAN JOE BEATY is a composer, concert pianist, and Professor of Music at Stephen F. Austin State University.

J. MASON BREWER is Texas' most distinguished Negro folklorist. He is presently on the English faculty at East Texas State University, Commerce.

JAMES W. BYRD is Professor of English at East Texas State University, Commerce. He is presently working on Black folklore under the auspices of an ETSU Faculty Research Grant.

INEZ CARDOZO-FREEMAN is with the Department of Comparative Literature on the Newark Campus of Ohio State University. She has done extensive research on Mexican folklore in Texas, Mexico, and the Southwest, as well as in her own area.

ANN CARPENTER is an assistant professor of English at Angelo State University, San Angelo, Texas, and is on a research grant studying the impact of the railroad on American folk music.

SARA CLARK works for the Encino Press in Austin.

ROBERT J. DUNCAN has worked in the research laboratory of St. Regis Paper

Co. in Dallas for the last twelve years. His interest in folklore began when he was a graduate student at North Texas State University.

MARTHA EMMONS of Waco, Texas, and of Irish ancestry, has taught in the public schools and colleges of Texas for fifty years. She retired from the faculty of Baylor University in 1971.

JULIA ESTILL (1882-1965) was an active member of the Society and a frequent contributor to its publications. She was a teacher and principal of Fredericksburg High School.

A. R. (DOLPH) FILLINGIM of Batson, Texas, was born and raised in the Big Thicket. He is a regular contributor of Thicket stories in *The Kountze News*.

JOE B. FRANTZ is professor of history at the University of Texas at Austin.

EDWIN W. GASTON, JR., is a professor of English at Stephen F. Austin State University and Treasurer of the Texas Folklore Society.

HARRY GORDON of Austin is a retired member of Exxon foreign service and was the organizer of the Texas Highland Games in Waco and of the Scottish Society of Texas, of which he is President Emeritus.

THOMAS A. GREEN, JR., is a doctoral candidate at The University of Texas. His two years of research at the Pueblo of Ysleta del Sur were supported by a grant from the Center of Urban Ethnography, University of Pennsylvania, at Philadelphia.

IAN F. HANCOCK is an assistant professor of English at The University of Texas and Secretary-General of the Komitia Lumiaki Romani.

JIM HARRIS is a teacher and doctoral candidate at East Texas State University at Commerce. His doctoral research is on folklore in modern southeastern fiction.

W. PHIL HEWITT is a research associate for the Institute of Texan Cultures. In addition to his Czech research, he was responsible for the Institute's pamphlet on the Italian Texans.

SADIE J. HOEL of Cranfills Gap, Texas, is a descendant of the original settlers of Bosque County, is a retired college and public school teacher, and is President Emeritus of the Bosque Memorial Museum, Clifton, Texas.

ALFREDA P. IGLEHART of the east side of Waco is a Master of Social Work from the Worden School of Social Service, Our Lady of the Lake College, San Antonio.

TERRY G. JORDAN is Chairman of the Geography Department at North Texas State University and is a specialist in Texas folk-geography.

LARRY LAUFMAN, who studied Near Eastern and Judaic languages and literature at the Hebrew University in Jerusalem, teaches Hebrew at the University of Houston.

SUSAN LUCAS (1947-1974) taught third grade in Austin and lived in the woods in Lee County. She died suddenly this summer, a few months after completing her contribution for this volume The world will sorely miss the gifts of her love and energy.

JO LYDAY teaches English at San Jacinto College in Pasadena, Texas, and is a doctoral candidate specializing in folklore at the University of Houston.

HOWARD N. MARTIN is the manager of the Research Department of the Houston Chamber of Commerce. He is presently serving as historical consultant for the Alabama-Coushatta Indians.

PATRICK B. MULLEN is a professor of English at Ohio State University and is an active and professional folklorist with the American Folklore Society, as well as a regular contributor to various state and local folklore societies.

JAMES P. MCGUIRE is a research associate for the Institute of Texan Cultures and has been responsible for the Institute's Lebanese and Syrian exhibits and publications.

GEORGE NIELSON studied and researched folklore as a graduate student at The University of Texas, and is presently at Concordia College, River Forest, Ill.

PALMER OLSEN of Clifton in Bosque County is a student of Norse folklore.

ALONSO M. PERALES is Director of the Bilingual Instruction Center for the San Antonio Independent District and a Fulbright Scholar in applied linguistics.

ERNESTINE PORCHER SEWELL is an associate professor of English at the University of Texas at Arlington and a descendant of the French settlers whom she writes about.

R. HENDERSON SHUFFLER is Executive Director of the Institute of Texan Cultures, San Antonio.

W. SILAS VANCE of Edinburg, Texas, is an author and scholar and a retired professor of English from Pan American University, where he taught American thought and literature.

KIT VAN CLEAVE is Editor of Publications for Baroid Division, NL Industries, Inc., Houston.

JOHN O. WEST is a professor of English at the University of Texas at El Paso and is the editor of the *American Folklore Newsletter*.

LORECE WILLIAMS is an author and professor with the Graduate School of Social Work at Our Lady of the Lake College, San Antonio.

GWENDOLYN WINGATE of Hamshire, Texas, is a rancher, rice farmer, and regular feature writer for the *Beaumont Enterprise*.

WILLIAM D. WITTLIFF is an author and artist and is the owner-director of Encino Press, Austin, Texas.

THOMAS M. WOODELL, the Assistant Dean of the Graduate School, University of Houston, is completing research on the culture of the Chinese in Houston.

ADINA DE ZAVALA (1861-1955) was the granddaughter of Lorenzo de Zavala, an active author-historian-folklorist, and was the founder and/or member of the most prestigious Texas-descendant societies.

TFS History

History

The Texas Folklore Society was founded jointly by John Avery Lomax and Leonidas Warren Payne, Jr. When Lomax returned in 1907 from his year at Harvard he brought with him George Lyman Kittredge's suggestion that he establish an organization for collecting Texas folklore. Payne, who had come to The University of Texas in 1906 to teach English, was interested in folk speech. Conversations between Payne and Lomax, then teaching at Texas A&M, led to the presentation at the 1909 meeting of the Texas State Teachers Association in Dallas of a resolution to form "The Folk-Lore Society of Texas." Payne became the first president and Lomax the first secretary, and together they worked out plans and details. By April 10 they had enrolled ninety-two charter members.

Next to the American Folklore Society, the Texas Folklore Society is the oldest folklore organization still functioning in the United States. The first meeting was held on the campus of The University of Texas in 1911. Mrs. Bess Brown Lomax was on the program with a paper on the now famous "Boll Weevil" song, which Lomax had collected in the Brazos bottom in 1909. (He had returned to The University in 1910.) Kittredge attended the third meeting and gave three talks. Annual meetings have continued regularly since 1911, except for interruptions in 1918-1921 and 1944-45 caused by the great wars or their aftereffects. The Society has stimulated the recording and study of the rich folk culture of Texas and the Southwest, has attracted both laymen and scholars, and has distributed its publications throughout America and the world.

Annual Meetings

The Society meets just before Easter, when members read papers on a variety of folklore subjects. On Thursday night there is a "sing" and on Friday night a dinner with an invited speaker. All sessions are open to the public. Occasionally the Society combines a meeting and an outing, as when it met in Alpine and visited the Big Bend.

Publications

In 1916 Stith Thompson, then secretary, oversaw the publication of the Society's first volume, for which Kittredge wrote the preface. This volume was entitled Publication No. I, and was reprinted in 1935 as *Round the Levee.* In 1923 J. Frank Dobie took over as secretary-treasurer, and in the following twenty years of his tenure edited an impressive collection of Texas and Mexican border lore in sixteen numbered volumes. Ever since Publication No. II was issued in 1923, the Society has sent out a book annually to its members, although some have not been numbered publications of its own.

The tradition established by J. Frank Dobie was continued by Mody C. Boatright when he assumed the office of secretary-editor in 1943. He had assisted Dobie in editing Dobie's last five volumes. Harry Ransom also participated in editing the last four. Boatright served for twenty years and produced fifteen volumes. He was succeeded by Wilson M. Hudson, who had been associate editor since 1951. In 1971 the Society's office was moved to the Stephen F. Austin State University campus in Nacogdoches, and Francis Edward Abernethy became the secretary-editor.

The volumes published by the Society contain many of the papers read at its meetings and other articles both volunteered and solicited. Most contributions are the product of original collection, and together they constitute a wealth of material in the various branches of folklore. Some topics dealt with in past publications are home remedies for man and beast, cowboy songs, Negro songs and tales, games, oil field lore, diction used in various occupations, tales of the border Mexicans, German customs, superstitions, weather signs, yarns about birds and snakes, Indian myths and legends, the origins of place names, lore of the high plains, of the Gulf coast, of the brush country, household rhymes, and traditional songs. *Texas Folk and Folklore* (1954) is made up of items that appeared in earlier volumes. In recent publications the amount of space devoted to folklore studies as distinguished from folklore collections has increased.

Membership

Although the Society was originated by college teachers and has always had its office on a university campus, it is not exclusively academic in its membership. Its members are doctors, lawyers, bankers, ranchers, farmers, businessmen, and housewives. Anyone may join, whether a resident of Texas or not. Libraries and other institutions belong to the Society and have continuation subscriptions to our publications.

Membership is recorded upon payment of the annual dues of $7.50, and members receive the annual publication or some other folklore book selected by the editors for distribution in the years when a book is not brought out by the Society.

This is a nonprofit organization; money received from dues pays the cost of printing or purchasing the annual volume. The small margin left over from the sale of books to nonmembers is applied to the expenses of the office.

Our emblem is the roadrunner, called *paisano* by border folk, which epitomizes the free spirit of the brush country. J. Frank Dobie chose the paisano for the Society—and for himself—years ago.

Manuscripts

Unsolicited manuscripts and art work are accepted from members only, and they cannot be returned unless they are accompanied by a self-addressed, stamped envelope. The editor will take every precaution to prevent loss of manuscripts, but no responsibility can be assumed for unsolicited materials.

Address communications to:

The Texas Folklore Society
University Station
Nacogdoches, Texas 75961

Index

POLES, THE: xxv-xxvi, 203-226
Pollock Foundation: ix
Portuguese: xxviii
Praha, Texas: 231ff
Prairieville: 246
Public Law 90-287: 16

Questad, Karl: 246
Questad, Martha: 249

Rabb's Creek: 295
Reierson, Johan: 246
Rienstra, Albert: 180
Rienstra, Dan: 179
Rienstra, George: 178
Rios, Don Domingo Terán de los: 29
Road of the Horse: 35-37
Roberts, Lillian: 191ff
Roosevelt, President Franklin D.: 285
Rose, Louis (Moses): 46-47
Rottle, Father James: 286
Roy, Edgar L., Jr.: ix
Rueg, Louis and Henry: xxvi
Rubi, Marquis de: 33
Russians: xxviii
Rystad, Rev. J. K.: 247

Saibara colony: 327
St. Denis, Louis Juchereau de: 29, 46
St. Elias Syrian Orthodox Church: 286
St. Jadwiga: 204
St. Nicholas Day: 232
St. Olaf's Rock Church: 247
St. Pe, Ethelda: 49
San Antonio: 204
San Francisco de los Tejas: 28
Santerre, François: 51
Santerre, Roy: 51
SCOTS, THE: xxiii, 169-173
Serbo-Lusatians: 295
Shea, William: 286
Shuffler, Henderson: vi, xi
Silvas, Pablo: 17
SLAVS, THE: xxviii, 277-280
Smetsers, Rose Lee: 83

Society of the Sons of Erin: 158
SPANISH, THE: xx, 27-39
Stappers, M. J.: 180
Steiner, Stan: 17
Stilwell, Arthur: 177
Swedes: xxvi
Swenson, Bervend: 246
Swiss: xxvi
Syrians: xxvii

Taro, Urashima: 332
Taylor Brethren Church: 235
Tejas: 11-16
Tellepsen Foundation: ix
Temple Foundation: ix
Terwey, Gerrit: 184
Terwey, Peter: 181
Texas Folklife Festival: vii
Texas Highland Games: 172
Thurber: 209
Thuringia: 153
Tigua: 16-19
Tvede, Elise: 246
Tweedmouth, Baron: xxiii

Villalobos, Don Gregorio de: 65

Waco: 129ff
Ward, Pegleg: xxiii, 159
Warenskjold, Wilhelm: 246
Wavell, Arthur: xxiii
WENDS, THE: xxviii, 295-300
Westphalia: 153
Wharton County: 191
WHITE ANGLO-SAXON PROTEST-
   ANTS, THE: 91-110
Williams, Hank: 60
Wilson, Stephen: xxiii
Wise County: 91
Wong Family Association: 319

Y'Barbo, Antonio Gil: 33-35
Yorktown: 204
Ysleta del Sur Pueblo: 16
Yugoslavians: xxviii